Democratic Politics in Spain:

Spanish Politics after Franco

Edited by
David S. Bell

 Frances Pinter (Publishers), London

First published in Great Britain in 1983 by
Frances Pinter (Publishers) Limited
5 Dryden Street, London WC2E 9NW

IBSN 0 86187 275 4

Typeset by Joshua Associates, Oxford
Printed by SRP Ltd., Exeter

CONTENTS

ABBREVIATIONS

ANE	*Acuerdo Nacional de Empleo*
AP	*Alianza Popular* (Fraga's conservative party)
CCOO	*Comisiones Obreras* (Workers' Commissions)
CEOE	*Confederación Española de Organizaciones Empresariales*
CDS	Centro Democrático y Social
CiU	Convergència i Unió (Catalan Nationalists)
EE	Euskadiko Ezkerra (Basque Left)
ERC	Esquerra Republicana de Catalunya
ETA	Euskadi Ta Askatasuna
FN	Fuerza Nueva
GRAPO	Grupo Revolucionario Anti Fascista Primero de Octubre
HB	Herri Batasuna
LOAPA	Ley Orgánica de Armonizatión del proceso Autonómico
ORGA	Organización Republicana Galleg Autónoma
PCE	Partido Comunista de España
PNV	Partido Nacionalistsa Vasco (Basque Nationalists)
PP	Partido Popular
PSA	Partido Socialista de Andalucía
PSP	Partido Socialista Popular
PSOE	Partido Socialista Obrero Español
PSUC	Partido Socialista Unificado de Cataluña
UCD	Unión de Centro Democrático
UGT	Unión General de Trabajadores

FOREWORD

Spain is another country: they do things differently there. One of the features of Spain's transition to democracy since the death of General Franco on 20 November 1975 has been the rapidity of the country's evolution towards a western European style of social democracy. This process is by no means complete and is not without its ambiguities (notably in the position of the army), nevertheless Spain can now be seen in the context of western Europe and has lost many of the so-called 'Latin' individual characteristics which made it the favourite of cultural analysts. In other words Spanish politics in the late 1970s and early 1980s was conducted with such a sureness of touch and a firmness of purpose that the democratic institutions were put in place within 6 years of Franco's death. Franco's supposedly indestructible insitutions were dismantled from within and replaced by a constitutional monarchy.

What, therefore, characterises the essays in this volume is not so much the peculiarity of Spain as the comparability with parallel trends and factors in other parts of western Europe. While Latin political culture and the differences in cultural development have often been cited to explain Spanish political instability and extremism, it will be interesting to see if this form of explanation can accommodate the moderate democratic Spain which has arisen from the transition. Anarchism, Republicanism, anti-clericalism, fascism, Carlism (the list could be extended indefinitely) have all left their traces but are no longer very active forces in Spanish politics. Naturally Spain has certain problems which are more acute than elsewhere as well as peculiarities of structure and environment which are not shared by other western European countries: these do not detract, however, from the essential comparability of its contemporary politics.

In Spain a two-party alternating party system has been under construction since 1976 when the PSOE and UCD started to emerge as the dominant parties and (although it is unwise to make predictions in politics) it looks as if this bi-polarity will continue with the Alianza Popular replacing UCD on the Right. Against many predictions Spain did not develop the symmetrical extremes of, say, Fourth Republic France, in which anti-system parties on the Left (the Communists) and the Right (ex-Francoists or quasi-fascists) attacked an unstable Centre which was forced to defend the country's institutions almost alone. In comparative electoral terms the extremes of Left and Right are no more significant in Spain than in the societies of northern Europe. In this sense Spain is 'northern European' and not 'Latin European': it is unlike France, Italy or Portugal in this respect. (Extremism within the institutions is, however, another matter.)

It is likely that the reciprocal two-party system will develop in Spain despite the collapse of the UCD. The Spanish Socialist Party now occupies the centre of the Spanish political stage. This means that electors who want to remove the government must unite and that electors who want to keep the government in must unite. Consequently there is a tendency for the big parties to be reinforced and for the small parties to be squeezed out (this has nothing to do with Spain's d'Hondt electoral system, it is an effect of the *party system*).

In the 1979 elections the competition was between the centrist UCD party of Prime Minister Suárez and González' PSOE; it was a competition for the centre, floating vote. Since 1979 Spanish politics has seen the startling collapse of the Centre UCD and the rise of the avowedly conservative Alianza Popular and, whilst the AP can be expected to make overtures to the Centre for electoral reasons the post-1982 position would appear to be more ideologically polarised. Unlike the UCD the AP, is led in a more authoritarian style and makes appeals to 'Reaganomics' rather than to Keynes. A system may well emerge which is more akin to West Germany with a moderate Socialist party and a big conservative party than to the *alternance douce* of 1979–82. This, however, is speculation and will depend on unforeseeable factors such as the problems faced by the PSOE government and the Alianza Popular's willingness to swap ideological commitment for vote maximisation. Whatever the case, Spain has an opposition grouped around a potential prime minister which is committed to parliamentary democracy and a Socialist government which is determined to continue the entrenchment of democratic institutions.

The party of the 'transition' is, of course, the UCD and Chapter 1 by José Amodia analyses the fate of this party which was virtually extinguished in the 1982 elections. The UCD, as José Amodia says, was a coalition of minor liberal, centre and left-centre parties around the figure of Adolfo Suárez whose creation it was. Centre democracy may have been an unstable construction from the outset (as MRP proved in France) because of the tension between its reform-minded leadership and its essentially conservative electorate. Nevertheless it was united by the need for rapid and effective transition to democracy and united behind Suárez as the best man to accomplish such a programme. Once the main democratic institutions were in place, and once democracy had been largely installed, the pressures which kept the alliance together were released, other issues became more pressing and these split the UCD apart: Suárez, when Prime Minister, had to deal with an increasingly unmanageable party which was split on a variety of issues from abortion to divorce-law reform to taxation policy. Suárez resigned because the party was divided thus removing a further reason for maintaining its existence. The new Prime Minister, Calvo-Sotelo had no greater success than Suárez and the further disintegration of the UCD was what precipitated the premature elections of 1982 in which the UCD was the principal loser. As has been said, the destruction of the big moderate centre UCD party is a tragedy for Spanish democracy and contributes to an unwanted heightening of ideological tone on the Right. Suárez left the UCD to found his own party, the CDS, but his popularity was insufficient to 'recreate' the UCD under a new banner.

In many ways the PSOE has taken over from the UCD. In the 1982 elections it was the obvious potential governing party: united, democratic and under the leadership of a popular potential prime minister, Felipe González. In the mid-1970s the PSOE did not appear quite in this light. It had atrophied somewhat during the 1960s leaving the role of the main opposition to Franco to the Communists and, it was not until the old Llops-leadership was overthrown by Felipe González and his associates that the PSOE began to re-emerge as the main party of the Spanish Left. Liz Nash, in Chapter 2, discusses the structure and politics of the PSOE and describes how it became what it is, a moderate socialist party under González' unchallenged control, despite a strong Marxist counter-current amongst the activists. Felipe González dominates the PSOE in a way which is unusual for a leader, although not unprecedented, in western socialist parties: the 1979 and 1982 election campaigns were Felipe's campaigns in which his personality and image were projected at some cost to the other PSOE politicians who did not muster equivalent publicity.

If the PSOE is not a one-man show, it is nevertheless firmly under the leadership's control after the Left's challenge of 1978–9 as Liz Nash shows. Difficulties which face the PSOE do not stem from its lack of a majority or internal splits but from the intractable problems of permanently hostile environment and a world recession which will prevent the realisation of the PSOE's plans to deal with unemployment within the space of a four-year legislative term. Hopes have been placed on the PSOE which it may not be able to fulfil and therein lies the great danger behind the sweeping victory of 1982.

However, there is no evidence that there is an extreme left-wing vote waiting to be captured by some party with the courage to move sharply leftwards. Extreme left-wing, republican, and pro-Soviet parties either performed indifferently or badly and the Workers' Commissions also lost ground to the Socialist-led UGT unions in 1982. (Unlike the 1930s, the recession of the 1980s has not produced extremist responses: the slogan that 'things were better' under Franco is patently false.) The Communist Party itself has fallen victim to the polarisation of Spanish politics but made its own position worse by a protracted internal power-struggle which was carried out with a brutality and lack of finesse unbecoming to a party which describes itself as 'Eurocommunist'. Chapter 3 raises the question of whether there remains any place in Spanish politics for the PCE.

Chapter 4 discusses some of the administrative and democratic norms of the new Spanish Constitution. The 1978 Constitution, drawn up by the Constituent Assembly of Spain tried to keep a balance between different principles of efficient administration and decentralised devolved, responsibility and has been marked by liberal ideas about how a civil service should operate. These principles are often ambiguous and came into frequent conflict with one another. In Chapter 4 Pierre Subra de Bieusses describes and analyses the implications of the Constitution in the light of modern administrative imperatives and in particular the human-rights aspect of Spain's new institutions as described by the Constitution.

Mike Newton, in Chapter 5, deals with the attendant problems of regional government. Nobody conversant with European politics of the last few years can fail to be aware of the difficulty of the regional problem in Spain and of the various complexities which it involves. The most critical of these is the Basque region with the ETA apparently disinclined to extend to the PSOE the 'honeymoon' period which is usual after the election of a new government. (One of the questions about the 1982 election victory is whether the PSOE has any new ideas on the Basque problem.) Terrorism has therefore continued in Spain and ETA has not been discouraged by the election of a Socialist Government.

But the Basque region is only one of many Spanish regional identities. The government was sensitive in its original approach to decentralisation, setting up pre-autonomy regional chambers to discuss and negotiate the extent of regional devolution with Madrid. This contrasts with the British approach to regional devolution in the Labour Government of 1974–9 in which statutes were handed-down from the centre on a 'take-it-or-leave-it' basis. Mike Newton discusses the situation in the various regions of Spain and concludes with the theme of overall Spanish 'unity in diversity'.

For the Socialist Government one of the problems of regional reform is that this issue is one over which the army is particularly sensitive. The

PSOE and the UCD together introduced a law restricting the extent of devolution in the immediate aftermath of the coup of 23 February. In Chapter 7 Dr Vilanova discusses the position of the army and its distinctive structure. The coup attempted by Lieutenant-Colonel Tejero was only one of a series of such plots (the latest of which was planned for the eve of the 1982 elections). The potential success of such coups lies not in widespread popular support for the extreme Right (as Tejero's 25,000 votes in the elections showed) but rather in the continuing and considerable influence of a small number of Franco's nominees in Spain's infrastructure.

The state of public opinion and the evolution of the political parties is described in Chapter 6 on the elections by Bruce Young. In it he examines the elections, the sociology of the new Spain and the issues which characterised the elections of 1982. These elections were bound to be crucial in the development of post-Franco Spain and the chapter devoted to them puts them into context, draws some conclusions about the future of Spanish politics and the probable course of the PSOE government.

One of the issues, though not a particularly prominent one, of the 1982 elections was the entry of Spain into the Common Market. Peter Holmes in Chapter 8 discusses the various problems involved in Spain's application to join the EEC and the consequences for Spain and the Community. Spain's request for membership is principally political and is, in effect, a request to be recognised as a full member of the club of western European liberal democratic societies. Franco made much of Spain's special relationship with Latin America and her distinctiveness from the rest of Europe. Application to join the EEC is therefore a rejection of that past and a recognition of cultural and social affinities with western Europe. The problem for Spain is that the EEC and particularly France will find it difficult to accommodate its application. The EEC has therefore been unresponsive to Spanish demands for membership and it is not clear that Spain is willing to wait indefinitely. However, there is another difficulty, namely the accession to the Community will not bring economic benefits of an immediately tangible nature: unless this is recognised by Spanish public opinion there could be political problems after Spain has joined.

It is hoped that this book will be of use not just to those interested in Spanish politics but also to those interested in other themes of comparative politics. There are lessons to be learnt in comparative studies from the Spanish attitudes to, and policies on, the issues of the 1970s and in the various ways in which regional, administrative and policy problems have been tackled. It is also likely that this book will interest students of political parties for, in this field, the Spanish experience is informative but sadly neglected.   *David S. Bell*

1 UNION OF THE DEMOCRATIC CENTRE

JOSÉ AMODIA

The Old Roots of a New Party

UCD (Unión de Centro Democrático) is a political organisation, which having started its life as a short-term and rather opportunistic electoral coalition early in 1977, was to become the ruling party after its success in the elections held in June of that same year. The understanding of UCD itself, of its heterogeneous ideology, and of the tensions and feuds which have been threatening its stability—and even its survival—to this day requires some historical perspective. On the one hand UCD encapsulates all the features of the process of democratisation that Spain underwent after Franco. It can be seen simultaneously as cause and effect of that process. On the other hand, UCD's roots go back deep into the Francoist period. Its origins can easily be traced back to the mid-sixties.

UCD emerges at the point of encounter of two forms of legitimacy, one based on the idea of continuity, and the other based on the idea of change. The former became a kind of bridge spanning the gap between the dictatorship which was being dismantled and the liberal–democratic system which was to replace it. Constitutional continuity made it possible for wide sectors of the Francoist ruling classes to survive politically. They crossed the bridge (some rather startling conversions to democracy taking place along the way), they organised themselves, and they continued to exercise power in the new democratic system, just as they had done under the previous authoritarian system with, of course, all the formal adjustments that such a radical transformation required.

At the same time UCD must be seen in the light of the legitimacy provided by change itself. Political reform was brought about and directed by many of those who would eventually become UCD leaders. It could be said the UCD was an attempt on the part of some political figures and groups to profit from the process of democratisation. It was a clever and well-timed way of exploiting the exceptional circumstances created by Franco's demise. The legitimacy that democratic change afforded them and the possibility of continuing to exercise power acted as catalysts to bring together a wide range of frondes, budding parties, and public figures, all of them Right of Centre in the ideological spectrum—the exceptions being very few and, once again, resulting from the unusual circumstances prevalent at the time.

UCD appeared as an electoral coalition in the spring of 1977. To be precise the coalition was set up on 3 May of that year, and in December, after the electoral success in the summer, it became a single party. But its origins go back much further. More than a decade previously, in the middle of the sixties, the mood in Spain was one of economic optimism and political concern. It was a period of fast economic growth, but, at the same time, Franco was showing signs of evident physical and mental decay, and the need to find a formula for political survival beyond Franco became an ever-present worry amongst the ruling groups. The problem was how to find a way to move from a dictatorial system based upon the idea of a single party to one which did not rely on a charismatic ruler and allowed some degree of political plurality, without losing control of the situation while bringing about the change. To a certain extent the Organic Law of the State of 1967—the last of Franco's Fundamental Laws— tried to be the official answer to the problem. Taking that law as a basis a number of attempts were made to set up political associations, as parties were euphemistically called. During the late sixties and early seventies the subject stimulated a great deal of interest and heated debate in the country. With hindsight, however, one can see the futility of it all. Political associations were no more than an official attempt at absorbing and controlling the emerging political pluralism. The formula was unworkable. They tried to confine pluralism within the narrow margins of the single party (or what remained of it), the so-called National Movement, and the efforts led to inevitable failure.[1]

But what is relevant to explain about the origins of UCD is not so much the official attempts at creating political associations in the sixties —even though some of the best known and most influential figures of UCD were directly involved in several of the associations—but the latent political pluralism which was at the root of such attempts. By the middle of the 1960s Spanish society had come a long way from the frightened and impoverished state it had experienced during the post-Civil War years. New generations of Spaniards, greater prosperity, increased social mobility, large-scale migration, improved education, etc., had not only given the country a different social texture and appearance, they had nurtured diversity. The idea of one single Spain, of such symbolic value to Francoist ideologues, gave way to many different Spains. Social plurality forced the acceptance of political plurality. Cracks became apparent on the regime's monolithic facade. The various groups and factions in the Francoist camp, or on its periphery, took advantage of the relative freedom provided by the Press Law of 1966 to seek some form of independent political identity. Their differences, their antagonisms, even, in some instances, their specific quarrels became known to the public at large. The pretence of ideological uniformity yielded, little by little, to this latent pluralism.

Needless to say this pluralism was rather limited in scope. The regime would tolerate personal dissidence, but it clamped down on any kind of organised opposition. It was not possible to organise openly for political purposes. Thus pluralism manifested itself in a very personalised way. Often factions were no more than small groups of individuals orbiting around a well-known public figure with little or no formal organisation to support them. Ministers, ex-ministers, and others who, having served the dictatorship in the past, later drifted away from it towards areas of mild opposition (what Linz called 'a-legal opposition')[2] and became the visible heads of small groups, often identified by the name of their leader. The term 'family', sometimes applied to these groups,[3] seems to convey their nature very appropriately.

But all this was not enough. As time went on the need to establish political organisations, essential for the power-struggle which lay ahead beyond Franco's life, became more and more pressing. By the late-sixties only the ultra-right wing groups would attach any value to the vacuous rhetoric of a totalitarian past: 'the unbreakable unity of Spanish peoples and lands', 'the permanent and unalterable nature of the Principles of the National Movement', 'organic democracy' or 'vertical syndicalism'. These were no more than empty shells, anachronistic remnants of a political system in an advanced state of disintegration. Change, plurality, open competition for power were imminent, and it was necessary to get ready for them. The assassination, in December 1973, of the prime minister, Admiral Carrero Blanco, the man chosen to guarantee the continuation of Francoism without Franco, brought added urgency to the situation.

In one way or another, during the period from 1967 to 1975, all the various forces in the Francoist camp started to prepare for the future, realising that it would inevitably have to be different, and that, therefore, a new approach to politics would be required. As they could not legally organise themselves outside the boundaries of the single party, they covered up their political aims with a varied and strange assortment of disguises. Of course, some were to avail themselves of the possibilities offered by the regime, setting up political associations in accordance with the principles laid down by the National Movement.[4] As mentioned earlier, these associations or pseudo-parties were condemned to failure, and fail they did, though some of them were eventually to dissolve, as it were, into the melting pot of UCD, providing in the process leaders as important as Rodolfo Martín Villa or Adolfo Suárez.

This was also the time when politics took on a gastronomic appearance. '*Cenas políticas*' (political dinner-parties) became fashionable, particularly in Madrid. A group of public figures would gather in one of the capital's most expensive restaurants, with the excuse of celebrating an anniversary or some other occasion. The after-dinner speeches and discussions would be used by political figures to spread their views for the future and to seek support for their plans. Amongst the guests—very appropriately called '*cenocentristas*', a name that suggested the political space they were aiming to occupy—at such occasions the names of future UCD leaders appear repeatedly.[5] Other politicians—and sometimes the same ones, for the differences between groups were never clear; they showed considerable affinities, and it was possible for the same person to identify with several of them—concealed their intentions by establishing cultural bodies or commercial enterprises whose names (*Godsa, Libra, Fedisa*, etc.) may now seem irrelevant, but at that time they were being nurtured by right-wing forces as the seedlings of future political parties. Others, again, were hiding behind journalistic pseudonyms. They used the press as a vehicle to make their presence known and to convey their message as openly as the circumstances allowed. Among these it is worth mentioning a group which in 1973 started publishing regular articles in Madrid's Catholic daily, *Ya*, using as a pseudonym the name of the Roman historian Tacitus.[6] Behind it there were some thirty right-wing members of the Christian Democracy which had grown in Spain as an offshoot of the close and long-standing relationship between the Vatican and Franco's regime. They were to play a major role in the setting up and development of UCD.

The roots of UCD are to be found then in that nebulous world where intentions were never openly declared and where organisations were always hiding their real nature. Many of the features of the UCD as a political party, many of the difficulties and crises it has experienced during the last five years can be traced back to its original polymorphism. It might be argued that this was inevitable. In terms of political organisation the Right was worse prepared than the Left for democracy. They had to improvise new parties, whereas the Left had kept theirs in exile or clandestinity. The Left could claim continuity with the republican period of the thirties. The Right had to start anew, or rather it had to carry out a profound conversion to turn large sections of the Francoist system into suitable components of democracy. As we shall see later many UCD leaders are survivors from the previous regime. They are the same politicians acting differently. Behind them one can easily detect the interests of the dominant classes at work. Having realised that the protective umbrella of Francoism had ceased to provide suitable cover they did not hesitate to transfer their allegiance and their financial support to the new parties, *Alianza Popular* first, and then *Unión de Centro Democrático*. Even the Catholic Church, which after the Second Vatican Council had moved away from the Franco regime and supposedly towards neutrality, was to offer some degree of sympathy and even moral support to UCD. In fact, of the three mainstays of Francoism—financial/industrial power, the Church and the armed forces—only the latter can be said not to have been directly involved in the UCD venture. As an institution the armed forces saw themselves (and to a large extent they still do) as the protectors of continuity and stability. Their attitude in relation to UCD was aloof, guarded, and mistrustful. They accepted change and the new ruling party so long as neither went too far too soon. From the outside they played an important part in shaping the organisation and behaviour of UCD.

The combination of all these factors, some new, most of them old ones recycled, determined the structure and ideology of the party which has been running Spain's new democracy for the last five years. Before we go on to analyse the nature of this organisation it seems, however, appropriate to say something about the idea of the political centre which forms part of the name of the party, and which is supposed to be symbolically represented by the two semi-circles, one green, one orange, that make up the party's emblem.

The Political Centre

Moderation was possibly the salient feature of the process of transition from dictatorship to democracy in Spain. Both the main political protagonists and the electorate at large displayed a considerable amount of commonsense and self-restraint. The decision to bring about change by constitutional means and the constant threat of military intervention at the slightest sign of deviation or radicalism imposed perforce a careful and deliberate tempo. All political parties, except for those on the extreme Right and the extreme Left, showed centripetal tendencies from very early on. They were offering themselves to the electorate for the first time in forty years. Socialists and Communists had lived since the Civil War in exile or clandestinity, and many Spaniards only knew them, through Francoist propaganda, as the destroyers of peace and order and as the enemies of Spain. Furthermore the Spanish electorate had altered considerably since the last democratic elections in 1936. Little or nothing was known about their political preferences after four decades of enforced silence, but it was assumed that the socio-economic transformation of the country, that is new middle classes, a global drifting of the economically-active population away from agriculture and towards industry and services, greater general prosperity, etc., and the fear of the unknown consequences any radical change might produce would incline Spaniards' support towards the more moderate electoral offers from either Right or Left.

Confronted by such a situation the PSOE, Spanish Socialist Party, and the PCE, Spanish Communist Party, were quick to adapt, diluting, or even rejecting, some of the more radical tenets of their programmes. They both renounced their traditional republicanism in favour of a monarchy which, although a major part of Franco's heritage, was increasing in popularity day by day. The Communist Party, which had for some years shown considerable independence from Moscow, gave up Leninism and its mythical goal: the dictatorship of the proletariat. Instead it presented itself as a party adapted to the national needs, not just Eurocommunist, but Hispano-communist. As for the PSOE, a socialist party with a long-standing claim to revolutionary goals, it moved openly towards the centre, shedding its Marxist label along the way and presenting itself to the electorate with the image of a Social-Democratic party.

If anything, these centripetal proclivities are even more apparent on the Right. Many politicians who had served the Franco regime during its later years would eventually find a means of survival by moving towards the centre of the political arena. Although the centrist banner finally fell into the hands of UCD, Fraga Iribarne was the first to realise that the way ahead for ex-Francoists lay in the Centre. Fraga Iribarne had been Minister of Information and Tourism from 1962 to 1969. In this latter year he fell from office in the aftermath of a gigantic financial scandal, the *Matesa* affair. From that moment on he started to distance himself from the regime he had served for so long, seeking to bury the memory of his past with a new image, that of a moderate and competent leader with the right blend of experience and democratic promise. He became Spanish ambassador in London and from there he published a number of books, far removed from his previous Francoist eulogies, offering solutions (and himself) for the future. He wrote 'the centre is the only way ahead for Spain'[7] because 'the centre is neither conservative nor revolutionary, but reformist. It does not reject the established order, nor does it accept it unconditionally; the man in the centre wishes to transform that order selectively— that is, certain sectors of it—and progressively—that is, step by step and without violence'.[8]

Back in Madrid Fraga Iribarne became one of the key figures in King Juan Carlos' first government, under the premiership of Arias Navarro. The failure of this government and of its limited reforms is well known.[9] The collapse of the government put an end to Fraga Iribarne's centrist aspirations. Together with his small party, *Reforma Democrática* he gave up his claim to the Centre. He moved towards a more conservative position, more in accordance with his beliefs and his temperament. Eventually in the autumn of 1976, he entered a coalition, *Alianza Popular*, with a number of small right-wing groups headed by others who, like him, had been Franco's ministers.

The appointment of Adolfo Suárez as President of the government to replace the dismissed Arias Navarro, in July 1976, came as a great disappointment to all those who were hoping for real change. It was seen as a grave error, or else, as an interim solution. However, Suárez' flexibility, his skill in manipulating the old system, and his undoubted conviction that change had become inevitable were to produce startling results. Once the Spanish people gave their approval to his project for reform in the referendum held in December 1976, Suárez ceased to be the political convert, who had made his career in the more reactionary institutions of the Franco regime, to become the man of the future. From his powerful position as head of the executive, and riding on the wave of democratic prestige provided by his bold reform programme, he decided to take over the centre position vacated by Fraga Iribarne. In order to do this he required around him an organisation, a party encompassing some other small groups and figures, with less of a Francoist past, which would allow him to put the final touches to his new centrist image. Thus UCD was born in the spring of 1977.

UCD is then, first and foremost, an organisation set up by those in power with the purpose of preserving that power. From the very beginning the launching of the new party relied heavily on the apparatus of the previous regime. The way in which political reform was carried out in Spain, i.e., slowly, from above, and with the legal mechanisms of Franco's Fundamental Laws, made it possible for Suárez and all those who gathered around him to benefit from it. The state-controlled press, radio, and, above all, television; the bureaucratic remnants of the single party; some important sectors of the civil service; all the complex network of local and provincial government, whose democratisation was delayed until the spring of 1979; and many other public bodies such as the Spanish Institute of Public Opinion, which provided valuable information about possible electoral behaviour, etc.; they were all skilfully used to help the new party on its way. A quick glance at the electoral campaign of 1977 should provide sufficient evidence to support this assertion.[10]

Secondly, UCD, although born as a coalition, had in Suárez its main axis. Without him, without his initial successes, without his popular and populist image UCD would have been something very different, or not existed at all. During the early period in the life of the party Suárez might very well have thought *'L'UCD, c'est moi'*. He, as head of government, together with the King had monopolised all the credit for the success of democratic reform. As public opinion showed at the time Suárez had become an invaluable electoral asset.

But at the same time it was equally clear that Suárez and his ministers could not by themselves set up a sufficiently powerful and convincing party to occupy the whole of the centre and displace Alianza Popular more towards the Right. During the months that preceded the formation of UCD, Alianza Popular was considered as the party of the 'establishment', the conservative alternative to the socialist option offered by the PSOE. So in order to insert himself between AP and PSOE Suárez conceived the idea of attracting to his side all the small groups which were emerging in the Centre, without as yet any definite identity. Individually none of them had sufficient weight to entertain any serious hope of electoral success, but put together they offered Suárez a handful of valuable names, the basis of future party cadres, a certain amount of experience, and, above all, a centrist image, which both Suárez and his ministers lacked. For their part, these budding parties, aware of their own weakness,[11] saw in Suárez' offer the opportunity to prosper, sharing in the prestige the President of the government enjoyed, and gaining access to the vast machinery of the state. This convergence of interests was to provide the necessary impetus to set up a new party.

It was Leopoldo Calvo Sotelo who was entrusted with the task of negotiating the necessary agreements. The Democratic Centre, a coalition which had brought together a number of these small parties at the beginning of 1977, was enlarged to form UCD. There is no need, for our purpose here, to explain the complex bargaining that took place.[12] It will suffice to outline the main ideological tendencies included in the new electoral coalition. For that is what it was intended as originally. All the electoral propaganda distributed by UCD during the 1977 electoral campaign referred to itself as an electoral coalition in which the main groups represented were those set out below.

The first and perhaps the most important part of the coalition were the Christian Democrats, many of them members of the group identified by the pseudonym 'Tacitus', mentioned earlier. They were closely linked to the

Catholic Church through their managerial or journalistic activities in the Catholic daily *Ya*, or in the publishing house Editorial Católica which, as the name suggests, is under Church control too. Some of them belonged, or had belonged in the past, to the Asociación Católica Nacional de Propagandistas, an exclusive coterie or club—very influential during the Franco years—whose founder, a Jesuit priest, had intended as a breeding ground for Catholic leaders. They represented for the most part the more conservative wing of Spanish Christian Democrats, although their ideological spread was soon to be broadened with the addition of new recruits when the more progressive wing, led by Ruiz-Giménez and Gil Robles, split up over the question of whether or not to join the new coalition. Quite a few of them eventually did.

There was then a liberal faction which gave UCD quite an attractive gloss. Just the word 'liberal', with its progressive connotations, was an asset in a post-dictatorial context, and the liberal leader, Joaquín Garrigues Walker, possessed undoubted charm and public appeal. But their impact had to be small because they lacked the weight of numbers or the influence of members with long-standing reputations. Only a few such as Joaquín Satrústegui, a liberal monarchist well-known for his opposition to Franco, had been heard of before. It could almost be said that the liberals were Joaquín Garrigues Walker and a few friends. When he died of leukaemia in July 1980 the liberals practically disappeared from UCD. The efforts that his brother, Antonio Garrigues Walker, with an approach to politics reminiscent of that of the Kennedy clan in the United States, is making to revive the liberal cause outside the framework of UCD corroborates this interpretation.

Thirdly there was a group that entered the coalition under the Social Democratic banner, a self-attributed position which lends itself to misinterpretation when comparisons are made to their homonyms in other European countries. If any group can claim this label in Spain, it is the PSOE, whose leadership and programme are clearly in the social democratic line. The so-called social democrats in UCD were, the same as the liberals, rather small in numbers, though their impact was considerably greater. Led by Francisco Fernández Ordóñez they were to be the main force behind some of the more advanced policies of UCD, such as fiscal reform or the legalisation of divorce. However, they would never feel entirely comfortable in the coalition, and a group of them, including their leader, finally left UCD during 1981 to set up a separate party under the initials PAD (Partido de Acción Democrática).

Lastly the group that, for lack of a more precise name, were referred to as independents, amongst whom, as the electoral pamphlets of 1977 put it, don Adolfo Suárez could be counted. This sector of the coalition was a ragbag of unclassifiable politicians. Next to President Suárez there was a residual assortment of more or less well-known figures including Martín Villa, Pío Cabanillas, Ricardo de la Cierva, Sancho Rof, Sánchez Terán, etc. who were masking their services to the previous regime under the independent label. Their ideological stance was rather ambiguous. They did not claim to share any specific set of principles. All they had in common was a certain populist attitude and a pragmatic acceptance of the inexorability of democratic change. Of course, their contribution to the UCD cause should not be measured in ideological terms, but rather in relation to their knowledge, experience and control of the machinery of government at both provincial and central level. Suárez himself, who had previously been a provincial governor, head of Spanish television and General Secretary of the National Movement, could be taken as the prototype in this group.

What Kind of Party?

As indicated earlier UCD was born as a loosely-knit coalition of minor groups and factions, to become, after the June 1977 general election, a unified organisation with some of the features of a mass party. Its history, though short, has been rather eventful. The coalition was hurriedly patched up at the beginning of May 1977, but the electoral success which followed soon created the need for a more unified structure in order to achieve greater co-ordination in governmental and parliamentary activities. In August of that same year UCD was entered in the special register of the Ministry of the Interior as an official party. In October it appointed its first executive committee, and a month later it published a document outlining its ideology. Finally, in December 1977 all the various groups within the coalition were dissolved and UCD officially became a single, united party. The time lapse was relatively short, some eight months, but the battle to achieve unity had hardly started. The structure and institutions of the new party were far from stable. The process of unification had been more apparent than real as the permanent dissension between ideological groups, between leaders, and between various party bodies were to show.

Both the small groups which initially formed the coalition and UCD itself after it became a single organisation can quite appropriately be termed cadre parties. It is not difficult to detect in them the features with which Duverger describes this type of party.[13] When Duverger writes:

The grouping of notabilities for the preparation of elections, conducting campaigns and maintaining contacts with the candidates. Influential persons, in the first place, whose name, prestige, and connections can provide a backing for the candidate and secure him votes; experts, in the second place, who know how to handle the electors and how to organise a campaign; last of all, financiers, who can bring the sinews of war. Quality is the most important factor: extent of prestige, skill in technique, size of fortune.[14]

His words are a befitting description of UCD. Undoubtedly the requirements of co-ordinated action on a national scale, and the demands of running broad electoral campaigns, both in the country as a whole and in the autonomous regions, altered somewhat the nature of UCD; it acquired some of the organisational traits of a mass party, but without ever losing what might be called its original or 'natural' proclivities towards elitism, quality selection, or its reliance upon caucuses of notables.

In accordance with its statutes, the party comprises an extensive and complex network of institutional bodies from the National Congress at the top to the provincial and local committees at its base. The Party Congress meets every two years. Two have been held so far, one in October 1978, and the other in February 1981. But all this, though essential to the running of a party, falls into the category of organisation or structural formalities, for UCD offers an ideal example of Michels' iron law of oligarchy in operation. Hardly surprising when one considers the way in which the party was devised and assembled from the highest echelons of power.

In UCD we have an organisation in which personalities are above institutions, the government controls the parliamentary party, and this, in turn, prevails over the non-parliamentary section of the party. These are tendencies present in most, some would say all, major parties; what is striking in UCD's case is the intensity of such hierarchical predominance. UCD is not so much a highly centralised party, as a party with a large head and somewhat stunted body. Having been created at the initiative of the government, and depending as it did on the aura which surrounded Suárez as the man who had made democracy possible, it was bound to become a presidential party. The holding of both the post of Prime Minister and that of Party President by the same person immediately established an all-powerful leadership, which, while in Suárez' hands, was further reinforced by the prestige he enjoyed. From that position, during the period he was in office (from 1976 to 1981) Suárez tried, not without success, to turn the party into the mainstay of his leadership, flooding the party's electoral lists and institutions with his own men. During those years he ran the party in a rather high-handed and personalistic manner, and with considerable disregard for its various committees and bodies. His attitude is succintly expressed by the title of a recent work on the subject: *UCD: La empresa que creó Adolfo Suárez* (*UCD: The Business Enterprise Created By Adolfo Suárez*).[15]

Paradoxically his might was to be the cause of his downfall. The surprising resignation of Suárez from office, as president of the government first, and later as party president (both occurring at the beginning of 1981) can, to a large extent, be attributed to the desire of the other groups and group leaders in UCD, particularly the Christian Democrats and Liberals, to curtail presidential power and have a greater say in running the affairs of the party and, in the final instance, of the government. The leadership crisis monopolised the attention of the delegates who attended the Second National Congress of the party in Majorca (6–9 February 1981) thus highlighting the internal contradictions of UCD. The coalition, as has been repeatedly said, was kept together by Suárez' transitory charisma, but once this charisma started to fade away his authority became weaker and weaker under the pressure of increasing demands for internal democratisation in the running of the party. On the other hand, and herein lay the contradiction, it was difficult to see how such an amalgam of divergent forces could be kept together without a very strong leadership. Suárez' response was to absorb the pressure by incorporating into his government some of the leaders (the figures who became known as the party barons) of the more vociferous and stronger factions. He only succeeded in postponing his downfall. After his resignation the party's second congress decided to abandon the presidential system. The posts of parliamentary leader and party leader were separated. The former was given to Leopoldo Calvo Sotelo, a compromise candidate whose past connected him with more than one of the UCD 'families'. But the new Chairman and the new General Secretary of the party were two men still very closely connected with Suárez, Rodríguez Sahagún and Calvo Ortega respectively.

It was no more than a temporary arrangement. Basic incompatabilities continued to upset the stability of the party. The main dissident voices within it (Christian Democrats and Liberals for the most part) had weakened the leadership without substantially increasing their own share in power. Suárez had fallen, but many of his men were still controlling key posts in the machinery of the party at all levels. Internal divisions had not disappeared, nor even been reduced, and Calvo Sotelo, with fewer powers and a less favourable political climate (UCD had by then ceased to enjoy the reputation of being the '*partido de la democratización*') was going to find holding the party together increasingly difficult. Some members disaffected from the Right to join the ranks of the Alianza Popular;[16] an even larger group abandoned UCD on the Left to set up an independent party under the leadership of Fernández Ordóñez, ex-minister of finance and ex-minister of justice, in November 1981. In the end Calvo Sotelo, after several government reshuffles, had to return to the presidential system. In November he forced the resignation of the party chairman, Rodríguez Sahagún, and became party leader himself. Suárez' influence was reduced even further when the General Secretary was replaced by Iñigo Cavero, a Christian Democrat, closer to Calvo Sotelo than his predecessor. But none of these changes would suffice to overcome internal dissension. The inherent contradictions of UCD did not disappear and the arguments between those in favour of a strong leadership and those favouring a more flexible structure and a wider distribution of power continue to this day.[17]

The caucuses, coteries or cliques we have been discussing constitute the essential ingredients of a cadre party or party of notables (either name seems appropriate) such as UCD, but the framework of the organisation has been growing in size and complexity, its electoral machinery has acquired vital significance, and its membership has extended, thus taking on some of the features of the mass parties. The question of membership is always a thorny one, made even more intractable by the unwillingness of parties to release verifiable information. Party allegiance can vary from rather passive electoral support to active militancy through participation in committee work and regular payment of membership fees. Electoral support is discussed elsewhere in this book.[18] As regards affiliation, UCD has obviously established in its statutes the formal requirements to become a member, but very little is known about the size or quality of its membership.

In general it can be said that the apparent political enthusiasm generated by Franco's demise and the subsequent process of democratisation has not been reflected in high levels of electoral participation or party militancy. All parties, of both Right and Left, have been reluctant to provide convincing evidence of their membership; their reluctance serving to mask an understandable tendency to blow up the figures. UCD has been no exception to this and the figures which follow must be interpreted in the light of it.

UCD is obviously a national party, with some 3,000 branches distributed throughout the country, and putting up candidates in all national, regional and local elections. The number of members appears to have been increasing slowly but steadily, although figures will vary widely from one source to another. In November 1977 the official news agency Cifra claimed 14,000 members for UCD.[19] At the time of its first congress, in October 1978, membership had jumped up to 80,000 according to another source.[20] A very slight increase occurred between this date and the general elections of March 1979, the figure going up by some 5,000 members.[21] And it appears that in spite of the serious crisis the party has been undergoing since then, membership continues to go up at an increasing rate. In March 1982 an official spokesman from the party's headquarters in Madrid claimed that 'UCD militancy exceeds 140,000 members, including in this figure the centrists of Catalonia'.[22]

All these figures can only be taken as indicative. Furthermore, they do not show the important differences which separate sympathisers, supporters, party members and militants. Even in their possibly inflated form they would not fare particularly well in any historical or international comparison. They corroborate the image of a cadre party, in which the membership plays a very limited role. This assessment is confirmed by the type of electorate that lends its support to UCD; made up to a large extent of older people, housewives and the more conservative sectors of the rural population, all of them social groups with a rather passive attitude to politics, and with very low levels of involvement in party affairs.[23]

A Sociological Profile of UCD Leadership

Having considered the party as a whole, let us now have a closer look at its leaders, the few dozen politicians who have sat in the Spanish cabinet since 1976. What kind of impression would one receive by reading an imaginary 'Who's Who of UCD'? To limit the answer to include only those members who held a ministerial portfolio since the formation of Suárez' first government in July 1976 simplifies the operation and it is methodologically acceptable, in view of the fact that UCD has been the party in government since its very beginning. It can be confidently assumed that the most important figures of UCD, at some time or other, were members of the government, and therefore, the sample will be sufficiently wide and representative to have general validity.

From July 1976 to December 1981 there were eight ministerial reshuffles in Spain, five under Adolfo Suárez and the other three under Calvo Sotelo. These eight different governments produced a total of sixty-four ministers. The figures are quite high considering that they only represent a period of five and a half years in government. They indicate a high degree of instability, partly explained by the inevitable fluctuations of a period of political transition, and partly too by the internecine tensions and struggles in the party discussed in previous sections.

Looking at the biographies of the sixty-four ministers as a whole, a kind of identikit picture of the typical UCD leader is clearly discernible.[24] It would be, more or less, like this: 'a male, born in Madrid, about forty-five years of age, Catholic, married with four children, a graduate in law, member of one of the elite corps in the civil service, and, last but not least, with political, and/or administrative, and/or managerial links with the Franco regime.'

᾿ Male predominance is no more than a repetition of what happens in all other sectors of Spanish society. Franco never had any female ministers. Of the sixty-four ministers under consideration only one is a woman, Soledad Becerril, and even her presence in one of the least politically relevant posts, the ministry of culture, can only be taken as a token gesture, for the presence and influence of women in UCD is minimal. In this they do not differ greatly from other parties. Taking the Cortes (as the Spanish parliament is called) as a whole, the number of women deputies and senators in both 1977 and 1979 parliaments did not exceed 4 per cent of the total.

Castile continues to be the political cradle of Spain. No fewer than thirty out of the sixty-four ministers, that is, 48 per cent were born in one of the Castilian provinces. Madrid, of course, was the birth place of the majority of this group, twenty-three to be exact; or, to put it another way, Madrid, with little more than 10 per cent of the Spanish population, produced 36 per cent of its ministers. By comparison, Barcelona, the second most important city in the country, only produced three of them. This pattern is simply a continuation of tendencies already prevalent under the previous regime and even before. In line with it too is the relatively high presence of Galician ministers, eight out of sixty-four. On the other hand, the number of Basques, quite considerable in Franco's governments, drops noticeably, two out of sixty-four. The serious problems affecting the Basque Country, and the pull of regional parties and of the autonomy issue (an argument applicable to Catalonia too) may account for this change.

As regards the more personal data, i.e. marital status, declared Catholicism, high number of children, some rather interesting deductions could be made from them. However, it will suffice to point out the high incidence of endogamy linking UCD's oligarchy with the previous regime. About 14 per cent of the politicians we are considering married daughters of important Francoist figures, mainly ministers. These endogamic connections extend to other levels of the party too.[25] More politically relevant still is the average age of the group. Forty-five (this calculation excludes the military ministers, all of them over sixty) is young in politics; a younger elite than Franco's. Most of the UCD leaders belong to what has become known as King Juan Carlos' generation (the King was born in 1938) and this means that the majority do not have personal experience or memories of that most tragic and divisive event in recent Spanish political history: the Civil War of 1936–39.

Their academic profile and professional record is very similar, in fact almost identical, to the one offered by the later generations of leaders in the previous regime. In this area there is no detectable break in continuity.[26] Following an old established legal approach to politics in Spain, 61 per cent of the group we are considering hold a law degree.[27] All sixty-four are university graduates, several holding more than one degree. No other academic qualification apart from law, not even political science, appears to be suitable to achieve success in public life. The outstanding feature of their profession outside politics is the high number who belong to one of the elite corps of the civil service or to some of the more exclusive of the liberal professions, in either case access can only be gained by means of competitive examinations known in Spanish as *oposiciones*. A brilliant academic record, and the corporate support and *esprit de corps* prevalent at the highest levels of the civil service have possibly been more important as a means of access to UCD's oligarchy than ideological identification with any of the groups in the coalition. It would be no exaggeration to say that UCD became the political organisation of the state bureaucracy, for, as we have said, most of its leaders have been recruited from the ranks of that bureaucracy. Among the sixty-four ministers, to give but a few numerical examples, eighteen are university professors (the privileged position and power of Spanish *catedráticos* are far above those of their British counterparts; the way in which Spanish professors have so far succeeded in stifling university reform bears witness to that power), five belong to the diplomatic corps, seven are state lawyers, seven are notaries, etc.

Finally, let us look at the political and administrative connections between the UCD elite and the Franco regime. They are considerable, even though nowadays most public figures in Spain try to play down their participation in the institutions of the previous regime, and those who do admit them tend to present their behaviour in as favourable a light as possible, adducing that the results did not coincide with their intentions at the time. The problem we have is similar to the one encountered by experts in the field of religious sociology to establish the differences between religious practice and true faith. For our purpose here we shall apply a purely mechanist formula, assuming that anyone who served Francoism in a post of authority identified with the system to some extent. There are three main ways in which these connections can be seen to exist: by the percentage of UCD leaders who sat in Franco's parliaments, by their acceptance of political appointments, and by the number of posts they held in state-owned or state-controlled firms. From all three angles the results indicate a considerable degree of continuity between Francoism and UCD.

The transfer of deputies from Franco's 'organic' Cortes to the new democratic parliament, and the many features shared by the two institutions have been highlighted in a recent study emanating from the University of Madrid.[28] Some 20 per cent of the parliamentarians elected in June 1977 had held political office with Franco. Needless to say, practically all of them are now members of either UCD or AP. It is worth mentioning too that the predominant characteristics amongst the 1977 deputies and senators coincide in general terms with the ones attributed earlier in this section to UCD's leaders. Turning our attention back to this group we see that out of the sixty-four ministers, nineteen held a seat in parliament during the Francoist period. This represents 30 per cent which is an even greater level of overlap between the Francoist parliament and the UCD's leadership than the one which has been detected between the two parliaments.

A second indicator of continuity is provided by the number of political appointments enjoyed by UCD ministers during the Franco period. To assess the connection in this area we have considered not just governmental appointments, but selection for political office at lower levels, such as heads of ministerial departments or provincial governors. The relationship thus established is much more intense than the previous one. Thirty-one out of sixty-four, or 48 per cent, were Franco's political appointees. The percentage goes up even further when the third link is taken into account. During the Franco years the highest posts in state-controlled enterprises and public monopolies served as a launching platform for future political careers, or as sinecures to reward services rendered to the regime. Many a minister, before joining the government or after leaving it, had a period as chairman or deputy chairman with firms such as RENFE, CAMPSA, Iberia, Tabacalera, INI, etc. These appointments had an obvious political significance, and in some ways they still do today. The number of UCD leaders who can be connected in this way with the Franco regime reaches the ratio of thirty/sixty-four, that is, 45 per cent of the whole group. Furthermore, in many instances the connections occur through more than one channel. Leaving aside the seven military ministers, who after all cannot be strictly speaking considered as members of UCD, only seventeen can be said not to have any links with the previous period.

Obviously, all the figures quoted above have a purely indicative nature, but they are sufficiently clear to show a startling degree of continuity in the ruling group, in spite of the change from dictatorship to democracy. Of course, there are detectable differences too. There has been a generational transfer, and the political attitudes have changed because the environment in which power is being exercised is not as it was with Franco. The very powerful figure of the minister, answerable only to Franco, supported by servile institutions and leading an alienated people, has given way to a very different type of politician, who has to face the challenge of opposition and submit to regular electoral judgement by the voters. In these new circumstances political behaviour had to alter, as had the ideological image from the moment that official dogma was no longer acceptable.

The Ideology of UCD

As a general rule, party ideologies, even when a party has long been established, are systems of ideas comprising a multiplicity of principles and aspirations whose real nature cannot be ascertained easily due to their often vague and incomplete definition. UCD's ideology certainly falls into this category; it could be taken as its prototype. In view of what has been said so far this was to be expected. UCD is not, as yet, a consolidated party. It is still undergoing a process of internal and external clarification, trying to develop an efficient and stable organisation while searching at the same time for its real ideological bearings in the political spectrum.

What one sees when looking at UCD's ideology is a considerable lack of definition or (and this amounts to the same thing) a confused amalgam of overlapping principles. The variety of ideological contributions by the various factions brought together by the initial coalition created a doctrinal combination, within one single programme, of principles which were not always compatible, and which in other western countries are to be found in opposing parties.[29] Ideological ambiguity was reinforced by the moderation and centripetal tendencies prevalent during the post-Franco years. This phenomenon tends to appear in any liberal democracy, as a result of parties trying to gain the middle ground, as Blondel and others have pointed out.[30] In the Spanish case this general drift towards the ideological centre was accelerated because the Centre, as has been repeatedly said, offered many politicians a way of overcoming their Francoist legacy, and because, in any case, UCD had to find some kind of ideological balance between various groups with centrist proclivities. The object was apparently to find the centre of the centre. Finally, the anomalous political conditions of the years during which UCD was established and developed favoured ideological ambiguity too. Parties were not so much expected to offer well-designed ideologies or specific programmes as to proclaim their general commitment or opposition to change away from Francoism and towards democracy.

A case can be made in favour of this lack of ideological definition, either because it is considered as something positive in itself or else on account of the fact that it is a feature common to most parties. Take this example from a study of the Spanish party system:

> What we have to ask ourselves is whether, in view of the present day problems in our society, ideological clarity is really necessary, and whether to run a country, either from the Right or the Left, things such as an efficient government programme, a leadership which inspires confidence, and the capacity to bring conflicting sides together are not much more important.[31]

A similar view in a wider context is expressed by Blondel when he writes:

> Ideologies are in fact as vague, and therefore as useless for the purpose of detailed policies, as the general goals which we all feel should be the basis of a 'good' party programme. In fact, ideology is merely another work for these goals and principles.[32]

But even the acceptance of this viewpoint (and one should be aware of its technocratic implications) does not help us a great deal to clarify what kind of doctrine or philosophy serves, in the final instance, as the basis or justification of UCD. Its electoral manifestos, such as they are, its governmental programmes, its concrete policies suffer from the same lack of clarity as its ideology. They veer haphazardly, sometimes to the Right, other times to the Left, in an attempt to follow an imaginary Centre line. Of course this centrist ambiguity may be necessary to hold the coalition together and, therefore, it could be intentional. When UCD proclaims its own ideology it does so with a set of principles which are no more than open-ended generalities. Official publications tell us that personalism, democracy, freedom, humanism, and equality are the ideological bases of the party, and that the party is democratic and progressive, an all-class organisation, that it defends security, social efficiency, and the quality of life, and that it is pro-European and is in favour of international solidarity.[33] Such a broad ideological umbrella could practically provide cover for any political party in the western world, save for those rooted in Marxist theory. The quotation which follows, taken from the same UCD publication, exemplifies even further this self-assumed vagueness: 'Finally, UCD believes that we live in a society in which the most realistic and pragmatic attitude is . . . a large dose of idealism.'[34]

However, in spite of all these obstacles, a wider view of UCD's goals, principles and interests should allow us to discern some of its ideological features. Possibly the most important ideological contribution is that of the Christian Democrats. It must be remembered that it is the more conservative sector of Christian Democracy. Some of their ideas appear rather outmoded based as they are on papal encyclicals and on the social doctrine of the Catholic Church. Their influence can be seen in the careful preservation of ecclesiastical privileges (privileges which have been reduced but are still considerable) in the protection of the traditional family; in the defence of private education, which in Spain largely means education provided by religious orders; and, in general, in a somewhat paternalistic attitude in matters relating to trade unions, labour relations, and other aspects of social policy.

Secondly, a kind of liberal humanism can be detected. This is what UCD publications call 'personalism', a term used in preference to others like individualism, from which a certain lack of solidarity might be inferred. In practice this means a greater emphasis on individual rights than on group rights. And to counter any possible accusation from the Left that such an attitude will inevitably amount to protecting the interests of those in the dominant and privileged groups UCD claims to be 'an all-class party, at the service of all the different peoples of Spain and of all the social, generational and human groups which are part of them.'[35] The language will have Francoist echoes for anybody familiar with the rhetoric of the previous regime.

Thirdly, UCD accepts and defends the general principles of a capitalist society. As UCD sees it freedom, in its widest sense, is only possible within a framework based on private initiative and the market economy. The state's role is purely subsidiary: to support and encourage the free forces of the market, to correct any overt abuses, and to operate compensatory mechanisms in cases of extreme inequality; but always keeping that intervention to the lowest possible level for, in the mixed economy, the private sector should take precedence over the public sector.

Up to here the general ideological principles outlined, except perhaps for those originating in the Christian Democratic sector of UCD, are common to most conservative parties in other countries. What is different is the context. Spain was moving from dictatorship to democracy and the party spearheading the change had to offer more advanced ideas and goals. These were provided by the Social Democrats and by those, who, like Adolfo Suárez himself, had brought with them into the party a kind of 'falangist populism', which combined a style reminiscent of the previous regime with a desire to show that their promises of change were genuine. At their behest, during its first few years in office, UCD shaped and implemented its most progressive policies: a new constitution, the long awaited reform of the tax system, or the setting in motion of the process of political and administrative decentralisation, to mention but a few.

The boundaries of the ideological space a party occupies are not just an internal matter. Those boundaries are drawn in relation to other sets of ideological principles external to the party itself, belonging to other parties. As important as what the ideology is, is what the ideology is not. Parties are always careful to show in which way they differ from their competitors. It is in this negative respect that the more right-wing pro-clivities of UCD become evident, especially after the formal completion of the process of democratisation, the replacement of Adolfo Suárez by Calvo Sotelo, and the subsequent desertion from the party of an impor-tant group of social democrats. Of late, little effort has been made by UCD leaders to raise any clear ideological barriers to separate themselves from Alianza Popular or from the regional conservative parties in Catalonia and the Basque Country, even though they have been competing with and losing to them in the more recent electoral contests. In that direction ideological continuity is more or less accepted. The deep ideological cleavage lies to the other side in relation to the PSOE and the PCE. In spite of the consensus politics of the late seventies which made democratic reform possible (transitory agreements and co-operation between UCD, PSOE, and PCE were not uncommon during this period) the fact is that UCD sees itself as something totally different from socialists or com-munists. UCD's ideological ambiguities are dispelled when the party looks to the Left. And although our arguments lead to a conclusion not dis-similar from García San Miguel's when he writes that 'the ideological physiognomy of UCD is so disconcerting and in a way so original as to make it rather problematic to classify',[36] some of these difficulties dis-appear when one considers what is outside the ideological space occupied by UCD. From that vantage point UCD falls clearly within what Fraga Iribarne calls '*la gran derecha*'.[37]

UCD, the Party System and the Future

The Spanish democratic system is still being run in. The new experience is not of sufficient length to discern established patterns of electoral or institutional behaviour. The people, under their new parliamentary monarchy and liberal democratic constitution, have been consulted in several referenda, and have had the chance to vote in two general elections (the third one appears now imminent), one local election, and four regional elections in Catalonia, the Basque Country, Galicia and Andalusia. And yet indulging in predictions would be foolhardy. Many of the democratic changes announced in the constitution await implementation and development. The party system is far from consolidated; an understandable state of affairs considering the relatively limited electoral experience and the fact that the electoral rules, so influential in the formation of the party system, which have been used until now are only provisional.

What can be said of the emerging party system is that it is a system of enormous complexity. National parties, by which one means the parties which operate electorally over the whole country, overlap with regional parties; democratic parties stand side by side with parties from both Right and Left opposed to the democratic system; the ruling party appears to be on the verge of collapse; the whole party system harbours a number of sub-systems as a result of the divergent electoral results in the autonomous regions. Linz, making use of the classification developed by Sartori, sees in the Spanish case a polarised multi-party system in which bipolar oppositions are in operation.[38] In relation to UCD this means that it has to face opposition both from the Left, from the PSOE and the PCE, and from the Right, from AP, not to mention the resistance offered by the small but influential presence of Catalan and Basque parties. In a more recent study Linz develops his theory further and continues to see UCD as a centre party within a polarised multi-party system, supporting his view with the following arguments:

(a) UCD's tendency to offer a synthesis of different ideological traditions;
(b) the central position of its voters in a Right–Left scale;
(c) the bipolar opposition mentioned above;
(d) the possibility of forming coalitions in either direction; to the right with AP, and to the left with PSOE;
(e) conversely, coalitions without UCD are extremely difficult;
(f) the moderating role of UCD makes political polarisation less likely.[39]

The line of our argument throughout this chapter questions the validity of the above assumptions. Some are inaccurate, for example, there is no ideological synthesis in UCD, only an overlapping of ill-defined goals and principles; others, like the ones referring to possible coalitions, suffer from a certain degree of functionalism and wishful thinking; above all, their major weakness is their transient nature. Party systems tend with time to become polarised. Duverger goes as far as saying that 'the centre does not exist in politics: there may well be a centre party but there is no centre tendency, no centre doctrine'.[40] Even without accepting Duverger's viewpoint in its entirety it can be argued that the Centre in politics is more positional than ideological, that it is transitory and circumstantial rather than permanent or deep-rooted. In the case of UCD this amounts to saying that UCD is not so much a centre party as a party which found itself in the centre of the political spectrum by the coincidental combination of exceptional historical circumstances. The initial pact to set up UCD, the development of its structures, its ideology, its behaviour as a party, the line it has followed in government can only be interpreted as centrist in relation to the process of democratic reform undergone by Spain. Now that the process has been completed, at least in its most formalistic aspects, the idea of UCD as a centre party has been largely devalued. Even its claims to party status are open to question. In the internal turmoil of the last few months the Prime Minister, Calvo Sotelo was forced to recognise that the crisis affecting UCD might be due to the fact 'that the coalition has never really become a single party'.[41] After the 1979 general election, and particularly after the resignation of Suárez as both Prime Minister and leader of the party, UCD started to show its true nature as an amalgam of new conservative forces and remnants of the previous regime. Its lack of internal coherence and its drift to the Right were therefore to be expected. In fact, the political clarification this change is bringing about can only be positive. There is no need to think that the polarisation of the party system towards two great blocks, each with one or two major parties, with perhaps some minor parties in between, will necessarily make democracy unworkable as some prophesy. The artificiality of UCD as a centre party cannot be sustained for long. The change required is not without risks, but that is the penalty to be paid for the way in which democratisation was carried out in Spain. In the words of a well-known Spanish journalist:

> The crisis of UCD is more than just the crisis of a political party. It is the crisis of the process of reform; it is the responsibility of a political class that was willing to dismantle—*ma non tropo*—the edifice of the old regime, but is now proving totally incapable of organising itself for democracy.[42]

Post-electoral Addendum

The results of the general elections held on 28 October 1982 have provided sufficient evidence to confirm (if confirmation was needed) the critical assessment and gloomy forecast made in the preceding pages about the short and eventful existence of UCD as a political party, and about its more than doubtful future. It is almost as if the party, having accomplished its task of providing the country with a democratic system, had suddenly become aware of its inadequacies to operate within that system. Even though the astonishing electoral results may require some careful analysis to single out and grade the most likely causes leading up to them, it would not be presumptuous to assume that the near total collapse of UCD was due primarily to its own internal contradictions and inherent limitations. As repeatedly argued in this chapter, UCD was a political coalition perfectly suited to the unique circumstances of the post-Franco years. It was remarkably successful at legitimising the complex process of constitutional reform and democratisation. Beyond that exceptional period UCD has been unable to organise itself as a stable parliamentary party or to run a reasonably efficient government as the ruling party. We might be witnessing the end of its existence: a transitory party in a transitional period.

There cannot have been many electoral reversals comparable to the one suffered by UCD in the October elections. Such a débacle is, in its own way, as unprecedented as the party's main success, the bizarre creation of a democracy with the remnants of the dictatorship. UCD had the majority in parliament, not an overall majority admittedly, but a working majority all the same; as the ruling party it was able to bring forward the date of the elections to suit its own interests; it had the support of important sectors of the mass media; it was able to run a very expensive electoral campaign,[43] and yet all these apparent advantages could not avert its total collapse at the polls. The bare figures offer a staggering picture. The 168 deputies and 119 senators of UCD elected in 1979 were reduced to thirteen and four respectively in 1982. Except for two ministers, Pío Cabanillas, Minister of Justice, and Luis Ortiz, Minister of Public Works, all the members of the government, Prime Minister Calvo Sotelo included, lost their seats. In 1979 UCD was the top party in thirty-nine out of fifty-two constituencies into which the country is divided, in 1982 it did not succeed in any of them. Its share of the vote decreased from 35 per cent to just over 7 per cent, and even though the turnout was considerably higher in the more recent elections UCD lost over 4.7 million votes, or to put it another way, some 75 per cent of the electoral support it had had in 1979 was, in 1982, transferred to other parties.

The above statistics speak for themselves. The electoral defeat of UCD predicted by the earliest public opinion polls eventually turned into a rout. The weeks of electoral campaigning only served to accentuate the decline. When UCD's electoral propaganda reminded the voters that 97 per cent of its founder members were still in the party it was implicitly recognizing the internal splits and continuous desertions. The departure in the summer of 1981 of Fernández Ordoñez and some other Social Democrats to set up a separate party that would end up entering an electoral coalition with the Socialists was to be followed by other important defections. A large part of the Christian Democrats, led by Oscar Alzaga, abandoned ship to form an independent party (PDP Popular Democratic Party) and support the cause of the more conservative Alianza Popular in the elections. Suárez himself was to apostatise. Unable to recover the control of UCD he decided to establish his own party (CDS Social and Democratic Centre) even though in ideological terms his electoral proposals to the voter were hardly distinguishable from those of the party he had renounced.

The appointment of the Christian Democrat, Landelino Lavilla as leader of UCD a few months before the elections took place did little, if anything, to stay the decline. He was given exceptional powers, forcing the Prime Minister, Calvo Sotelo, into a secondary position. The whole electoral campaign was mounted around the figure and words of Lavilla. He steadfastly refused to accept any kind of electoral alliance with Fraga's AP, even though the opinion polls, some sectors of his own party, and the CEOE (the Spanish equivalent of the Confederation of British Industry) were pushing him in that direction. He fought a losing battle. His centrist claims were in competition with those of the other parties which had broken away from the original UCD nucleus. And even worse, the centrist offer had lost its appeal for wide sections of the electorate.

Democracy is still a tender plant in Spain and it will remain so for some time to come. Many reforms are still required but power has to be exercised with great care. The situation is extremely fluid. It would be foolhardy to forecast events even in the short term. However, the signs do not augur well for UCD and other centrist parties. Their proliferation is indicative of their own weakness. The election held on 28 October altered the political map of Spain. For the first time in their long history the Socialists have an overall majority in parliament and with it the chance of forming a reformist government to bring about some of the changes that the successive UCD governments could not, or were unwilling to, implement. Opposing them is AP, which has become the main opposition party. With the electoral failure of the PCE to counterbalance, at least in part, that of UCD, the political map has taken on the appearance of a two party system, with, of course, more complex sub-systems in the Basque Country and Catalonia.

Whether this pattern will become stable is difficult to say. It will partly depend on the success of the Socialist policies, and partly too on the parliamentary behaviour of AP, a party whose adherence to democratic principles cannot yet be put beyond doubt. Nevertheless, AP has taken over from UCD as the main representative of bourgeois interest and this may prove a stabilising factor. As for UCD, it has become a party without a role. It has lost its *raison d'être*. Its moment has passed. An alliance with AP as requested, and even demanded, by some influential members may be the way out. Some have gone as far as to suggest abandoning the initials UCD.[44] Were this to happen and the party fizzle out quietly the most apt epitaph might well be 'UCD, the party that never was'.

Notes

1. For a fuller discussion of this question see J. Amodia, 'El asociacionismo político en España: aborto inevitable', *Iberian Studies*, 3 (1974), pp. 9–15.
2. J. J. Linz, 'Opposition in and under an Authoritarian Regime: The Case of Spain', in R. Dahl (ed.), *Regimes and Oppositions*, Yale University Press, New Haven, Conn., 1973, pp. 171–259.
3. A. de Miguel, *Sociología del franquismo*, Euros, Madrid, 1975, pp. 143–233.
4. On the subject of political associations see, for instance, J. Conte Barrera, *Las asociaciones políticas*, A.T.E., Barcelona, 1976, and Equipo de Estudios, *Lucha política por el poder*, E. Querejeta, Madrid, 1976.
5. On the subject of the *'cenas políticas'* see M. del Mazo *et al.*, *Los cenocentristas. Radiografía política de una cenas*, np, Bilbao, 1970.
6. These articles were later published in book form: *Tácito*, Ibérico Europea de Ediciones, Madrid, 1975.
7. 'Teoría del Centro' in *Legitimidad y representación*, Grijalbo, Madrid, 1975.
8. Ibid., pp. 240–1.
9. Amongst the many books on the subject R. Carr and J. P. Fusi offer a brief and balanced view of those months in *España, de la dictadura a la democracia*, Planeta, Barcelona, 1979, pp. 269–80.
10. On the 1977 elections see P. Ramírez, *Así se ganaron las elecciones*, Planeta, Barcelona, 1977, and F. González Ledesma *et al.*, *Las elecciones del cambio*, Plaza y Janés, Barcelona, 1977.
11. It is said that the late Joaquín Garrigues Walker, leader of one such liberal group, used to refer to them as 'taxi-parties' because all the members could travel in one taxi.
12. For a fairly detailed account see F. Jáuregui and M. Soriano, *La otra historia de UCD*, E. Escolar, Madrid, 1980, pp. 39–74, and E. Chamorro, *Viaje al centro de UCD*, Planeta, Barcelona, 1981, pp. 113–74.
13. M. Duverger, *Political Parties*, Methuen, London, 1950, pp. 62–71.
14. Ibid., p. 64.
15. J. Figuero, *UCD: La empresa que creó Adolfo Suárez. Historia, sociología y familias del suarismo*, Grijalbo, Barcelona, 1981.
16. Amongst them two of the best known names in the party: M. Herrero de Miñón, at one time parliamentary spokesman of UCD, and the Francoist historian and for a brief period UCD's minister of culture, R. de la Cierva.

17. At the time of writing this section Calvo Sotelo has just volunteered his resignation as Chairman of the party.
18. See Chapter 9.
19. F. Jáuregui and M. Soriano, op. cit., p. 85.
20. E. Chamorro, op. cit., p. 182.
21. Figure quoted in E. Espín, 'Las fuerzas políticas concurrentes', in J. de Esteban *et al., Las elecciones legislativas del 1 de marzo de 1979*, Centro de Investigaciones Sociológicas, Madrid, 1979, p. 80. The exact figure given by Espín is 85,621.
22. In a letter to the author dated 8 March 1982.
23. For an exhaustive analysis of UCD electoral support see J. J. Linz *et al., Informe sociológico sobre el cambio político en España, 1975-1981*, Euramérica, Madrid, 1981, pp. 463-502.
24. All the data which follow were taken from the ministerial profiles published in the Spanish press, and from the biographies of deputies and senators in Equipo de Documentación Política, *Radiografía de las nuevas Cortes*, Sedmay, Madrid, 1977. I have also made use of the sociological analysis of Suárez' UCD by J. Figuero, op. cit., pp. 105-202.
25. J. Figuero, op. cit., pp. 127-33.
26. For an academic/professional profile of Franco's ministers see A. de Miguel, *Sociología del franquismo*, Euros, Madrid, 1975, pp. 91-127; and, by the same author, *La herencia del franquismo*, Editorial Cambio 16, Madrid, 1976, pp. 61-80.
27. This partly explains the obsession with constitutional reforms, to the detriment of more specifically political changes, during these last few years in Spain.
28. M. Baena del Alcázar and J. M. García Madaria, 'Elite franquista y burocracia en las Cortes actuales', *Sistema*, **28** (January 1979), pp. 99-104.
29. To illustrate the point contrast, for instance, the publications of two important UCD figures: the Christian Democrat J. L. Alvarez, *España desde el Centro*, Espasa-Calpe, Madrid, 1978 and the social democrat F. Fernández Ordóñez, *La España necesaria*, Taurus, Madrid, 1980.
30. J. Blondel, *Political Parties*, Wildwood House, London, 1978, pp. 99-104.
31. J. J. Linz *et al., Informe sociológico sobre . . .*, p. 465.
32. J. Blondel, op. cit., p. 109.
33. From the official UCD pamphlet *Principios ideológicos y modelo de sociedad de UCD*, Madrid, 1980.
34. Ibid., p. 18.
35. Ibid., p. 7.
36. L. García San Miguel, 'Las ideologías políticas en la España actual', *Sistema*, **40** (January 1981), p. 65.
37. Fraga Iribarne, leader of *Alianza Popular*, has, as a result of the improved performance of his party in the regional elections in Galicia and Andalusia, been propounding the idea of a grand right-wing coalition which he likes to call 'la mayoría natural'.
38. J. J. Linz, 'The New Spanish Party System', in R. Rose (ed.), *Electoral Participation. A Comparative Analysis*, Sage Publications, London, 1980. pp. 101-89.
39. J. J. Linz *et al., Informe sociológico sobre . . .*, p. 468.
40. M. Duverger, op. cit., p. 215.
41. *El País*, 30 June 1982.
42. P. Altares, 'Kamikazes de la democracia', *El País*, 10 July 1982.
43. Given the limited accountability of parties in matters of electoral expenditure it is not possible to find reliable information. The Spanish press has consistently placed UCD's electoral budget at the top of the list. The figure most often quoted is 1.800 million pesetas. It has been calculated by some to be as high as

5.000 million (*El País*, 5 November 1982) although this latter figure must undoubtedly be taken as a highly inflated estimate.
44. Opinion expressed by some members during the first post-electoral meeting held
by the party executive. *El País*, 5 November 1982.

2   THE SPANISH SOCIALIST PARTY SINCE FRANCO: FROM CLANDESTINITY TO GOVERNMENT: 1976–82

ELIZABETH NASH

Introduction: A Socialist Election Victory

On 28 October 1982 the Spanish Socialist Workers' Party (PSOE) won a landslide election victory just seven years after the death of the dictator Franco in November 1975. The most noticeable feature of this election, the third since the fall of Francoism, was the spectacular collapse of the ruling Union of Centre Democrats, hitherto the strongest party. This was a defeat unprecedented for any ruling party in Europe since The Second World War. The sheer scale and conclusiveness of the Socialists' victory helps consolidate Spain's gradual and halting process of democratisation. They won 202 of the 350 seats in Congress, with 46 per cent of the vote. To all appearances the Socialists in a majority parliament with party general secretary Felipe González as Prime Minister are now well-placed to carry out the political programme on which they were elected.

They are not, however, home and dry: there was a dramatic upsurge of the right-wing conservative party Alianza Popular led by Manuel Fraga. This party which had thirteen seats before the election won 106 on 28 October making it by far the largest opposition party. Socialists and right-wing conservatives are now the two major parliamentary forces in Spain; between them they account for 306 seats. The remaining forty-two are shared among ten different parties.

The shattering defeat of the ruling UCD thus marks a new polarisation of political life in Spain, bringing to an end the period of consensus based on a pragmatic and ultimately ineffectual political alliance on the centre-right. Former Prime Minister Leopoldo Calvo Sotelo lost his seat. The Spanish people concluded that such a government was a recipe for stalemate and paralysis and decided to opt for one side or the other. Former UCD voters swung either to AP or PSOE. The PSOE won former UCD voters genuinely seeking moderate change. These included important gains among poor rural workers in traditionally conservative strongholds like Castille. Those turning away from the UCD to the AP were no doubt expressing more honestly their real political interests. The artificial and contradictory nature of the centrist alliance is now clear to see.

It would be tempting to conclude that Spain is moving towards a 'two-party model' of democracy where stability is guaranteed through the prospect of a peaceful alternation of clearly defined parties of government and opposition. But in Spain today the issues of political debate are not simply different policies within a framework of shared democratic values implied in the idealised 'Westminster model'. They involve fundamental questions about the role of the state, whether it is to be centralised or federal, and the role of the army and security forces in civilian life. Commitment to democratic institutions on the part of the conservatives can never be taken for granted, although it is possible that the increased strength of the Right within parliament may discourage activities of those outside it.

Military conspiracies and rumours of coups abounded throughout the election campaign, and although the threat of military intervention appears to have abated, it can never be entirely discounted whilst the structures of the army and security forces remain unreformed since the days of Franco.

Socialists benefited from the sharp decline of the Communist vote. The PCE won only five seats compared with the twenty-three they had before, and their vote declined by two-thirds from 10.8 per cent to less than 4 per cent. Their support collapsed in the industrial heartlands of Madrid and Catalonia. Serious internal crisis was largely responsible. The party faced the elections weakened by mistakes made by Santiago Carrillo's authoritarian leadership, expulsions, splits and bitter internal battles. The CP which emerged from Francoism as a political force of some significance based on its brave record of resistance and industrial militancy under conditions of dictatorship, has suffered an increasingly rapid decline of influence, as the fortunes of the PSOE have soared.

Since the PSOE emerged from the conditions of repression and illegality of the Franco period, its popularity has never been in doubt. In the first general election after the fall of Franco, in June 1977, the Party which three months earlier was illegal won 30 per cent of the popular vote. What was more doubtful at this stage was their ability to govern. Political inexperience, internal divisions, the continued unrest within the armed forces, and the need for the ruling UCD to have enough time to discredit itself totally were factors which led many socialists to hope privately that they would not win the next general elections called in 1979 and that the UCD government would complete its term of office.

A major factor contributing to the Socialists victory in 1982 was undoubtedly the disenchantment generated by the UCD. But there were important elements, deliberately fostered and developed by the party which enabled the Socialists to take advantage of that disenchantment, and effectively to replace the UCD as the only political force in Spain speaking for the people as a whole. These were first, that the PSOE could present itself as internally united with a capable, talented and homogeneous leadership, in contrast to the UCD and the PCE which were riven with discord. Secondly, its programme 'for change', 'for fresh air', promised continuous moderate progress, real but not revolutionary transformation. This responded to the desires of the Spanish people who wanted neither the paralysis of the Centre nor the return to the past of the far Right. The moderate content and deliberately low-key presentation of a programme of cautious change aroused hope without generating hostility or fear. It genuinely appealed to everyone, *(catch-all)*.

Finally, there are the undeniable personal qualities of Felipe González, General Secretary of the PSOE, now Prime Minister of Spain, who presents a leadership style unknown in Spain's political history. He is attractive in appearance and manner but is not upper class, does not come from Madrid; as a speaker he is fluent but not demagogic, he speaks to people in the form of a dialogue with equals, does not talk down to people or harangue or patronise them. He criticises in the content of what he says but never in harsh or sneering language. His political and personal past is clean, untainted with Francoism. He claims no great political feats of bravery or imprisonment under Francoism—a background and personal life with whom the ordinary Spaniard can readily identify. He gives the impression of being straight, honest and sensible, motivated by ethical considerations and ideals but pragmatic with his feet on the ground.

He has for several years now been the most popular and well-known politician in Spain, and there is no doubt that the socialists' electoral success owed much to the deliberate emphasis on the charismatic figure of Felipe as party leader and future Prime Minister. This exploitation of Felipe as an electoral asset has been present from the early days of democracy, and has been considerably helped by that other key figure in the PSOE, Alfonso Guerra, Deputy General Secretary, now deputy Prime Minister and close comrade of González for more than twenty years. Guerra is everything González is not: ruthless, arousing strong antipathies by his abrasive and contemptuous manner with opponents; 'the hatchet man', tirelessly concerned with the minutiae of day-to-day political organisation, unable to delegate, politically left-wing. He has readily taken on the unpleasant tasks behind the scenes, leaving Felipe free to concentrate on projecting the party outward.

After the election victory, González defined the three major tasks confronting the Socialist government: to consolidate democracy, to combat the economic crisis, and to build a state respecting autonomies (devolution of power to regions and nationalities). Many factors affecting these issue lie outside the control of a Socialist government, even a majority one, and it is premature to speculate on its prospects for success. In particular, the new government has been cautious in its promises to intervene in the economy and in the armed forces. On the road to power the PSOE has made compromises and abandoned or modified many Socialist policies and principles to help consolidate Spain's fragile democracy and to respond to Spain's more heterogeneous social structure, no longer divided crudely between workers and bosses.

Many within the party remain critical that the party's pragmatic approach, which serves to win votes will not consolidate Socialist policies; and that without firm commitment to transforming society, it will not be possible to improve conditions for working people. The debate on party strategy, and ideology, the conflict of opinions about what kind of party the PSOE should be, has run strongly throughout the party's history. The form it has taken over the last seven crucial years is important in understanding the nature of the party today; while democracy remains, the debate will certainly continue.

Part One: From Clandestinity to Democratic Opposition 1976–78

The PSOE which emerged from the forty-year-old dictatorship of Franco was at the same time both an old and a new party. Originally founded in 1879 by Pablo Iglesias, a young metalworker encouraged by Marx's son Paul Lafargue, the Spanish Socialist Workers' party is the oldest political party in Spain. It traces its origins back to the formation of the industrial working class in Spain and to Karl Marx himself. But as it reappeared in the twilight of Francoism, it was a young party with a young leadership and fresh ideas offering a new alternative to a generation of Spaniards for whom Franco was the only political experience. In contrast to the UCD which was intimately linked to the vestiges of Francoism, the PSOE could boast a clean break from the Francoist past, it could also match the CP in its roots in the Republic and beyond. If its leaders had less impressive records in the struggle in clandestinity and prison than CP leaders it only made them more identifiable to ordinary Spainiards. Besides, the PSOE also boasted its own party veterans who backed up, but did not supplant the young untried party leadership. The idea of 'the old and new party' was an important part of the party's image as it reappeared on the political scene in the mid-1970s. [1].

The main political opposition within Spain throughout the Franco period had been provided by the Communist Party. Leaders of the Socialist Party were mainly in exile, gradually losing touch with the political situation in Spain. But in 1970 the situation began to change, as representatives of groups within the country won a majority on the party's executive committee. Two years later, following the party's twelfth congress held in Toulouse, the leadership moved back into Spain. This had two effects. The party became more radical, freed from the control of a bureaucracy influenced primarily by anti-communism. Membership swelled, as the socialist movement within Spain now had an organisation around which to rally.[2] At the party's thirteenth congress at Suresnes, near Paris, in 1974, the last to be held in exile, Felipe González (aged 32) was elected General Secretary. He represented the Seville federation, and was a compromise candidate acceptable to the two other main areas of Socialist activity, Asturias and the Basque Country.[3] He represented a new political generation of Spanish Socialists for whom democratic government was unknown, the popular front not even a memory, and whose formative political experiences were the sharpening class struggles of Spain's developing industrial capitalism of the 1960s.

A similar process was occurring within the socialist trade-union organisation, the General Workers Union, UGT, whose new executive elected in 1971 included a majority of leaders representing areas inside Spain. This strengthened the prospect of reorganising the PSOE within the country, and of projecting an alternative vision of Socialism to that offered by the Communist Party. The reorganised UGT began to gather strength and to expand from its traditional heartlands in the steelworks and engineering plants of the Basque Country, and the mines of Asturias. With some 2,000 members within Spain,[4] the PSOE began to pull together the disparate groupings in the country into a coherent organisation, to recruit new members and to prepare for the end of the dictatorship, which by 1974 was no longer a remote dream but a real possibility.

The PSOE held its first congress in Spain since the fall of the Republic forty years before in Madrid in December 1976; it was still illegal (see Table 2.1). The PSOE reappeared as a radical Socialist party, defining itself as 'a class party, and therefore a mass party, Marxist and democratic'. It rejected 'any form of accommodation to capitalism or the simple reform of the system' and sought 'the supersession of the capitalist mode of production through the conquest of political and economic power, and the socialisation of the means of production, distribution and exchange by the working class.' The ten largest banks were to be nationalised, together with fifty of the largest firms. Participation democracy was to be extended beyond the limits of the capitalist state and parliamentary actions were to be combined with popular mobilisations.[5]

Table 2.1   PSOE executive committee elected at 27th Congress, December 1976

President	Ramón Rubial
First Secretary	Felipe Gonzalez
Organisation Secretary	Alfonso Guerra
Political Relations Secretary	Enrique Múgica
International Relations Secretary	Luis Yañez
Education ('Formación') & Documentation Secretary	Luis Gomez Llorente
Propaganda Secretary	Guillermo Galeote
Press Secretary	Javier Solana
Trade Union Secretary	Eduardo López
Youth Relations Secretary	José María Benegas
Administrative Secretary	Carmen García Bleise
Emigration Secretary	Joseph Luis Albinyana

Spokesman (Vocales)

Nicolás Redondo	Luis Fajardo
Antonio García Miralles	Carlos Cigarrán
Rafael Ballesteros	José María Triginer

It was soon to establish a position well to the left of the Communist Party, which was trying to play down its militant past and present itself as a pillar of moderation. The youthful image of the Socialist Party and its explicit declaration of its socialist credentials and emphasis on 'socialism is liberty' were a refreshing contrast to the aged CP leadership represented by Santiago Carrillo and La Pasionaria. For all their commitment to the democratisation of Spanish society (epitomised in the CP election slogan in 1977 'to vote communist is to vote democracy') the old CP leadership continued to retain an iron grip on the party's internal life. In its desire to assert its democratic credentials and ingratiate itself with the UCD government, the CP began to deny its socialist character altogether; Santiago Carrillo's elaboration of the ideas of Eurocommunism[6] revealed a moderation and reformism which fell far short of the aims of even middle of the road members of the PSOE.

In that first exuberant general election of June 1977, it was the casual campaigning style of the Socialists and the open-necked shirts and floppy locks of a youthful Felipe González that caught the popular mood. The PSOE won 28.7 per cent of the vote and became Spain's second largest party and main opposition force. It won comfortably in every major city and in most of the crucial industrial areas including the Basque Provinces. It grew rapidly into a mass party as its membership swelled to over 200,000.

Felipe González shot to prominence and became a figure of national popularity. He was then 35 years old, but already had fifteen years experience of working in the PSOE. He was born in Seville of a family of modest means. His father worked for a landowning family. At university he studied law and in 1966 he opened the first labour advice centre in Seville, defending the rights of workers involved in the many industrial disputes.[7]

The spectacular growth of the PSOE after the June elections brought its own problems: in absorbing and educating its new recruits and in maintaining a democratic internal structure. Full policy discussion with party members proved impossible and important political decisions were taken without rank-and-file consultation.

This was the case with the Moncloa Pact, an agreement signed by the Communist and Socialist Parties with the UCD government.[8] It was agreed that a 22 per cent wage-ceiling would exist for a year in return for reforms including greater trade-union freedoms. The trade unions and the employers' federations were between them expected to implement the pact, even though neither had actually taken part in its formulation. Carrillo seemed the more seduced by the constant to-ings and fro-ings to the Moncloa Palace for discussions with Premier Adolfo Suárez; he was later to claim the whole thing was his own idea. Neither party had any qualms, however, about commiting their respective union organisations to delivering on the agreement.

The 22 per cent wage-ceiling was in general observed over the following year, although many strikes took place over wages and conditions. The trade-union leaders carried the main responsibility for restraining their members in the interests of the pact; but union leaders' popularity suffered as a result and in some areas smaller unions gained in popularity at the expense of both the socialist UGT and the communist-led Comisiones Obreras. The unions came under increasing pressure to assert their independence from their respective parties and show greater willingness to defend their members even when this cut across party strategy.

Trade-union elections took place from January to March 1978. They revealed that the PSOE's industrial strength did not match up to its electoral strength, and that the important role of the PCE in opposition to Francoism was perhaps more accurately reflected in the 35.8 per cent vote for the communist-led workers' commissions, than in the CP's disappointing 9.2 per cent vote in the general elections. The socialist UGT won 22.7 per cent of the vote. The UGT fared better in large firms with more than 250 workers, the CCOO in smaller plants. The UGT did well in the Basque Country, particularly Viscaya, the Asturian mines, eastern Andalusia and Old Castile, while the workers' commissions were strongest in Madrid, Catalonia, Valencia and western Andalusia.[9]

Trade unionism in general remained weak, however, since these results related only to one-quarter of the active population and excluded agricultural workers. It was to become clear over the next few years that these respective positions of the CCOO and the UGT were to shift dramatically. For the UGT this was their benchmark from which they were to advance, for the CCOO their high-point from which they were to decline. Trade unions were to remain weak within the economy as a whole, however, as the economic recession deepened.

Following the Moncloa Pact all parliamentary parties collaborated to draft Spain's new Constitution in a climate of political consensus, in which the Socialist Party shifted perceptibly to the Right. The approval of the Constitution by referendum on 6 December 1978 was the most important political event in Spain since the death of Franco, and (in replacing Franco's assortment of authoritarian laws and decrees) marked the end of the '*ad hoc*' stage of the transition to democracy opened by the general elections of 15 June. The new Constitution was drafted by a committee representing all parties in the Cortes and reflected the spirit of compromise in which it was drawn up. The Socialists (and Communists) made important concessions on two matters of principle: the monarchy and the church.

The Constitution describes Spain as a 'parliamentary monarchy', whose government is answerable to a lower House of Parliament elected by universal suffrage. The role of the King is largely symbolic: he nominates the prime minister but only with the approval of Parliament which selects the candidate. Both the Socialists and the Communists broke with their republican tradition by agreeing to this[10]—an act which was to prove less than traumatic since republicanism soon became virtually a dead issue, except on the far Left.

The Constitution separates church and state but specifically recognises the Catholic nature of Spain. This was another major compromise of the Left,[11] important because it spilt over into the field of education (50 per cent of private education was in church hands) and the questions of divorce and abortion. The Constitution was approved by Parliament in October 1978 and was supported by most parties except the far Left, the far Right and the Basques. As expected it was overwhelmingly approved by referendum with 87.79 per cent in favour and only 7.91 per cent against. Nevertheless the abstention rate of 32.48 per cent was unexpectedly high, mainly in the Basque Country.

Suárez did not regard the referendum result as a sufficiently fervent endorsement of the UCD government so he called general elections for 1 March 1979, *before* the municipal elections which were announced for 3 April. This was the strategy most likely to favour his own party since local authorities remained in the hands of Franco appointees. The Socialists were clearly outmanoeuvred on the question of the municipal elections. These had been expected since early 1978 and the left-wing parties had constantly protested at their delay, demanding that they precede the general elections. Socialists and Communists were confident of substantial victories especially in the big cities and industrial areas.

Throughout the period from the signing of the Moncloa Pact (October 1977) to the Constitutional Referendum (December 1978) the politics of consensus predominated in the actions of the PSOE. Felipe González spoke of his hopes of putting together a Left–Centre coalition with fragments of the UCD, Basque Nationalists and Catalan Democrats.[12] He felt a more moderate approach was necessary to consolidate Spain's fragile democracy and to broaden the party's appeal. Sections of the UCD were responsive to this approach and several ministers in Suárez' government approached the PSOE to sound out which members of the UCD they would be prepared to govern with.

The campaign for the March 1979 general elections revealed the ambiguity of the PSOE's position: by presenting themselves as the most sincere supporters of Spanish democracy, they inevitably appeared as apologists for the Suárez government. They had to attack Suárez' record, as part of the campaign, but were at the same time keen to take credit for their participation in key aspects of it, like the Moncloa Pact and the constitutional process.

The PSOE's election slogan 'A firm government for a secure country' and grave portraits of Felipe with greying temples were designed to reinforce the image of the party as a serious contender for power. The approach was premature however, and the outcome of the March 1979 general elections was practically a repeat of those in 1977 but with a higher proportion of abstentions. Suárez slightly improved his lead and the Socialists gathered only 229,349 new voters despite the fusion with the Popular Socialist Party (PSP, which had taken 4 per cent of the votes in

1977) and the existence of 3 million first-time voters. The PSP was a small but significant grouping of Marxists and intellectuals founded in 1954 by philosophy professor Enrique Tierno Galván. It won 4 per cent of the vote in the June 1977 elections, after which the PSP and the PSOE opened up discussions on eventual fusion. In April 1978 a PSP congress voted to join the PSOE, and on 30 April the two parties fused. Galván became President of Honour of the PSOE and subsequently Mayor of Madrid. The majority of the PSP members were absorbed painlessly within the PSOE, adding some intellectual weight to the thousands of raw young recruits flocking to the party for the first time. Many in the party were relieved that the PSOE did not have to take on the responsibility of office at this early stage of its development. Even in opposition the party continued to move uneasily between its responsibility to attack and expose the weaknesses of the Suárez administration and its reluctance to be seen to be threatening or disrespectful to the fragile democratic institutions of parliamentary government.

Within the party the debate about alliances with other political forces (couched in terms of electoral arithmetic) began to rage more strongly. Whilst González saw the need to capture the middle ground by softening the radicalism of the party's programme, those on the Left pointed out that in the 1977 election the parties of the Left, the PSOE, PCE and PSP won 42.2 per cent of the vote (and 144 seats) while the Right and Centre–Right, the Alianza Popular and the UCD won 42.1 per cent (but 181 seats). They argued that a more rational electoral calculation would involve deepening and consolidating a majority left-wing alliance under Socialist hegemony; to try to reach for the centre ground would be to compete unsuccessfully with the UCD at their own game and risk losing the support of a large section of the Left vote.

Inevitably the debate centred on the prospect of workers' unity 'a union of the Left' or an inter-class alliance, a rapprochement with sections of the UCD. Ironically both the main Left parties, the PCE and the PSOE were keener on reaching out to the centre for their electoral support than to each other. The long-standing hostility between them persisted throughout the transition to democracy. Each feared that a French-style 'union of the Left' would be too reminiscent of the Popular Front and would be a provocation to the Spanish right.

Additionally, as José Maravall has shown,[13] the two parties were competing with each other for mass working-class support: the PSOE may have had greater electoral appeal than the PCE but the Communists were, in the opening period of Spain's new democracy, stronger in the trade unions. The conventional wisdom applicable to the history of the labour movement in Britain, that without a strong base in the unions, a party's parliamentary presence cannot be sustained, seems to have been reversed in Spain, where the steady ascent of the PSOE followed the rising popularity of the UGT. The decline of the CCOO was in turn precipitated by the failing fortunes of the Communist Party. The decline of the CP itself clearly owes as much to its own internal crises as to competition from the PSOE. In both cases however, in conditions where the role of trade unions in general remained weak, it was the political parties' political and parliamentary records that determined success or failure at trade-union level, rather than the other way round.

With the disappointing result at the March 1979 poll, and the reassertion of a more radical approach, the PSOE gradually began to thaw out its relations with the Communist Party.

Arguments in favour of a Left unity strategy appeared to be strengthened by the results of the local government elections in April 1979. Socialists and Communists between them swept the board in all Spain's major cities including Madrid and Barcelona. The two parties then made an agreement, a 'pact of progress', to support the Left candidate for mayor with the highest vote in each locality, to unite the left vote.[14] A Socialist mayor was elected by 1,039 municipalities and a Communist one by about 150 as a result of co-operation between the two parties. Over 70 per cent of the Spanish people had left-wing local authorities.

But Socialists were quick to reject accusations that 'pacts of progress' were divisive and smacked of the Popular Front. They emphasised the Left parties' separate identities and said that negotiations between them to form stable and effective majorities in town halls were justifiable attempts to consolidate democracy. On the contrary, they insisted that it was the Right, with its contempt for democratic institutions which sought to polarise society and perpetuate Francoism.

To summarise then, the party which had re-emerged in 1976 with strong left-wing views and projected a lively, open and progressive image to attract a generation of Spaniards experiencing political life for the first time, adopted, after the general elections of June 1977 a moderate consensus style of politics which lasted until March 1979 when the election results showed this strategy to have been unsuccessful in winning more votes.

After March, the party began to reassert a more left-wing stance, but within the party discontent was brewing over the party's record over the previous two years. This was to be revealed at the party's twenty-eighth congress held in May 1979.

Part Two: 1979—the Defeat of the PSOE Left

1979 was a critical year for the PSOE. The 28th Congress held in May reaffirmed the party's radical programme but resulted in the resignation of González as General Secretary. An extraordinary congress held in October toned down the party's commitment to Marxism, restored González and strengthened his authority, and marked the eclipse of the party's left wing as a coherent organised force.

The two congresses mark a watershed in the PSOE's recent history, revealing and prefiguring many of its future developments.

The 28th Congress

Many of the 1,018 delegates who thronged the huge Palace of Congresses in Madrid in May came with two main grievances which had arisen over the previous two years. First, that party members were not consulted about important changes in party policy and activity, and secondly that too many compromises had been made with the Suárez government. But it was clear that the main dispute was to be over whether or not the party defined itself as 'Marxist'. The congress slogan 'Building in Liberty' was regarded by some as referring more to the party's role in Spanish political life than to its inner workings.

The PSOE undoubtedly had a strong Marxist tradition, although December 1976 was the first occasion on which the word actually appeared in the party's programme. Felipe González never concealed his belief that the term was inappropriate to a party seeking to consolidate a fragile democracy and win over the mass of the Spanish people. He first stated publicly that he wanted to see Marxism abandoned in May 1978. This caused an outcry in the party. Even Alfonso Guerra, Felipe's loyal number two who has never been known to cross his colleague in public, did not conceal his surprise at the move, and remarked that the matter had not been discussed in the party leadership. To most people's relief González did not pursue it. But ten days before the opening of the congress, he repeated in a public meeting in Gijon that he would like the Marxist label dropped. This virtually guaranteed that it would be a major point of dispute.

From the start emotions ran high at the 3,000 strong congress. Most delegates, two-thirds of whom had only a few months' experience in the party, were in rebellious mood and determined to teach the leadership a lesson. The first sign of the strength of feeling came during the opening speech of Tierno Galván, former leader of the PSP, in his new capacity as Mayor of Madrid. 'We are in conditions to assimilate all our ideological past . . .', he said, 'To abandon any ideological aspects or the vigour of our ideals would be to abandon a space which today must not be in hands other than those of the socialists'. This, interpreted as an endorsement of the party's Marxist label, provoked tumultuous applause and a fervent rendering of the Internationale.

There followed elections to conference committee, the party's sovereign body during conferences between the resignation of the old executive and the election of a new one.[15] The official candidate for conference chairman, Gregorio Peces-Barba, secretary of the PSOE parliamentary group was defeated in favour of José Federico Carvajal, ex-president of the Senate constitutional commission and considered to have Marxist sympathies. This too was warmly hailed by most delegates who were keen to make a show of strength in the opening session.

Felipe González opened the conference debate by presenting the outgoing executive's report on the party's activity in the last two years. This he did in a low-key manner. He admitted the leadership had made mistakes but said that on balance the record was positive. He emphasised the party's Marxist heritage and said he wanted to rescue Marx from those who made him a dogma. He rejected the idea that Marx should form the dividing line between true and false, just and unjust, those supporting and those not supporting the party. Society was more complex today he said, although the persistence of class conflict justified maintaining a strong socialist ideal. He expressed disappointment that the PSOE, which had been able to win 30 per cent of the vote in the June 1977 elections, could not improve on this in the elections of March 1979 with a membership of 200,000. 'In a year and a half of political struggle we could not integrate new social sectors into our political project.' Yet the last two years were the most important in the life of the party. It now had 5½ million votes, 121 deputies, 70 senators and 15,000 councillors and mayors (more than the number of party members two years before). From clandestinity it had become the most important force on the Left. Formerly under authoritarian rule, Spain now had a Constitution guaranteeing basic rights and liberties which the PSOE fully supported.

Referring to the period of political consensus, he said 'this was not exactly the policy we socialists had wanted but it was imposed on us by circumstances and benefited Spanish society as a whole.' He admitted it had several drawbacks. For a start 'the party should have been more demanding in its desire for social change. They should have insisted on the holding of municipal elections as part of the agreement.' Instead the support of the Left legitimised the UCD government without creating conditions for strengthening the Left's own position. Secondly he acknowledged that the PSOE had failed to mobilise people outside parliament and the party in support of its ideas and activities. This led to passivity, abstensionism and a recovery of the Right. Finally, internal party matters were neglected in favour of activities directed towards government, at a time when the party was in a 'permanent crisis of growth'. He further admitted the PSOE's performance in the March elections had failed to fulfill expectations and conceded that the party had neglected its trade-union work at a time when the still-fragile unions were in need of active support.

The hail of criticisms which followed was due partly to the structure of PSOE conferences which traditionally allows only those with criticisms to speak on the executive report.[16] It was the opportunity for party members to air their grievances. The main protest was that the leadership had not kept members informed about decisions taken. Delegates complained that they learned what was going on in the party by reading, not their own paper *El Socialista*, but the 'bourgeois press'. They said there was inadequate education for new members, overemphasis on parliamentary activities and a tendency to solve political disputes within the party by resort to organisational measures like expulsions. Alfonso Guerra as Organisation Secretary came under severe personal attack on this count.

Felipe González recouped the situation somewhat in his reply on behalf of the outgoing executive and remarked prophetically 'no-one in this party is indispensible'. When it came to the vote 68 per cent of the delegates supported the report, 21 per cent abstained and only 10 per cent opposed it. The leadership considered this a satisfactory endorsement, although they were concerned at the number of abstentions. Delegates too were pleased at the degree of open criticism the conference permitted.

Attention then focused on the workshop discussions, *'ponencias'*,[17] particularly the one on the 'political resolutions'. Felipe González took part in the discussion behind closed doors and argued 'like any other party activist' against calling the party Marxist. Discussion was apparently sharp: at one point Felipe accused the radicals of turning the party into a 'party of frustrated petty-bourgeois', expressing surprise that only the intellectuals insisted on maintaining an exclusively Marxist party. Inevitably an Asturian miner injected *'yo soy obrero y marxista'* ('I am a worker and a Marxist') and this tipped the balance in favour of the left-wing 'critical' sector.

The radicals or so-called *'sector critico'* emerged as an identifiable force following González' first public suggestion that Marxism be dropped from the party programme. It reflected a broad section of party membership but never succeeded in consolidating itself organisationally. Its main leaders were Pablo Castellano, Luís Gomez Llorente and Fransisco Bustelo, all from Madrid, who campaigned to retain the party's full-blooded socialist character in the face of what they regarded as the right-wing Social Democratic drift pursued by Felipe González. They won substantial support at the 28th Congress, where the question of ideological purity became linked with matters of internal party democracy. The debates between 'the *criticos*' and supporters of Felipe González and the existing leadership 'the *felipistas*', were wide-ranging, dealing with all aspects of the question of the nature of the PSOE as a socialist party. At Spanish Socialist Party conferences the looseness of the timetable and the importance attached to workshop discussions outside the main plenary conference tends to reinforce the impression that most of the business that really matters is conducted in the corridors, at night. Certainly when the political resolution was finally agreed in the workshop (*ponencia*) and brought to the floor of the full conference it was already eleven o'clock on Saturday evening. It stated 'the PSOE reaffirmed its character as a class, mass party, Marxist, democratic and federal', a formulation proposed by the Asturian delegation. Under the heading 'Principles' the resolution asserted the class contradiction between proletariat and bourgeoisie, the need for the working class to take power, for the socialisation of private property and the abolition of class society. It rejected accommodation without reform of capitalism.

A later section, 'Analysis of the Political Situation', says that the Moncloa Pact helped consolidate the transition to democracy and that the PSOE would defend the constitution as a guarantee of democratic liberties and a step towards socialism. A final section, 'Strategy', emphasised socialism's democratic content and commits the party to 'deepen democracy' by measures including workers' self-management, political decentralisation and the creation of citizens' associations.

Joaquín Almunia from the Sevillian delegation, identified with González, proposed an amendment deleting the first section altogether and referring to the party's varied socialist tradition and to its aim of serving a broad bloc of classes, not just the working class. Fransisco Bustelo, 46-year-old economics professor, senator for Madrid and leader of the 'radicals' vigorously defended the Marxist position and said the PSOE must not give the impression of a shameful swing to the Right. 'If today we add a little water to the old wine, tomorrow we'll add a little more and in five years' time there'll be no more wine', he said.

In the early hours of Sunday morning the amendment was defeated with 61 per cent voting against it, 31 per cent in favour and 6 per cent abstaining. In the heat of the moment no vote was taken on the substantive resolution as it stood. The Left at this point believed they had won; and no-one was prepared for Felipe González' decision to resign as party leader.

Certainly for the *criticos* González' resignation was a bombshell. They had come to congress determined to castigate the leadership and impose a clear Marxist line to arrest what they regarded as the social democratisation of the party under Felipe's influence. González wanted to ensure that if the party was to accept his leadership then the radicals had to recognise that Marxist solutions were in his view unrealistic in the changed circumstances of a democratic Spain. The problem was that neither had a fallback position; but while González acted fully conscious of the consequences of what he was doing his opponents did not. Following the defeat of the González line, the *criticos* clearly had no plan to assume control of the party executive themselves. Having won the political argument, they seemed not to have considered following through by presenting an alternative leadership. In fact the PSOE without Felipe was the last thing they wanted.

On Sunday afternoon, long after the congress was due to have closed, Felipe explained his position. Since he could not agree with the majority decision it was his duty 'ethically, morally and democratically' to withdraw from the leadership and argue his position from the rank and file. His farewell speech was cheered and applauded and interrupted by cries of 'Stay, Felipe!' by the same delegates who had inflicted on him such a crushing defeat the night before.

Fransisco Bustelo, Pablo Castellano and Luís Gomez Llorente, the *criticos*' main spokesmen tried to scratch together an alternative Left ticket, with the benevolent support of Enrique Tierno Galván. Not a single candidate was put forward;[18] if Felipe wouldn't stand, no-one would.

Finally it was agreed to elect a steering committee, comprising Carvajal, ex-administrative secretary Carmen García and three veteran PSOE notables, Ramón Rubial, Antonio García and José Prat. The committee was empowered to carry out the day-to-day running of the party until an extraordinary congress was held later in the year. Meanwhile the party's political leadership was entrusted temporarily to the parliamentary group, led by Felipe González.

'Marxist or not' became the dominant issue of the congress. Everything else was pushed to one side and other important decisions such as the decision not to recognise tendencies in the party, not to support the legalisation of abortion, and to abolish the post of international secretary within the party, were taken in a casual and off-hand way.

Felipe González took personal responsibility for having provoked the debate and admitted he had presented it badly. Certainly the way he expressed his wish to the party to abandon Marxism, on both occasions at a public meeting, without opening discussions within the party first, was bound to arouse the anger of conference delegates who already felt that the leadership was doing too much on its own account. So 'Marxist or not' provided the focus for complaints that the leadership had made serious compromises during the last two years and was heading rapidly down the road to social democracy. González' resignation left the party in serious disarray, facing the prospect of a bitter power struggle between the *felipistas* and the *criticos*. But there was no doubt of the positive impact of his action on the Spanish population at large, to whom the concept of resignation is utterly alien. There was speculation at the time that the whole exercise was a deliberate device to throw the Left into confusion and imprint his authority indelibly on the party. There is still no conclusive evidence that this was so, but in retrospect it is clear that the months between the 28th and the extraordinary congresses marked a turning point in the party's internal life and that the Left's opportunity had slipped, perhaps for good.

But in the aftermath of the 28th congress the *criticos* appeared in confident mood, although they displayed a certain unease about the enormity of what they had done. Fransisco Bustelo announced he would stand for the executive alongside Gomez Llorente and Castellano. 'What we want', he said, 'is for the PSOE to maintain the position it has had throughout its hundred years' history, and turn neither to the Right nor Left. We're not radicals. It's the others, Felipe González and Alfonso Guerra who have become moderates. I have a lot of respect for social democracy but it's not what we want here. We suspect that Felipe González and Guerra want to tilt the party towards social democracy.'

Pablo Castellano wanted 'to deepen internal democracy in the party and give it a truly federal character'. In 1976 he said, 'the PSOE was defined as a federal organisation, but the outgoing leadership didn't respect that principle. They never stopped intervening in the life of the federations.'

But no sooner had the Left defined its position and objectives then it began to melt away. In the crucial months before the Extraordinary Congress González launched energetically into a tour of the country to whip up support in all regions. The party summer school, the young Socialists' congress and the usual congresses of the regional federations were all suspended until after the extraordinary congress; this was seen by many as an attempt to eliminate debate. In fact the struggle between Left and Right never materialised, due to the efficiency of the pre-emptive measures taken by the party leadership. At the crucial moment the Left was defeated by its organisational weakness and lack of nerve. When it came to the crunch they were reluctant to consider the future of the PSOE without Felipe González as leader.

The Extraordinary Congress September 1979

The Extraordinary Congress took place not in the stadium-like Palace of Congresses but in the oppressive and pretentious opulence of the Hotel Melia Castilla. Its purpose was to resolve the impasse produced at the 28th Congress, agree party policy and elect a new leadership. Felipe González had carefully prepared the ground during the summer for a successful comeback.

But more importantly, in accordance with a decision hastily taken in the concluding chaos of the 28th Congress, delegates were this time elected by regional federation, not by local grouping as before. As a result the number of delegates was much smaller (about 420 compared with over 1,000 in May). Furthermore, those elected were mainly people with positions of authority within the party rather than rank-and-file members. Most were regional leaders, MPs, mayors or councillors; of the 420, twelve were women. A party survey showed that the social composition of the delegates had shifted between the two congresses in favour of the middle class (see Table 2.2). In addition only the eighty-six 'heads of delegations' could vote. Naturally they voted for the majority view of their delegation, leaving the minority unrepresented.[19]

The result of this severe filtering was that the critical sector, whose strength in the party was estimated at about 40 per cent, had less than

Table 2.2   PSOE: survey of social composition (percentages) of delegates to 28th and Extraordinary Congresses, 1979 (quoted from *Systema*)

	28th Congress	Extra-ordinary
Manual workers	16	7.5
Students	5.4	1.9
Office workers	14.3	7.4
Functionaries	13	22.6
Professional and Technical	24.7	29
Proprietors of trade and industry	4	5.3
PSOE employees	3	4.5

10 per cent of congress support. The powerful Andalusian delegation was by far the largest and accounted for 25 per cent of the delegates. The delegation leader, *jefe de delegacion*, who controlled with his single vote one-quarter of the whole conference was none other than Alfonso Guerra.

The political debates and power struggles of importance had already taken place, in the regional party congresses called to adopt political resolutions for submission to congress, and to elect delegates. There is no doubt that the Left were completely outmanoeuvred in this period; the 'neutral' steering committee enabled the former executive to organise matters satisfactorily in their favour. Flabbergasted by González' resignation in May the radicals lost the opportunity presented to them by failing to present an alternative slate. They continued to be undecided about whether they should now present a complete opposition slate or, in the event of an acceptable compromise being reached on the programme, favour what they called an integrated slate.

For the *felipistas* the crucial issue was who should lead the party. They were in no doubt of their position: they were completely opposed to an integrated slate, or 'committee of synthesis' saying that it would be unworkable. They realised that behind the esoteric debate about Marxism lay fundamental divergencies in strategy which could not easily be reconciled. They were prepared to make concessions on the programme if a 'homogeneous' team remained in control.

The atmosphere of the Extraordinary Congress was low-key ('not that extraordinary' was the wry assessment of *El País*' cartoonist) and no surprises were expected. Three main issues were however resolved up to a point. First, the role of Marxism in the party's ideological principles; secondly internal organisational guarantees for decentralisation and internal debate; and thirdly alliances with other political forces. Not a great deal of light was thrown on these issues by the congress debate itself. But it became clear that they were all reflections of the general point of contention: what kind of party should the PSOE aspire to be in the transformed conditions of Spanish democracy? Should it discard the old ideological baggage that had served it well for forty years of clandestinity and confrontation with the state? Or should it reaffirm its long-standing radical, even revolutionary, commitment so that the attractions of parliamentary democracy would not lead the party to abandon its aim of overthrowing capitalism? This counter position is rather crude. There is after all much common ground between the two sides, such as the importance of parliamentary democracy in the transition to socialism. But the Left's main fear was that the party was becoming 'social democratic' by which they meant electoralist, centralist, elitist and class-collaborationist.

As far as the role of Marxism is concerned, the new programme approved at the Extraordinary Congress describes the PSOE as a 'class, mass, democratic and federal party'. It goes on: 'The PSOE adopts Marxism as a theoretical, critical and non-dogmatic instrument for the analysis and transformation of social reality, accepting the various contributions, Marxist and non-Marxist that have gone to make socialism the great emancipating alternative of our time and respecting personal convictions.'

'Marxist' was dropped from the list of the party's defining characteristics but the PSOE 'understands Marxism as a non-dogmatic method' and 'accepts critically the contributions of all socialist thinkers.' The new wording, by accepting non-Marxist 'contribution', could no longer be interpreted as excluding non-Marxists which was Felipe's chief objection, since he openly admitted he was not a Marxist. The barrier preventing the PSOE from attracting those broad sectors of Spanish society necessary to win a parliamentary majority, as Felipe and his supporters saw it, was thus removed.

The critical sector attributed the whole Marxism controversy to González' electoralism; his desire to water down the programme in the belief that this would make it acceptable to larger numbers of voters who would enable the party to attain government office. González's attitude has always been that this is nothing to be ashamed of. In his opening speech to congress he openly expressed his esteem of the Swedish Social Democratic Party and his wish to see the PSOE move in this direction. But the Left feared that if this happened the party would have to become so compromised that it would be unable to present itself even as a credible alternative to the Right—let alone fulfil its aim of overthrowing capitalist society.[20]

The question of political alliances was part of the same argument. González always dismissed the idea of a common front of the Left—in practice an alliance with the Communist Party—on the grounds that it would never bring the PSOE to power. The *criticos* favoured a strategy of Left unity, arguing that only the Right benefited from a divided workers' movement. They also disputed the electoral arithmetic that dictated that the middle ground, the so-called 'broad social majority', offers more votes than unity on the Left. They feared the PSOE was contemplating an alliance with the UCD, a fear only partly allayed at the Extraordinary Congress. The statement on Strategy and Political Objectives says the party 'has to maintain an autonomous and independent policy . . . in circumstances of democratic normality. . . . Only in a situation of extreme threat to the survival of the democratic system would the socialist party have to make the sacrifice of collaborating with other democratic forces in a policy of defending the democratic framework.'

This would be strictly limited in time and programmatic content and would have to be approved by the party's federal committee (which has rank-and-file representation). The *criticos* were prepared to accept the possibility of such an alliance, i.e. with the Centre and Right, but wanted it to be approved by an extraordinary congress. Meanwhile they proposed a policy of 'understanding' with parties on the Left. This was dismissed by the *felipistas*, who said an extraordinary congress would be impractical under the conditions of extreme emergency under which such an alliance were to be contemplated; and 'understanding' as a term applied to relations with left-wing parties was regarded as too vague to be acceptable.

The party leadership were already confident that the PSOE by itself had a good chance of becoming Spain's majority party, and wanted to take a pragmatic stance towards alliances with other forces. The *criticos* feared rejection of Left unity in favour of an 'autonomous' policy might lead to a centre-Right coalition, and took cold comfort from assurances that the PSOE would not accept a 'subordinate' position in government. This whole discussion was shot through with the anti-communism which still characterises the PSOE, a historical legacy which was sustained by the fierce competition between the two parties.

On organisational matters, the congress took a small step towards the recognition of tendencies. Party statutes said: 'Complete freedom of internal discussion is guaranteed, although the formation of organised tendencies will not be permitted.'[21] The statement adopted by Congress, however, on 'Model of the Party' says: 'Freedom of expression must be absolute at all levels of the party guaranteeing respect for different currents of opinion which may be expressed in various forms of internal theoretical political activity.' This was little more than a recognition of what had been happening in recent months, and appeared to give some organisational substance to González' promises that there would be no 'witch-hunts' against the Left.

Felipe González was triumphantly returned as general secretary of the party with an overwhelming 85 per cent of the vote. This and the election of a new, uniformly *felipista* executive committee (see Table 2.2) marked a crushing defeat for the *criticos*. Even González' most loyal supporters were uncomfortably aware that his return had been overeffectively guaranteed. No sooner was the unexpectedly conclusive victory announced than assurances were made to the Left that they would not be routed. There was a strong desire on all sides to maintain party unity and heal the discords. Fernando Carvajal in his concluding speech as Congress Chairman stressed: 'there are no winners or losers . . . we are all comrades'. González assured Castellano that the Left would be free to operate. Castellano seemed reconciled, saying 'we'll just have to keep fighting for our ideas; we must remain a united party'. Another *critico* remarked 'we will be the Left minority like the Ceres in the French Socialist Party'. Unlike Ceres, however, the PSOE Left had no voice on the new executive. Luís Gomez Llorente the only *critico* on the previous executive, declined the offer of a place on the new one. Enrique Tierno Galván, 'the old professor', who had supported the *criticos* in May, sank without trace as his post of Honorary President was quietly eliminated.

The Extraordinary Congress had achieved the feat of removing the voice of the Left from the party leadership, in a manner which appeared to be offering reconciliation. It remained only for the 29th Congress in 1981 to complete the process by eliminating the voice of the Left from party congress altogether, enabling the leadership to put aside distracting internal disputes and concentrate on preparing for power (see Table 2.3).

Part Three: 1980–82 Preparing for Power

As the party began to recover from the trauma of the two congresses in 1979 it turned its attention towards two important areas of political activity which had been rather neglected: supporting the trade-union activity of the UGT and attacking the UCD government.

The UGT took the step of signing an agreement with the employers' federation, the CEOE, which met the main UGT demand for union recognition in factories and the elimination of state intervention in collective negotiations. The move was bitterly denounced by the *comisiones obreras*, the most powerful union, as having taken place behind its back. It demonstrated the aim of both the UGT and PSOE of building up their strength in the workplaces by a policy of participation rather than confrontation. The UGT admitted that the section on workers' rights, guaranteeing a 43-hour week and 23 days of paid holiday, could have been stronger, whilst the *comisiones* criticised the clause which strengthened the employers' hitherto limited ability to lay off workers. Another important difference between the UGT and *comisiones* was the former's insistence on the trade unions themselves as the negotiating partner. The CCOO had always favoured the factory committees, elected by all workers, not just unionised ones, and these were frequently dominated by the numerically superior Communists.

Nicolás Redondo was decisively returned as general secretary of the UGT at its congress in April 1980, and the union elections in November

Table 2.3   PSOE Executive Committee elected at Extraordinary
Congress, September 1979

President	Ramón Rubial
General Secretary	Felipe González
Vice-General Secretary	Alfonso Guerra
Organisation Secretary	Carmen García Bloise
Administration Secretary	Emilio Alonso Sarmiento
Secretary of Education ('Formacion')	José María Maravall
Secretary of Studies and Programmes	Javier Solana
Secretary of Sectoral Policy	Ciriaco de Vicente
Press and Propaganda Secretary	Guillermo Galeote
Secretary of Municipal Policy	Luis Fajardo
Secretary of Political Relations (with other parties)	Enrique Mújica
Youth Secretary	Juan Antonio Barragán
Autonomies Secretary	Maria Izquierdo
Secretary of Trade Union	Joaquín Almunia (nominated by UGT)
Policy Emigration*	Fransisco Lopez Real
Culture	Ignacio Sotelo

Spokesmen (Vocales)

Carlos Cigarran	José María Obiols
Gregorio Peces-Barba	Pedro Bofill
José Federico de Carvajal	Txiqui Benegas
Donato Fuejo	José Angel Villa

*Responsible for the substantial numbers of overseas PSOE members.

confirmed the UGT as the trade-union organisation responding most
accurately to the wishes of the Spanish labour movement. The UGT's
position improved dramatically, to become neck and neck with the CCOO.
It won 32.8 per cent of the vote (compared with 21.6 per cent in 1978)
whilst the CCOO with 33.3 per cent slightly lost ground in comparison
with a 34.5 per cent vote in the previous elections.

Within the party, the victory of the *felipistas* at the extraordinary congress was matched by similar victories, albeit bitterly won, at the congresses
of the Madrid and Andalusia federations in December 1979, confirming
the organisational eclipse of the *criticos*. Problems remained however in
the Catalan party.

But by the time the PSOE's federal committee, the chief organ of the party between congresses,[22] met in January 1980, the organisational dispute was to all intents and purposes over.

For the first time the PSOE began to give detailed attention to the question of economic policy in which the 40-year-old tradition of bargaining for higher wages was modified to put emphasis on issues like housing, education, health, transport, taxation and employment. A policy document said: 'The socialist proposal is to displace the process of redistributing the surplus towards obtaining collective services and facilities, limiting wage claims to the maintenance of existing purchasing powers'.[23] Pressure, in other words, was to be diverted to other terrain than that of wages. The main priority was the creation of jobs, the second the strengthening of the unions and the third the improvement of the social wage, like housing. Tax reform is proposed, but not nationalisation.

Meanwhile the popularity of the PSOE and of Felipe González as leader continues to rise among the population at large. A survey carried out in March found that 64.1 per cent of Spaniards considered González would be as good as or better than Adolfo Suárez as Prime Minister.

A further boost to the party's popularity and its public profile in general was provided by the motion of censure which the PSOE proposed in parliament in May 1980. It was relayed on TV and radio for a week and became the common talk of everyday life. It lost, of course, by 166 votes to 152, but in the course of the debate the socialists were able to publicly attack the government for corruption, incompetence and its disastrous economic policies. It also revealed that the ruling UCD was unable to rally one single extra vote outside its own ranks.

Throughout 1980 the UCD continued to drift badly without vision or direction. The economic situation deteriorated, with unemployment mounting, and the question of regional autonomy continuing to catch the government (and it must be said the opposition too) on the hop. Irresistible popular pressure which grew during the year forced the UCD grudgingly to accelerate a process of regional autonomy, much against its inclinations. As it happens, the UCD, CP and PSOE were all in various ways wary of the autonomies process devolving power to the regions, because of its association with armed actions which they all deplored; because of the threat it posed to the parliamentary majority of the nationally organised parties by the proliferation of smaller regional ones, and in the case of the two workers' parties, because of their reluctance to allow regional or national interests to outweigh the common class considerations of working people throughout the country. Regional contradictions inevitably reverberated within the organisations of their own federal structures, and conflicts between the centre and the regions were as acutely reflected within the PSOE and the PCE as within the Spanish State itself.

Neither the PCE nor the PSOE were to present a convincing critique or alternative to the UCD's handling of the regional devolution question. Autonomies and the economic crisis were the two major issues facing the UCD and it was incapable of tackling either of them. When Adolfo Suárez resigned as Prime Minister on 29 January 1981 the minority government he had led entered a prolonged crisis which lasted until and undoubtedly contributed to the coup attempt of 23 February. Between those two events various incidents took place which revealed the extent of the crisis that had been brewing and indicated that the date the generals chose to attempt their coup was not random but carefully selected.

Less than a week after Suárez' resignation, on 3 February, King Juan Carlos made his first visit to the Basque Country (against Suárez' advice) and endorsed the principle of devolving power to the nationalities. On 6 February a young engineer was killed by the Basque separatist organisation ETA precipitating massive protests and demonstrations. On 13 February a suspected ETA member was tortured to death after nine days interrogation by police in Carabanchel prison. The Basque Country was gripped by general strikes. In response ETA kidnapped three consuls in San Sebastian on 20 February.

This succession of events was regarded by the army and the security forces as a provocative threat to their sacred creed of a single unified Spanish state in which the regions paid full obeisance to Madrid. Meanwhile in Madrid, Parliament could not agree on the new Prime Minister to succeed Suárez. It is hardly surprising that the generals thought their moment had come. Lieutenant-colonel Antonio Tejero's coup, as we know, failed, but few doubt that Spain's 5-year-old democracy survived only by a very narrow margin. The only factor preventing military take-over was the refusal of the king to back the rebel officers. Tejero himself was only the front man for General Armada, second in command of the armed forces, an old Francoist who had fought alongside Hitler in the Second World War and now saw himself as Spain's new military ruler. Many other generals throughout the country, poised for action, only wavered in their resolve when it became clear that the King was not joining the action.

The coup attempt highlighted the extreme fragility of Spain's democratic structures, which in most cases remained only skin deep. Key institutions like the army, the courts, above all the police and the civil guard, remained intact and unreformed since the rule of Franco. The UCD feared that clearing out Franco's old guard would provoke a coup, and since it counted amongst its number a motley assortment of ex-Francoists it was reluctant to press the point. But so long as the armed forces remained in the hands of fascist hardliners the threat of a coup was ever-present. After the coup's collapse, the immediate response among Spaniards of all shades of opinion to the Left of Franco, was an overwhelming desire for unity.

The PSOE made a formal offer to the UCD government to join them in a coalition, believing that a broad parliamentary majority was necessary to prevent the next coup attempt from being successful. At its federal committee meeting on 28 February the PSOE stated that considering the risk to the country's democratic institutions, 'Spain needs the formation of a government with a broad parliamentary majority and extensive social support'. The federal committee therefore 'reiterates the offer made by the PSOE to the party in government and other parliamentary forces in the Congress of deputies to agree a programme of government action with an agreed timetable for carrying it out.'

It noted that 'the serious seditious attitudes against constitutional order cannot be confused with the general behaviour of the armed forces and security services who responded to the mission assigned to them by the constitution.' It also commended the role played by the king 'as a firm guarantor of democratic freedoms'.

The new Prime Minister, Leopoldo Calvo Sotelo, nevertheless declined the socialists' offer, perhaps fortunately for the PSOE which stood to be dangerously compromised by coalition with the UCD, particularly as no conditions were imposed in this case by the party in return for its support.

In the immediate aftermath of the coup then, the PSOE effectively abandoned its role as parliamentary opposition and took a much more co-operative attitude towards the government. Politicians of all hues were severely unnerved by 23 February; they closed ranks in a remarkable fashion and moved smartly to the Right. The government sought to placate the armed forces in a number of ways: a generalised campaign portrayed them as loyal to the constitution, explaining that the coup attempt was the work of a small group. The trial and eventual sentence of those implicated showed a leniency which demonstrated the reluctance to put too much pressure on the armed forces, lest it be regarded as a provocation for further military actions. New provisions strengthening the anti-terrorist laws were introduced. In the months that followed, the PSOE continued to place the defence of democracy over considerations of party advantage. It argued that a more representative government, displaying the unity of parliamentary forces as a whole, would strengthen parliament itself. Felipe González said he was less concerned about winning the next general elections, scheduled for 1983, than that they should take place.

The danger was, however, that the Spanish people, suspecting that there was little difference between the two main parties, would lose interest in both, and in parliamentary government in general. This popular disenchantment with the workings of democratic government could provide the most fertile breeding ground of all for successful military adventures. It was the PSOE which had most to lose by shoring up a weak and dithering minority government. The PSOE was by now the most popular party in Spain and the only one with a modicum of internal unity and coherence. The UCD in contrast was, by mid-1981, in a state of terminal collapse. It was clear by now that in an election campaign the UCD would fall apart and virtually disappear. Towards the second half of the year, therefore, there arose a growing awareness within the PSOE that a prolonged pact with the government would be damaging to the party's electoral prospects and that they must offer a clear alternative if they wished to retain popular support. An emerging 'socialist Left' insisted that apart from a thorough clean-up of the army and the police, bolder economic measures including nationalisations and a more active public sector were necessary.

In June the party produced a policy document designed as a response to the current situation,[23] '*El PSOE ante la situación política*'. It concerned itself mainly with terrorism, the autonomies process and the economy. Its intention, of providing a programme of government action, was to put some distance between the PSOE and the UCD and to offer a kind of ultimatum to force the government to reach a formal agreement with the socialists. The document steered clear of the controversial, albeit central, problem of cleaning up the army and of extending civil liberties in a situation where armed forces and security forces still remained unreformed.

In September 1981 the PSOE launched its campaign against entering NATO. PSOE policy was not against NATO as such, but was opposed to Spain joining it, putting an end to its long tradition of neutrality. The party was careful to distinguish its position from that of the CP which was for the abolition of NATO. Spain's membership of NATO would in the PSOE's view upset the balance of power in Europe and would offer no guarantee that the Spanish armed forces would act in a more democratic way in the future. Felipe González drew on the examples of Turkey and Greece to disprove this idea.[24]

Spain was in any case linked to the Atlantic Alliance via a bilateral treaty with the US which the socialists were quite happy to renegotiate.

The party demanded a referendum on the issue and polls indicated that while the Spanish public were not greatly mobilised on the issue, they were mostly against Spain joining. González promised to conduct a referendum on NATO membership if the Socialists came to power.[25] The anti-NATO campaign disturbed the government but in no way affected their determination to join, under strong encouragement from other NATO members, and the decision to join NATO was approved by parliament towards the end of 1981.

The 29th Congress, October 1981

The party leadership wanted a peaceful congress, which would show the party as one of unity and responsibility. It chose the innocuous slogan 'Roots for Democracy'. This was to be the last congress before the next general election and every effort was made to show the country that the PSOE was a serious contender for power and that its leader Felipe González was the best candidate for premiership. Already in June Guerra was making overtures to the Left in an attempt to prevent further divisions. Sectors of the far Left in Spain continued to be attracted to the PSOE which increasingly came to be seen as the main arena for socialist activists of all persuasions. Various left-wing groupings within the party continued to emerge, notably *Izquierda Socialista*, the original *criticos* led by Gomez Llorente and Pablo Castellano, and *Reflexiones Socialistas*, arguing for a democratisation of the party's internal workings, particularly concerning the selection of congress delegates (by *agrupación* local grouping) and their voting methods (one delegate one vote).

The election victory of the Greek Socialist Party PASOK in October, on the eve of Congress, was added to the May 1981 socialist victory in France as an example to the PSOE of an apparent socialist tide sweeping the Mediterranean. All this contributed to making the 29th Congress little more than a spring-board for the forthcoming election campaign. Alfonso Guerra said 'the problem of the next congress is whether or not the socialists offer an image of ability to govern'.[26] González, launching the Congress at a press conference was even more explicit: 'it must be normal, peaceful and able to project itself outwards, above internal considerations'.[27]

A further objective, in which it was largely successful, was to project the PSOE as a party opening wide its doors so that Spanish society as a whole was more fully represented in its ranks.

The trauma of the February coup attempt overshadowed the whole proceedings. It revealed, as Felipe González said in his opening speech, what had existed since 1976 as a constant underlying threat to Spanish democracy. His message was that only the Socialists were capable of genuinely deepening democracy, and strengthening the country's fragile democratic institutions was to be the party's main priority. González' account of the party's work over the past two years revealed the dilemma which faced it since the emergence of a framework of democracy: on the one hand, faced with the incompetence and disarray of the UCD government it was essential to show by acting as a critical opposition that the PSOE offered a clear alternative. On the other hand, the commitment to democracy was something which overrode party advantage and González defended the party's decision to join with the UCD on issues like the autonomies process, trying to rationalise the various demands of the regions and nationalities for self-rule, and in agreeing an economic pact with the employers.

The pursuit of unity within the party was so successfully achieved that it produced an almost Eastern-bloc style unanimity. The executive report was approved by 99.4 per cent and Felipe González was re-elected general secretary by a 100 per cent vote. The high degree of uniformity and the elimination of the critical 'socialist Left' from among the delegations was due partly to effective pre-emptive action by the party apparatus which had succeeded in dislodging most *criticos* from positions of importance within the party since the last congress, and partly to two organisational characteristics which operated against them.

The first was the two-tier system of electing delegates, whereby delegates are elected by specially convened regional congresses and not by local group, as before. The intention was to strengthen the party's federal character and weaken the power of the Centre. But as González noted, the effect was to take power away from the rank-and-file party members in favour of regional officials. Secondly, once at Congress, only heads of delegations had the right to vote, so that minorities on delegations went unrepresented. Congress decided to make no change to this tradition of majority rule.

The two leaders of the party's Left wing, Gomez Llorente and Castellano had argued strongly for representation of tendencies within the party and for the right of individual vote. They were defeated on this count and as a result did not take part in the congress at all and the Left's voice was simply not heard. The ideological battle, which had raged so fiercely in the last two congresses was practically extinguished. A perplexed fraternal delegate from the National Executive of the British Labour Party stopped Guerra to ask him why the left was not present at the congress. '*Yo soy la izquierda. Estoy aquí*', 'I am the Left. I am here' was the calm response.

'And how do you justify the 100 per cent vote for Felipe González?' he was pressed. No more than Michael Foot received. But in response to one question he was cynically direct: 'What's going on then?' '*No pasa nada . . . o si pasa algo, no importa.*' 'Nothing . . . or if it is it's not important'.

As far as the party's political strategy was concerned, the 29th Congress marked a perceptible moderation of policy. 'The objective of socialism' began the main political resolution 'is to achieve the social conditions which will permit the happiness of man.' The party aims to lead a broad alliance of classes and social groups united by their experience of oppression and their desire for change. This alliance would include more than workers and more than socialists, in fact all those opposed to big business and the far Right. The transformation of society would be achieved by deepening liberties and eliminating economic obstacles to social emancipation.

Some favoured a coalition with the UCD, others a link with breakaway sections of it. But Congress stuck by the idea of an 'autonomous socialist project', i.e. the prospect of an outright socialist majority government. The socialist Left's policy of a Left alliance with the Communists was not even considered.

On economic policy, proposals for wage controls were successfully resisted by the UGT delegates. A policy of 'responsibility' on wages was approved however. Financial and energy sectors of the economy were considered targets for nationalisation, specifically 40 per cent of the financial system. Food, pharmaceutical and electronic industries also 'required a strong presence of the public sector'. But no firm commitments were made. Proposals for administrative and financial reform were agreed, including the setting up of a state bank and the socialisation of savings banks.

Formal congress sessions were among the dullest since the party became legal, and it was truer than ever that the most important business took place outside them. This was mainly to do with the composition of the new executive. An official list of candidates was drawn up in the usual way, by a process of energetic negotiation amongst existing executive members and heads of the main delegations.

At the 29th Congress a new permanent commission of nine was established within the executive commission including the President, General Secretary and his Deputy (Ramón Rubial, Felipe González and Alfonso Guerra). The function of this new secretariat was to conduct the day-to-day business of the party. The idea was put forward by Felipe and criticised by some delegates as an excessive concentration of power. Members of the executive not in the new secretariat were to be allocated their responsibilities by the General Secretary and effectively declined in status relative to the members of the 'permanent commission'.

Most of the new members of the executive were drawn from regional parties. Carmen Mestre's presence reflects a recognition of the importance of women's issues, but women in the PSOE continue to fight for the creation of a women's organiser. In appearance and in political content, the congress was almost entirely male-dominated. Luís Yanez, the ex-International Secretary seeking reinstatement, fought unsuccessfully for the restoration of the post which had been suppressed at the 28th Congress. International affairs continue to be handled directly by the General Secretary.

Table 2.4 PSOE Executive committee elected at the 29th Congress, October 1981 (with percentages of votes received)

President	Ramón Rubial (99.5)
General Secretary	Felipe González (100)
Vice General Secretary	Alfonso Guerra
Area Secretaries	
Social Action	Ciriaco de Vicente (90.8)
Image (formerly Press and Propaganda)	Guillermo Galeite (89.7)
Finance and Administration	Emilio Alonso (88.5)
Culture	José María Maravall (86.2)
Studies and Programmes	Joaquín Almunia (84.9)
Organisation	Carmen García Bloise (68.1)

Executive Secretaries

Maria Izquierdo (92.6)	Salvador Fernandez (81.7)
Carmen Mestre (92.1)	Joan Lerma (80.4)
Javier Saenz Consculluela (91.7)	José Angel F. Villa (80.1)
José Mariá (*'Txiki'*) Benegas (91.3)	Javier Solana (76.7)
Manuel Chavez (88.5)	Luis Fajardo (73.1)
Pedro Bofill (88.2)	Enrique Múgica (68.3)
Salvador Clotas (86.5)	José María Obiols (67.1)
Fransisco Lopez Real (83.3)	Joan Prat (65.7)

Provisional Conclusion

The 29th Congress of the PSOE showed the party to be deliberately preparing itself for government and adopting a pragmatic attitude towards its conception of socialism and towards the social sectors of political allies to whom it appealed. It confirmed the party leadership as one that was united, talented and hardworking, though already, in its short experience of free operation in democratic conditions, showing signs of remoteness from its rank-and-file—what Felipe called the 'oligarchisation' of the party. All that was required was the passage of time to complete the perfection of the party's image as attractive to all Spaniards, and to accomplish the almost total collapse of the credibility of the UCD, a vital component in the Socialists' electoral victory. Felipe González, unchallenged in his authority over the party, continued to rise irresistably as the most popular political figure in Spain.

The programme which the PSOE developed for the 1982 election campaign was not a particularly radical one, and did not figure prominently in the campaign. Its main commitment, to create over 800,000 jobs in four years was however a major gesture in response to the main concern to the Spanish electorate.[28] With 2 million unemployed, a rate of 16 per cent, Spain's unemployment situation was by 1982 the worst in Europe.

The aim was to promise gradual continuity of change, without radical transformation to the Left or Right; to promise in effect little more than what the UCD had promised but been unable to deliver. The private sector of the economy was to remain virtually untouched and was to be supported by government policies to create the bulk of the new jobs. Only the electricity supply was to be nationalised. The socialist programme won cautious approval from employers.

It was left to the UGT to insist on the inclusion within the programme of measures benefiting the labour movement such as the reduction of retirement age to 64, the forty-hour week, 30 days paid holiday and increased unemployment benefit.[29]

Administrative reform is another key element in the socialist programme, with the aim of eliminating corruption and inefficiency in public life, particularly the traditional Spanish practice of '*pluriempleo*' multiple jobs in public service. The aim of the programme was to give hope to everyone, and antagonise no-one. It will be a formidable task for the government to fulfill the hopes it has generated, but there is no doubt of the strength of popular support and enthusiasm which it enjoys at the outset. Equally there is no doubt that the PSOE will continue to play a major political role in Spain.

Notes

1. Felipe González and Alfonso Guerra, *El PSOE*, Ediciones Alba, Bilbao, 1977, p. 11. *Este Viejo y Nuevo Partido*, Secretaria Federal de Organisacion, Madrid, 1979,PSOE, Editorial Pablo Iglesias.
2. 'Spain, Eurocommunism and Socialism', in *The Dilemma of Eurocommunism*, The Labour Party, 1980, p. 54.
3. José Maravall, *The Transition to Democracy in Spain*, Croom Helm, London, 1982, p. 145.
4. Ibid., p. 146.
5. Ibid., p. 151.
6. Santiago Carrillo, *Eurocommunism and the State*, Lawrence and Wishart, London, 1977.
7. M. A. Aguilar and E. Chamorro, *Felipe González: Perfil Humano y Político*, Editorial Cambio 16, Madrid, 1977.
8. *Los Pactos de la Moncloa*, Servicio Central de Publicaciones, Madrid, 1977.
9. *The Dilemma of Eurocommunism*, op. cit., p. 56.
10. 'We are not monarchists . . . A republican state is more responsive to the wishes of the Spanish people for participation and liberty.
    In these moments of transition from authoritarianism to democracy, the issue of the monarchy or the republic is not a priority.
    If . . . the people support . . . the institution of monarchy we socialists will accept the popular decision, although we will continue not to be monarchists.'
    El PSOE, op. cit., p. 71.
11. 'A confessional state today is a medieval relic. A state which represents the jurdico-political superstructure of a whole collectivity cannot and should not uphold a particular religious creed. The state must therefore be secular. It is the only way to respect citizens' differing religious beliefs or their lack of them.'
    Ibid., p. 125.
12. Interview in *In These Times*, September 1978.
13. José Maravall, op. cit.
14. Text of PSOE–PCE pact on Municipal Policy quoted in full *Este Viejo y Nuevo Partido*, pp. 310–12.
15. Article 11, *Reglamento de Congresos*, PSOE, n.d.
16. Article 23 (b), *Reglamento de Congresos*. 'After the executive report has been moved the Congress Chairman will open the debate, asking for contributions from delegations not in agreement with all or part of the report.'
17. Article 25, *Reglamento de Congresos*. 'Ponencias (workshops) will be constituted by delegates in proportion to the size of delegations. An individual delegate cannot register in more than one workshop. Members of the Federal Executive Commission can participate in all ponencias but cannot vote . . .'
    Article 26: 'The purpose of the workshop is to draw up a statement to be presented to the Congress plenary session; the mover of the statement is to be elected by the participants in the workshop.'
    In practice the word *'ponencia'* refers both to the workshop itself *and* the resolution it presents to the full congress; it is, in other words, both the statement and the process by which it is elaborated.
18. There is nothing in the party rules relating to the nomination of candidates for the executive commission. Accordingly they 'emerge' in an apparently informal fashion, as a result of lobbying, negotiation and log-rolling amongst existing national and federal party leaders.
19. Article 20, *Reglamento de Congresos*. On Social Composition see Table 2.1.
20. The debate is explored in some detail in a special edition of *Zona Abierta*, **20**, May–August 1979, especially contributions by Fernando Claudín, Luis Gomez Llorente, Antonio Santasmeses, Enrique Gomariz and José Maravall.

62   *Elizabeth Nash*

21. Article 3(b), *Estatutos*, PSOE n.d.
22. The federal committee comprises: the federal executive commission, general secretaries of party federations in the regions, a young socialists' representative and regional delegates from the federations. It meets at least every four months or when called by one-third of the executive commission. It is the party's main policy making body between congresses and is responsible to party congress. Article 28, *Estatutos*.
23. *El PSOE ante la situacion politica*, 30 September 1981.
24. Speech to Labour MPs, House of Commons, March 1981. *El País*, 21 October 1981.
25. *50 Preguntas sobre la OTAN*, PSOE, Madrid, p. 134. *Por El Cambio*, Programa Electoral PSOE, 1981. *El País*, 21 October 1981.
26. *El País*, 18 October 1981.
27. *El País*, 21 October 1981.
28. *Por El Cambio*, p. 7.
29. Ibid. and *Cambio 16*, 20 September 1982.

Appendix: Social Composition of the PSOE

(based on a survey conducted by the party of its member (*Los Afiliados Socialistas*, PSOE, May 1981) quoted *Cambio 16*, 15 August 1981)

The survey showed that most members were satisfied with the internal workings of the party, that there were no significant and internal divisions and that the party, with 101,082 members, could now be considered a mass party. The average age of party members was 48 years. Only 1.8 per cent of the party's votes in elections came from party members, a very low proportion compared with other European socialist parties.

Its social composition is, however, quite similar: just over one-third of the party's members were manual workers, 21 per cent were pensioners. It has very few public servants as members.

Eighty per cent of members joined the party after the death of Franco, 5 per cent during Francoism and 13 per cent joined during the Republic, before Franco came to power. Only 39 per cent have religious beliefs.

Only 9 per cent of members are women, although their educational level is higher than that of the average male party-member. (32 per cent of the women have higher education qualifications compared with 18 per cent of the men.)

Most members are of modest income (64 per cent earn less than 50,000 pesetas a month). Recent recruits tend to belong to the 'new middle class', professionals, office workers, etc. and very few members (6 per cent) have had university education.

The majority (61 per cent) are satisfied with the internal workings of the party: 10 per cent see it negatively. More than 80 per cent of members pay their dues and attend party meetings, but less than 50 per cent regard themselves as active members. Most think there should be more discipline in the party.

3 THE SPANISH COMMUNIST PARTY IN THE TRANSITION

DAVID S. BELL

Resorting to a device that many others have found useful, the PCE (Partido Communista de España) adopted a journalistic term 'Eurocommunism'. Because this word was associated with the 'liberal' trend in western European Communism the Spanish Communist Party and its Catalan branch (Partido Socialista Univicat de Catalunya—PSUC) have attracted more than their due share of attention. However in retrospect Euro-communism appears less historic than it did in the mid-1970s, when the big Communist parties of Italy and France seemed poised to move into government and, with hindsight, it is possible to say that the changes are less significant than was once thought. Hence, although the PCE differs in degree from the Italian Communist Party and in kind from the French Communists, it is still a part of the international Communist movement, and has been unwilling to deny the epithet 'Socialist' to the Eastern-bloc regimes.[1] This lack of thoroughgoing self-liberation and hesitant support for Russia has been a factor in the PCE's internal troubles,[2] but it also makes the PCE less interesting than when it appeared to be breaking new ground.

Just as for Herbert Morrison 'Socialism is what a Labour government does', Santiago Carrillo appropriated the vogue term Eurocommunism as the label for their political line. Before other western Communists had become aware of it, Eurocommunism had been adroitly used to fill the vacuum of Spanish Communist strategy and ideology in post-Franco Spain, the Spain of political democratisation. Although Eurocommunism was a handy slogan it was no more than that and could not answer the questions asked by activists and voters, who increasingly demanded answers on matters of democracy (inside and outside the PCE), and policy, which the Party could not face. Moreover in 1977 the arrival on the stage of the large and electorally attractive Socialist Party effectively cut away the regions of support amongst floating or moderate voters to which the PCE was trying to appeal.

Party Structure

A Communist Party is, above all, its central organisation. After the 'bolshe-visation' of the Communist parties in the 1920s, when the European parties were submitted to Third International discipline, the hierarchical structure and responsiveness of the dedicated 'vanguard' nucleus became their distinctive characteristics. In order to place the PCE in some kind of inter-national perspective, and to bring out the importance of the Spanish model, a digression on Communist theory and on party structure is therefore necessary. It has, for example, been suggested that the Spanish Communist Party innovated in the following areas: it has abandoned 'dictatorship of the proletariat'; it has become non-violent; it has moved away from the Soviet model of society towards a specifically Spanish vision; and it is no longer Leninist. Although there is some truth in all of those points the first is trivial but the last is crucial.

For doctrinaire Marxists the theory (if it can be dignified with such a name) of the 'dictatorship of the proletariat' may be vital but its status in Communist doctrine is much more ambiguous and in practice it appears to be one of those pieces of ideological ballast which can be thrown over-board whenever a party needs some lift. Stalin himself obliged the British Party to abandon this notion in 1947 (the CPGB remained as servile to Moscow as before), the Portuguese Communists dropped the term and then participated in a *coup d'état*, the French Communist Party abandoned the concept but soon afterwards entered one of its hard-line phases: in sum the term can be dropped without effect on a party's subsequent action and the absence of the phrase is neither new, nor a significant guide to future behaviour.

Similarly a non-violent outlook is no innovation in Western Europe. State Monopoly Capitalism (SMC), the orthodox doctrine of western Communism, states that violent revolution is off the agenda for the fore-seeable future in capitalist countries. SMC, which emerged as a standard Communist 'teaching' in the early 1960s, merely makes explicit what the Yalta agreement and the 'balance of terror' in Europe have made inevit-able: Communists behind the capitalist lines would have to find their own way to power, through the pluralist system where possible. But, for orthodox Communists, SMC was to lead to Socialism defined as the model revealed by the Soviet Union. It was on this point that, in the mid-1970s the PCE appeared to be genuinely innovatory though not quite to an 'unprecedented' extent: Carrillo in *'Eurocommunism' and the State* exten-sively criticised the USSR, in particular for the lack of freedom, and it was even hinted that Eastern Europe was not 'Socialist'.[3] This was not developed: Carrillo's book turned out to be the flood tide for criticism of Russia inside the PCE; Spanish Communists still refer to 'Socialist' Countries and the PCE has not gone as far as the Italian Party in dissociating itself from Jaruzelski's regime in Poland or from the main Russian movement.

For reasons of domestic politics the PCE found it prudent to distance itself from the Russian system but it was reacting to events not making root and branch condemnations of Russian behaviour. The development of a specific Spanish route to Socialism need not be dwelt upon, for the originality of a non-revolutionary strategy is not (as has been noted) confined to Spain. Moreover the western Communists have taken many different routes since Stalin's death: it is the destination which matters and that remains a variant of Moscow-style Socialism.

The view that the PCE is no longer 'Leninist' is more misleading. 'Leninism' can mean many things but one of the meanings is that of a group of 'professional revolutionaries' and the PCE is a hierarchy structured around a core of some 300 or so Party functionaries—professional revolutionaries. All Communist parties are essentially this nucleus of full-time, dedicated, party professionals—it is where the power lies and the person who controls the apparatus controls the party. In Spain the controller was Carrillo but the struggle to retain and expand his control explains to a large extent the post-1979 upheaval in the PCF.

Leninism is sometimes identified with the concept of 'democratic centralism', a principal to which all Communist parties are supposedly wedded but which in Spain works rather differently from the traditional model. Unlike French Communism, Spanish Communism is not a party of unanimous votes, nomination from above, or of arbitrary changes of direction, but then neither does it fall into the category of what, for want of a better term, can be called the 'social democratic model' of activist participation in policy-making and decision-making. The Spanish Communist Party is neither run like a continental Socialist party nor like an orthodox Communist party.

Democratic centralism in the Spanish Party means strict party discipline and the subordination of the minority to the majority: a wide enough definition, but one which does allow for competitive elections for posts although its consequences are ultimately those which Trotsky pointed out in 1906: a dictatorship over the Party. The PCE became Carrillo's party in a way which was inevitable given the emphasis on the professional organisation of the Party and the strict obedience of members to the hierarchy. The Party hierarchy was, of course, staffed by Carrillo's placemen but there are minority groups within the PCE which have their own power bases, although they are not in a favoured position when faced with the leadership machine. The PCE is less strict in discipline than say the French Party, but it is none the less centralised.

Even if the Spanish Communist Party is Leninist in its centralised structure and control it is not a revolutionary party. Spanish Communism has abandoned the cell structure for the territorial unit of the *agrupación*. As has been pointed out this change from revolutionary cell to territorial *agrupación* was no innocent concession to democracy but a well-timed organisational manoeuvre which broke-up the solidifying alliances of intellectuals in the mid-1970s PCE.[4]

The non-revolutionary disciplined structure, although not enforced by nominations, ensures control by the leadership and indirect elections are used to assure domination by the Secretariat. The principal body in the Party, the Congress, is held every three years. *Agrupacións* elect delegates to provincial conferences which in turn elect delegates to regional conferences and it is this level which elects delegates to the National Congress. Since elections for delegates are by majority vote, minorities are unrepresented unless (sometimes the case) an agreement is reached with minorities and this means that the leadership usually takes the mandates. Where the leadership has a slight advantage over its opponents they have preponderant weight in the choice of delegates, there is thus a multiplier effect which works in the leadership's favour. Official delegates are also assisted by the prestige of the Secretariat, their control of the organisation, the fact that they are full-time politicians against what are usually part-time activists, and the restriction of the main organs of Party Communication (like the PCE's *Mundo Obrevo*) to the leadership under the heading of the prohibition of 'factions'. Whereas the leadership can organise its supporters there are no (official) means of forming a current of opinion in the Party (like CERES in the French Socialist Party, or Labour's *Tribune*).

At the National Congress a Central Committee of 104 (before 1981 it was 161) is elected and this in turn elects a President, a Secretary General and an Executive Committee.[5] A Central Committee election is decided by a list vote: the composition of the lists is decided by a committee of candidates which draws up the names of those on whom there is agreement. Minorities in whom there is no agreement go on to a separate list and because the system requires the displacement of votes to dissidents *en bloc* it is difficult (though not impossible) for minorities to get elected. The Secretariat is elected by the Central Committee which is composed of the leadership supporters plus representatives from the unions and regional parties.

In effect the PCE is a party which is commanded from the centre, which is not federal, but which does have minority currents opposed to the Secretariat. The size, strength and originality of the opposition has slowly been reduced since 1977 to the benefit of Carrillo and this, in large part, was because Carrillo had neither the flexibility of François Mitterrand who held the fissiparous French Socialist Party together nor the standard Communist machine of a leader like Georges Marchais. Although the rout of the PCE in the 1982 elections led to Carrillo's resignation and his replacement by Iglesias and although a further rally by those who want a more open organisation could be expected, the establishment put in place during the intra-Party fights should be able to control any situation which develops. Carrillo's use of power means that the new Secretary General has been surrounded by Carrillo supporters.

A Communist party which has debates and votes as open as the PCE cannot be considered normal in international Communist terms. When Carrillo was less firmly in control (on his return from Paris) the IXth and Xth National Congresses and the Vth PSUC Congress presented spectacles more in keeping with Social Democracy than with Communism. Now that the 'schismatics' and intellectuals of the anti-Franco years have been expelled the exuberance of and freedom of expression of the years 1977–79 have only a very weak contemporary echo. After the Xth Party Congress in July 1981 the leadership began to impose much tighter limits in the Party's internal debate and the minorities have since lost their main positions at the top of the Party.

The Spanish Communist Party in the Unions

Like all Communist parties the PCE has a special position in the unions but the Party's power is less than might appear and it is doubtful that Spanish Communists can use the Workers' Commissions to lever themselves back into favour with the electorate. There are two major trade-union confederations in Spain: the Comisiones Obreras (CCOO—Workers' Commissions) are Communists and the UGT (Union General de Traba-jadores) are Socialist. In the 1978 elections for factory delegates the Workers' Commissions were the largest (34.43 per cent to the UGT's 21.7 per cent) but since that time, when they benefited from their anti-Franco vote and their reputation, their position has been eroded. It is possible that in 1981–2 the two big unions were about level which is none the less a tribute to the skills of the CCOO which has resisted the pro-Socialist swing visible elsewhere in politics.

Communists have played the leading role in the Workers' Commissions almost since their foundation but it does not follow that they can deliver a Communist vote. It is none the less a major resource for the PCE and its leaders are all Communists. Marcelino Camacho leads a forty-two member Executive of whom only two are not PCE.[6] Given the discipline of Communist activists this produces a relationship which is at the least very close and which recalls the traditional 'Leninist' relationship with the union as 'transmission belt' to the working class more than a new form of relationship. It is principally the discipline and organisation of the Communists which enables them to retain control over the mainly non-Communist rank and file.

Thus the Party can, and does, control union strategy for its own purposes. According to Carrillo, and standard Communist view, the Party is the vanguard and the unions job is to organise the members. Party members are expected to join the Workers' Commissions which are themselves, expected to recruit for the Party: the inter-exchange of personnel is frequent. But if the CCOO–PCE tandem does not reflect the French Communists' domination of their *Confédération Générale du Travail* unions, this is because the Spanish Communists have taken a much more moderate political line and because their position in the working class is much weaker and subject to Socialist competition. Whatever Eurocommunism may mean in organisational terms, for the unions it means a reassertion of the 'Leninist' role. Camacho and other CCOO leaders have not been completely dominated by the Party, but at some cost: Camacho resigned from the PCE executive as an expression of dissent at the growing domination of the leadership over subordinate organs. But Communists retain their hegemonic position in the Workers' Commissions only at the cost of restraint and if they asserted the PCE line too strongly the CCOO would suffer severely: the Workers' Commissions National Congress is not overwhelmingly Communist, it includes and tolerates many different currents.

The Transitional PCE

Although the Spanish Communist Party was the principal force in the clandestine opposition to Franco, its history since its legalisation in Easter 1977 has been one of almost consistent decline.[7] Because of its historic role the PCE emerged from clandestinity with considerable advantages: a large number of enthusiastic activists (in the region of 200,000), an appreciable intellectual backing, support amongst the professional classes, a large union organisation (the Comisiones Obreras—CCOO the Workers' Commissions), a fully funded organisation, and the prestige arising from its anti-Franco struggle. In a few short years the Party had dissipated this inheritance largely because of its organisational inadaptability and its essential irrelevance to the central questions of Spanish politics.

The PCE's 9.4 per cent vote in 1977, the first democratic elections, belied the prognostications of many commentators who believed that it would emerge as first party of the Spanish Left (a place which went to the Socialists). An implicit analogy was being made with the big Resistance parties of Italy and France in 1945, an analogy which was misleading because the PCE did not bring Franco down, because the dictatorship was dismantled by centre politicians and the King and because the PCE was handicapped by its association with Moscow in a social climate which was far from revolutionary. However there is an important parallel with the French Communists in 1945: the Party had recruited from quite diverse milieux amongst people whose principal aim was to oppose the dictator-ship. These recruits had a quite different conception of the nature and role of the Party from the exile leadership who, on their return from abroad, were fixed with an ebullient but refractory Party. Re-establishment of leadership control over the Party operations meant disruption on a major scale against the internal 'resistance' activists and the pro-Soviet groups. Carrillo returned from Paris, surrounded himself with loyal supporters (so-called 'Parisians' as most had been in exile), and took over a Party base which was heterogenous, which had accepted discipline as a necessity of clandestinity but which was calling for a more open structure, and which had few romantic notions about 'Socialist' Russia.

Carrillo's first moves were to make him master in his own house, to set out the Party's democratic credentials, and to underline the Party's freedom of action by striking at the pro-Soviet current: this strategy, which in a publicity *coup de force* was baptised 'Eurocommunist', entailed public criticism of the least palatable aspects of the USSR and gave the Party a role in post-Franco politics through its very moderation (its acceptance of the monarchy, and of the Moncloa pacts of October 1977 establishing wage control, etc.)[8] but which gave it no tangible returns.

Eurocommunism, or political moderation, made sense when the PCE expected to emerge as the principal party on the Left, but in June 1977 it polled only 9.4 per cent to the PSOE's 29.9 per cent and this barely improved to 10.4 per cent in 1979. Furthermore the Communists faced a better organised Socialist Party, they were still distrusted by a large section of Spanish public opinion, and the leadership (in a Spanish political elite which was very young) was a living reminder of the Civil War. Disillusion amongst Party activists set in with the low vote and the Party began to use up its capital as principal opposition to Franco at an increasing rate. Carrillo nevertheless persisted with a 'moderate' role, possibly calculating that a radical position would destabilise Spanish democracy and that there was no extreme-Left constituency to which it could appeal, so that abandonment of Eurocommunism would end any potential the PCE had to influence events. Carrillo nevertheless played the Eurocommunist card with a flair and *élan* which disguised the PCE's weakness and gave it an international audience beyond what would be expected for a marginal party of that size.

Thus the Party's IXth Congress in April 1978, which dropped the reference to Leninism from the statutes, was a consolidation of the moderate Eurocommunist line, although it was not ambitious enough for some groups and the lines of future strife were already evident both in the regions (the Catalan delegation was split) and amongst the intellectuals, who expected a looser and more ideologically adventurous Party (for example Pilar Brabo clashed with Carrillo over the feminist issue). But the IXth Congress was not a difficult one for the Party leadership, who 'modernised' the PCE's view of Russia, and it represented a 'holding operation' for Carrillo, who still needed time to settle his supporters into the apparatus.[9]

Clashes in the PCE during the run-up to the IXth Congress gave the Party a more open image, but they were the harbingers of future divisions. Three broad currents are identifiable in the PCE after 1977: they are the pro-Soviets, many of whom, like Enrique Lister, left to form their own party; the 'renovators', mainly intellectual and middle classes who wanted faster liberalisation and a looser Party structure; and the Carrillo leadership which used the term 'Eurocommunist'. As is customary in Communist parties the power struggle for control of the PCE was conducted in Marxist language and by reference to points of doctrine and it went on from 1977 to 1982 when it ended with the complete victory of the Carrillo supporters but also with the virtual obliteration of Spanish Communism at the polls.

Although there had been problems for the leadership in Catalonia (where the pro-Soviets mounted a strong challenge) and in some other areas where the IXth Congress 'Draft Theses' had caused quarrels, internal organisation and structure, regional freedom of Party branches, and political orientation had all been questioned. After the IXth Congress the PCE continued to perform badly in the polls and it made very little progress in its attitudes to the USSR.[10] Carrillo's disastrous experiment with a daily *Mundo Obrero* cost the Party an indeterminately large sum and the leadership never really admitted the error. Moreover challenges from the Basque and Catalan regional parties began to gain and, ironically, the Party's international policy (run by 'renovator' Manual Azcárate) was instrumental in provoking difficulties with pro-Soviets because of the condemnation of the Russian invasion of Afghanistan (hence 'Afghans' as the name for the pro-Soviet group in Catalonia).

Pre-1979 clashes in the PCE were minor affairs compared with the full-fledged fight of 1981–82. The broad chronology of events was: the Fifth PSUC Congress of January 1981 which installed an anti-leadership faction in charge of the Party's Catalan branch but which was followed by a PSUC Congress in May 1981 which reversed the pro-Soviet positions of January and prepared the extraordinary PSUC Congress of May 1982 which gave Carrillo complete control of the Catalan Communist Party. Alongside the Catalan problem ran difficulties in Madrid and the Basque country and with pro-Soviets so that before the Xth Congress of July 1981 and afterwards there were continuous expulsions (the pro-Soviet Francisco Garcia Salve '*padré Paco*' for example). But the Xth Congress was bitter but decisive in the last instance although the difficulties continued afterwards. Thus in November 1981 the Basque Party tried to assert its freedom of action and was dissolved, something which proved to be a signal for the expulsion of renovators who had approved of the Basque Party's position. At this time ten Madrid councillors were expelled followed by forty or so provincial councillors who had shown sympathy with them. The Worker's Commissions which had not been too greatly involved in the disputes displayed some agreement with the renovators but, in a move emphasising the CCOO's autonomy, Marcelino Camacho (secretary general) and Nicolas Sartorius resigned from the PCE Executive. Thus was the ground prepared for the elections of October 1982.

Trouble in Catalonia

The Fifth PSUC congress in January 1981 came as an unwelcome shock to the leadership, although it was preceded by signals of Catalan dissidence like the circulation of amendments to the outgoing leader Grutiérrez' statement, the 'Draft Theses' (which were watered down to suit the pro-Soviets in PSUC). Opposition was organised by the pro-Soviet 'Afghan' faction but it is not necessary to invoke the 'hand of Moscow' to explain the anti-Madrid feeling in a PSUC of old-style activists who were both nationalist and troubled by the apparent failure of Eurocommunism to make gains. Eurocommunism was designed as a strategy for Madrid's benefit and the opposition to the Eurocommunist leadership led to the unlikely alliance of pro-Soviet 'last-ditchers', trade-union 'Leninists' and various nationalists. The defeat of the leadership's desire to retain this word Eurocommunist in the PSUC statutes caused the resignation of Secretary General Gutiérrez and President López Raimundo. Their posts passed to Fransisco Frutos and Pere Ardiaca in what was a set-back for Carrillo, though not, as Madrid tended to imply, a straight pro-Russian victory.[11]

Carrillo's response to the defeat of the leadership's supporters in Catalonia was to call for another extraordinary Congress before the main Xth PCE Congress.[12] With unquestionable energy, but with questionable impatience, Carrillo and his supporters set about the undoing of the Fifth PSUC Congress; a feat which was finally achieved with the extraordinary Congress of March 1982. After March 1982 there were a series of expulsions, exclusions and hasty departures from PSUC resulting in a fall in the number of Catalonian activists from about 30,000 to about 10,000 with many party workers moving over to the pro-Soviet Partit dels Communists de Catalunya (PCC). Antoni Gutiérrez moved back into the post of secretary general.[13] Events after the extraordinary Congress showed how 'democratic centralism' could be invoked against minorities in a way which would be highly unusual in a Socialist party: the leadership, now claiming to represent the 'majority', found its old opponents (the outgoing Executive) to be in breach of Party discipline and Pere Ardiaca, amongst others, was expelled.

The Xth National PCE Congress—28 July 1981

Problems between the leadership, the renovators and the pro-Soviets continued to simmer between Congresses but came to a head at the Xth Congress. There was no reconciliation at the Xth Congress through consensus but the dispute was resolved in the sense that afterwards the Eurocommunist leadership held the main posts without significant challenge from within the organisation. After the Xth Congress the weight of the Madrid bureaucracy could be thrown against isolated opponents.

Carrillo's intention to secure his grasp on the Party was announced from the outset: *Nuestra Bandera* (edited by Azcárate) was accused of factional activity. Francisco Garciá Salve was expelled for pro-Soviet views, and Carrillo gave a combative, uncompromising speech criticising 'nihilists' who wanted to legalise 'currents' within the Party. *Mundo Obrero*, for its part, announced that the Congress would be tough because there were both anti-Eurocommunist (i.e., pro-Soviet) and 'social democratic' (i.e., renovator) forces at work. Although Julio Anguita the 'renovator' mayor of Cordoba was present, the platform was almost entirely composed of Carrillo's supporters, who therefore started with the advantage of co-ordinated activity from the centre.

In the first indicative vote, Basque CP-leader Lertxundi, who emerged as a leading renovator, gave the opposition a victory by lowering the threshold which minorities had to pass to be able to speak from 33 per cent to 25 per cent. Envenomed in-fighting took place in delegations some of which, like Madrid, took refuge in abstention but at stake were some very different conceptions of the Party ranging from the Federal structure proposed by Aragon's José Luis Martinez, through the freedom of expression for currents demanded by the renovators, to the outright suppression of differences demanded by the Valencia delegation. For the renovators the war was lost when the Congress rejected by 651 votes to 273 (133 abstentions) the proposal to allow the existence of organised groups of opinion in the Party, i.e. the so-called 'horizontal' groupings.

In the candidature Committee of thirty, which meets to decide the lists for the Central Committee, only three renovators were present, a procedure which enabled the reduction of renovators on the Central Committee from the 30 per cent or so in the body of the Congress to 13 per cent in Party organs. For example Carrillo's supporters were included but in the Basque delegation; despite the renovator majority, three were 'Eurocommunist' and two were Lertxundi's supporters. In the Congress vote three renovators not on the official list were surprisngly elected (Chemi, Pilar Pérez, and Jordi Bórza), many renovators getting a higher vote than Carrillo's supporters so that the final Central Committee included eighty-eight Eurocommunists and sixteen renovators: the Central Committee used its Eurocommunist majority to purge the Executive Committee (which it elects) of the unruly. Azcárate was thrown off the *Nuestra Bandera* editorial board and the secretariat was staffed by Carrillo's nominees in preparation for the final struggle.

Much the same dispute was replayed a few months later in the Basque Party, where the desire for local autonomy and a strategy somewhat different from Madrid on opposition to Carrillo became manifest. Madrid refused to allow the Basque Communists to negotiate a fusion with the Basque left-wing party Euskadiko Ezkerra which would have meant the loss of control over its Basque branch in an organisation not predominantly Communist. Basque Communists had only one deputy in the regional parliament, Roberto Lertxundi, and the majority in the Basque Party saw this fusion as a way of revising their position, but it assumed a freedom of action which, ultimately, they did not have. Carrillo had Lertxundi's opponent in the Basque Party Ormazábal made leader by the Central Party in Madrid and then expelled Lertxundi and his supporters (who in fact constituted the bulk of Communists in the Basque Country). Euskadiko Ezkerra has maintained some influence in Basque political life but the reorganised Basque Communists are a tiny group.

Basque Communist difficulties brought the problem of the remaining renovators in the Party to a head. This was particularly so in Madrid, a section that was composed of a preponderance of lawyers, doctors, professional people, middle management and 'intellectuals', who had concentrated in the Party during the anti-Franco years. As a result the Madrid Federation was one of the most open to new ideas and the least amenable to the leadership imposed from outside by Carrillo's supporters. Amongst the first to leave were Eugenio Triana and Madrid deputy Ramón Tamames, although the complaints about the Party's internal autocracy continued long after their departure in May 1981.

In the run-up to the Xth Congress both Madrid and Valencia provincial conferences took up positions in favour of a more relaxed Party structure, but, once again evoking the subordination of the minority to the majority Carrillo stated that 'some order was needed' within the Party and the renovators either had to comply or were summarily disciplined. After Lertxundi's announcement that the Basque Communist Party would fuse with Euskadiko Ezkerra, renovators in the party gave their public support for the move. Carrillo and his supporters used this as an opportunity to discipline the Madrid Party: ten councillors were immediately expelled including, Pilar Arroyo, Pilar Brabo, Manual Azcárate etc., and the federation was thrown into turmoil. During the winter of 1981–82 the Madrid federation was thoroughly purged to the extent that in some areas it almost ceased to exist and it probably lost about three-quarters of its activists.[14] As an added twist to 'democratic centralism' only the leadership view of affairs was given in *Mundo Obrero* and, unlike *Treball* (the PSUC's weekly) in the weeks prior to the Vth PSUC Congress, the debate was kept frankly under Carrillo's control.[15] Communist activists voted with their feet elsewhere in Spain so that by 1982 the official figure of 160,000 Party members was certainly incorrect and the so-called renovators were replaced along with the 'pro-Soviets' to the benefit of Carrillo's supporters in the central apparatus. Unlike the Italian Communists the Spanish Party has proved itself incapable of maintaining central discipline and the loyalty of the middle classes in a modern society. This inability to hold the intellectuals it had recruited during the resistance to Franco is partially a result of the PCE's weak and marginal position in Spanish politics but it is also a result of the leadership's inflexible and unimaginative use of 'democratic centralism' against minorities.

Conclusion

The victory of Carrillo over both the pro-Soviet section of the PCE and the renovators opened up a future of leadership domination and almost limitless tactical flexibility. Spanish Communism became disciplined and more like the rest of the continental Communist movement. Internal dissidence, squabbles, explosions, and the shedding, in the full glare of publicity, of the PCE's most prestigious figures no doubt contributed to the lessening of the Spanish Communists' popularity but the problem goes much deeper. Neither Carrillo nor the other Communists have been able to give a convincing reason for voting Communist in contemporary Spain. The manipulation of the term Eurocommunism disguised this difficulty in the early stages but it has never been overcome. In broad terms if the PCE becomes more 'liberal' it enters a competition with the PSOE which it cannot win, but any return to a hard-line position will leave it equally marginal (there was no evidence in the 1982 election of a vote to the Left of the PCE waiting to be picked up—the extreme Left also did badly).

This strategic *impasse* was evident during the 1982 elections when, despite an active well-planned, well-run campaign the PCE received a decisive rejection at the polls. The Party's manifesto 'So that nobody is out of work' contained one or two demagogic elements (such as the objection to the restrictions on devolution) and did not mention Poland (in a concession to pro-Soviets). The aim seemed to be to reinforce the Socialist message, not to outflank the Socialists; but it was an attempt to carry some Socialist proposals slightly further (to create one million jobs in place of the PSOE's proposed 800,000). In Catalonia the PSUC ran a particularly active campaign which started with a motion of censure on the Catalan Nationalist administration in the regional assembly, which predictably failed because an attempt had been made to gain wider support, but here too the Party fell before the PSOE tidal wave.

In the west the PCE vote fell by over a million from 1,900,000 to 840,000 (from 10.4 per cent to 3.8 per cent) and the number of deputies from twenty-three to five. Those deputies elected were: Santiago Carrillo in Madrid; where PSUC once had eight deputies; only López Raimundo from Barcelona was returned; Horacio Fernández Inguanzo from Asturias; Ferrando Pérez Royo from Seville; and, from Valencia, Antonio Palomares (the PCE had no Senate seats). But the PCE lost across the board; very little in the way of an identifiable social base remains to a Party which is now a collection of scattered individuals who have residual support in some working-class areas. Carrillo found himself having to deny resignation rumours on the night of the elections, Sortorius[16] attacked Carrillo indirectly the day after the poll and on 6 November Carrillo resigned to make way for his own nominee Gerardo Iglesias. But the leadership's grip on an attenuated organisation (deserted by activists opposed to Carrillo) has tightened and the Eurocommunists should be able to see off any contenders through the use of the Party apparatus.[17] It is not clear whether Carrillo's resignation is a genuine stepping down or whether he intends to run the Party through the person of Gerardo Iglesias, a somewhat grey figure beholden to Carrillo. In any case neither Carrillo nor Iglesias have the resources to revive the Party, they can at best hope for the Socialist government to make mistakes.[18]

In conclusion, it should be pointed out that the PCE's place in history is assured because of its role during the transition to democracy. The moderation of the PCE deprived the Right of an argument against democratisation and de-radicalised the entire political spectrum. Thus the lack of a radical Communist Party meant that left-wing groups inside the Socialist Party have had much less power and, unlike CERES in the French Socialist Party, their position has been marginal. At crucial times the PCE, by expressing its support for the democratic system in Spain, has enabled the growth of a securely-routed constitutional system. From the PCE's point of view, this is troublesome since the system which has arisen is more akin to Northern Europe than to Southern Europe: a large Socialist Party faces a Conservative Party in an increasingly bi-polar confrontation and in which Communism has no place. Spain has come to be an essentially Downsian competition for the political middle ground for which Communist Parties are by their very nature ill-equipped.

Notes

1. Within the voluminous literature in 'Eurocommunism' this point is substantiated in Manual Azcárate, *Crisis del Eurocommunismo*, Argos Vergara, Barcelona, 1982, p. 291 ff. Santiago Carrillo went quite far in his *'Eurocommunism' and the State*, Lawrence and Wishart, London, 1977 and see S. K. Holland, 'The Economics of Eurocommunism', in E. Mortimer (ed.), *Eurocommunism*, Penguin, London, 1980 and F. S. Kissin, *Communists: All Revisionists Now?*, Fabian pamphlet 299.
2. Pedro Vega and Peru Erroteta, *Los Herejes del PCE*, Planeta Barcelona, 1982.
3. Santiago Carrillo, op. cit., p. 164, 'the October Revolution produced a state which is evidently not a bourgeois state but neither is it a genuine workers' democracy'. However the criticisms of Russia in the International Report of the Xth Congress were toned down and eventually abandoned.
4. P. Varga and P. Erroteta, op. cit., p. 25.
5. About twelve are appointed *'ex-officio'* by the unions and regional parties. See M. Azcárate, op. cit. p. 225 ff.
6. *El País*, 25 April 1978.

7. Joan Estruch Tobella, *El PCE en la Clandestinidad, 1936-56*, Siglo *XXI* (Madrid) 1982. Clandestine membership of the PCE in the mid-1960s may have been in the region of 2,000-3,000. See Guy Hermet, *The Spanish Communists*, Saxon House, London, 1971, p. 116.

8. Eusebion M. Mujal-León, 'The Domestic and International Evolution of the Spanish Communist Party', in R. L. Tökés (ed.), *Eurocommunism and Détente*, New York University Press, New York, 1978, pp. 204-70.

9. The IXth National PCE Congress is reported in *Noveno Congress del Partido Communista de España, 18-23 April 1978*, Editorial Critica, Madrid, 1978.

10. Ramón Tamames, 'Renovarse o Morir' in *El Viejo Topo*, 11 (December 1980), pp. 21-6. Structural rigidity is given as the main reason for his leaving the PCE.

11. The leadership reply was given in G, López Raimundo and A. Gutiérrez Díaz, *El PSUC y el Eurocommunismo*, Grijalbo, Barcelona, 1981.

12. *El País*, 6 January 1981 and Sortorius' reply to the 'pro-Soviets' in *El País*, 14 April 1982.

13. *El País*, 23 March 1982.

14. *El País*, 18 December 1981. Article by F. Claudín, *Le Monde*, 27 July 1981.

15. José Maravall, *The Transition to Democracy in Spain*, Croom Helm, London, 1982, especially Part 3, and Peter McDonough, Antonio López Pina and Samuel H. Barnes, 'The Spanish Public in Political Transition', *British Journal of Political Science*, 11 (1981), pp. 49-79, on the moderation of the electorate. A severe attack on the strategy of Carrillo's PCE can be found in *Franco est mort dans son lit*, Hachette, Paris, 1980 by C. S. Maura.

16. *El País*, 28 September 1982.

17. *El País*, 8 November 1982.

18. Since this chapter was written the PCE's number of deputies was reduced to four.

4 CONSTITUTIONAL NORMS AND CENTRAL ADMINISTRATION: REFLECTIONS ON SOME OF THE ARTICLES OF THE 29 DECEMBER 1978 CONSTITUTION

PIERRE SUBRA DE BIEUSSES

Other than in minor details, Spanish public administration remained practically unreformed during the transition period. Up until the end of 1978 the complex administrative organisation of the dictatorship remained intact: adaption to the new political situation was not undertaken. The nature of the State, as it is outlined in the Constitution of the 12 December 1978, differs fundamentally from that of the Franco-state, there is therefore an imperative need for an adaption of the State's organic structures (and hence of its administration) to the new supreme law and to the political realities of which it is but the expression. In fact it is difficult to ignore any longer the evident relationship between the political and administrative contexts: a relationship which implies, in the present case, an articulation of the administrative organs to adapt them to function for the needs of a democracy, and the need not only to look at the administrative structures in themselves but to examine them with a specific object in mind. In the terms of the first Article of the Constitution: 'Spain is in law a social and democratic State, which upholds as the supreme values of its juridical order, liberty, justice and political pluralism' and, according to Article 23, 'citizens have the right to participate in public affairs.'

Given a society with such a basis, the Spanish administration will have to promote those values which are the stated objective. If constitutional precepts are not to remain a dead letter, it is important to 'conceive of and to make possible an administration that is no longer dominated by a few people dug-in behind the barricades of power, but one that is a collaboration between public authorities open to all suggestions and groups and individuals participating actively so as to satisfy social needs.'[1] This is the only way in which the declarations of Constitutional principle can become effective since 'it is the public authorities, [according to Article 9 of the Constitution] which have the power to bring about the conditions that will make real and effective the liberty and equality of individuals and of the groups to which they belong and to clear away the obstacles which inhibit or make difficult their full exercise.' It is important that these public authorities can work through the medium of organisations conceived with that function in view, in the framework of a pluralism which is not only that of the Society, but of the State itself within which co-exist diverse entities which have power and authority by virtue of the autonomy principle. It is thus possible to see that the administration of democratic Spain should be intrinsically different from the previous one.

Having said that, Spain's problems were not solved instantly by the adoption of the new Constitution. Whilst the Constitution lays down which reforms should be undertaken, it is obviously left to the legislature to organise and implement them. Thus the arrangements currently written into the Constitution are under review, and therefore only the areas of administration envisaged by the Constitutional law are considered here. However, even the theme thus delimited would be far too large to be seriously tackled within the compass of a short chapter.

Given the new pluralist nature of the State which has just been mentioned, there is no longer, as with the preceding fundamental laws, a monolithic public administration, or a State organisation in a single bloc which only recognises subordinate legal entities. The administrative bodies which will develop and be organised in Spain will be reduced since Title VIII of the Constitution establishes the existence of the real devolved authority—which is not the same as the central State: the commune, the province and the autonomous community. Their examination would need a special study which, for the reasons of space mentioned above, cannot be dealt with in the current discussion. Moreover, it should be noted that Spanish doctrine[2] is generally agreed on the point that Article 103 (which deals with the principles which inspire the action of the public administration) concerns only the central State: the central civil service; the military administration; the security forces. With regard to the very specific characteristics of these two last types of administration, a general all encompassing analysis would hardly be coherent; it is therefore only the central civil service which will be examined in the following expanded comments. First, one should establish what is meant by that.

The first point poses no difficulties. Contrary to what happened under General Franco to the basic law of the regime of State administration which included the Head of State in the 'high administrative authorities', and to what is the case in the institutions of a large number of other countries, no executive power has been given to the King of Spain; instead it has been given as a whole to the government by Article 97 of the Constitution. That aside, the question that has just been posed could, *a priori*, seem somewhat superfluous if the general consensus that the central State administration is composed of all the authorities which form the executive were taken into account; these authorities have a political role, which brings their study into that of constitutional law, and an administrative role, under which title they belong to administrative law. None the less it is important to stop at that point where the analysis by some Spanish commentators moves on to questions of the unity or duality of concepts of government and of administration.[3]

Under the preceding system the law on the conduct of the administrative State explicitly linked the civil service with a series of authorities and organs integrated into the government; the head of State, the Cabinet, the Prime Minister and the ministers. But now, as, for example thinks Professor Baena del Alcazar,[4] 'everything appears to indicate that the Constitution distinguishes between government and administration', to the extent that one is led to ask whether the latter comes from the former. The differentiation had already appeared under the heading of Title IV: 'Of the government and of the administration.' It is confirmed by the fact that the legal system of these entities depends, not on one, but on two articles.[5] Finally Article 97 leaves no doubt as to the superior and distinct character of the government relative to the administration to the extent that it allows that 'the government directs . . . the civil administration'. From the organic point of view, government and administration are two different things.

In fact, it is not clear exactly how these facts led the doctrine mentioned above to a dualism of concepts, and it is even less convincing if, going beyond the limited examination of Title IV, one looks at the whole range of constitutional arrangements capable of shedding light on the matter. One example will enable a rapid clarification of this. On the point about the reasons for the ineligibility and incompatibility of deputies and senators, Article 70-I-B alludes to 'The high authorities of the administration which the law enumerates, with the exception of members of the government.' It follows, therefore, from that formula that members of the government are also high administrative authorities. The connection between the government and the administration is effected through the ministers, these being at the same time members of the government, and placed at the head of the ministries which are as a matter of fact the highest organs of the administration. There is nothing out of the ordinary in this and it is consistent with points which comparative law can clarify. André de Laubadère[6] makes clear that 'the central administration is made up of all the authorities which form the executive power.' Professor R. Entreña Cuesta[7] notes about the current Spanish system that 'the cabinet constitutes the most important of the collective organs of our working administration.' As to its composition, it is stated in Article 98(I) that 'the government is composed of the Prime Minister, and below that level of the deputy Prime Ministers, of ministers and of other members envisaged by the law.'[8]

It goes without saying that, in terms of Article 97, the government exercises statutory power. Ministers can only take statutory powers under legislative delegation, or on the basis of an agreement given by statutory decree from the government, and the other administrative authorities are limited to the internal regulation of services. Apart from the power of statute which comes from Article 97, the government is also empowered by the Constitution to pass 'legislative decrees' (Article 85) under the delegation of the general Cortes (Article 82), and, in the case of 'extraordinary and urgent necessity', legislative measures in the form of decree laws (Article 82).

In Spain, as in all other countries, it has evidently always been impossible, and it has become even more inconceivable, for a complete management of the national public services to be provided from the capital by the central administrative authorities. The central administration must therefore necessarily have a territorial aspect, the country being divided into areas which serve as the framework for the local administrative authorities. Traditionally called 'peripheral' administration,[9] this, until the present, was composed of civil governors who were the 'permanent representatives of the nation's government' in each province, and, in the provincial framework, there is always a delegate from the different administrative Ministerial Departments of State, under whose authority the peripheral services of the Minister concerned are grouped together. In view of the 1978 Constitutional text, it may be doubted that such a peripheral State administration should continue to exist. First because the State authorities which should be exercised throughout the entire territory continue to be maintained. But also because this type of administration is explicitly designated in Article 154 dealing with its co-ordination with the administration of autonomous devolved local communities. Moreover, the same article creates a new peripheral authority in the person of the central administration's delegate in the autonomous communities. Given the silence of the supreme law on civil governors, some people have suggested their eventual disappearance. However, the designation by Article 141(I) of the province as the territorial unit of division of the State already leads to the supposition that it will not be so; doubts were raised by the Royal Decree of 10 October 1980, which not only maintained the institution, but reinforced the position of civil governors by ensuring that the government delegates exercise their powers through the intermediary of the governor. Because of their diversity, these few introductory remarks have already led to the reference to a large number of articles from the 29 December 1978, constitution. To attempt an exhaustive investigation that ignored none of the range of Constitutional matters (of unequal importance) which touch on central State administration, would lead to an excessively long, rather incoherent article lost in the detail of much minutiae. By isolating a few fundamental articles, the discussion has been limited to an examination of the principles which should inspire administrative organisations: arrangements made to encourage the participation of the citizen in administrative work, or to guarantee the effective subordination of the administration to the law.

The Principles of Administrative Organisation

In the terms of the first line of Article 103, 'The public administration[10] serves with disinterest[11] the general good and acts in conformity with the principles of efficiency, hierarchy, decentralisation, devolution and co-ordination in entire subordination to the law and to right'. Not limited to the constitutionalisation, in itself advisable, of the principle of the compliance of the administration to the law and to right,[12] the Spanish Constitution inserts diverse principles of administrative organisation into the supreme law. On this last point, the precise formulation used is certainly not above criticism and seems to run alongside principles as intrinsically opposed as hierarchy and decentralisation. Equally ambiguous is the fact that concepts applying to very distinct preoccupations and of a noncomparable legal content are situated on the same level. The importance and the interest of these dispositions should not be under-estimated, however.

At first sight the mention of the principle of efficiency appears gratuitous and, in consequence, debatable. Indeed, even if precedents in comparative law do exist, why should a mere wish be given constitutional rank? What is the use of this constitutionalisation which is nonsensical, since it is necessarily deprived of any legal consequence? Even if the Constitution remains silent, an inefficient administration will never be anything but a bad administration.

One example will demonstrate that, in our view, it would be erroneous to support such an interpretation of the situation. Line three of Article 103, which was not quoted above, states that 'The law will determine the status of civil servants and the details of the right to union organisation'. According to Article 28 (lines i and ii), the same law determines the details of the right of union organisation for public servants, and on the issue of the right to strike, 'establishes the precise guarantees assuring the continuity of services essential to the community'. It is therefore discernible that the legislator whose conception of the efficiency of administration leads him to view the civil servant as a citizen apart but subject to exorbitant rights and obligations under common law, would find in the first line of Article 103 the indisputable constitutional base for a legislation which restricts and violates the freedom of union affairs and the freedom of the right to strike for public servants. Having said that, the following principles are those which should be given most attention: hierarchy, decentralisation and co-ordination.

Hierarchy

This may seem a surprising first choice in that the hierarchic option is here deprived of all originality and all innovative character. It is known that it implies a system of central administrative organisation which has traditionally been characteristic of Spain and which, after the manner of the French model, is typical of the administrations of a large number of countries. It would therefore be superfluous to explain that the choice to which it bears witnesses is that of a Spanish administration in which the power of decision will remain largely concentrated at the top of the hierarchy, that is in the hands of the minister. In this the subordinate strata only serve to transmit and to execute: to transmit questions from the territory of origin up to the level of the competent minister who reaches a decision about them, to transmit in the reverse direction the ministerial decision, and, finally to execute the concrete tasks according to the orders handed down. The important thing is not this, but rather the very unusual and debatable system of constitutionalisation.

In elevating the principle of hierarchy to that of the highest norm, it is thereby given the maximum legal authority, that is, it is imposed on the legislators themselves. (It is only thus ranked that the latter can organise within narrow limits, given the principle regarding the characteristics of administrative organisation.) The system is thus extraordinarily rigid; Spain cannot change its administrative model without any constitutional revision. It might be surmised that such an enshrinement of principle does not necessarily imply acceptance.

The Spanish State of the democratic Constitution of 1978 evidently differs profoundly from that which preceded it. The logical result of all this is, that there appears an imperative need of means to adapt the structures and thus the administration to the new political and social conditions. Now, as it is clearly stated in the doctrine,[13] the inevitable enforcement

of hierarchy in this area leads to the maintenance of bureaucratic organisation, that is to say leads to the status quo, to the persistence of the bureaucratic power which emerged from Franco's regime. Recalling the content
of the law on the State's administrative regime of 26 July 1977, Professor
Garrido Falla notes that with regard to the constitutionalisation of the
principle, there is no need to modify the previous commentaries as far as
the positive law is concerned.[14] Beyond that specific point it is worth
reminding oneself of the long-term implications of solidifying a system
founded on hierarchical relations and susceptible only to slight modernisation (by management, by the search for further rationalisation and for
more devolution) beside the appearance of another form of administration
where the legitimacy of power will come from the top but also where
each agent of the public service could participate in the administration of
his branch.

Decentralisation[15]

By contrast with the preceding remarks, the reference to the principle of
decentralisation should be regarded as positive. One of the key articles of
the constitution is, without doubt, Article 2 which deals with the matter
of national unity and the autonomy of nationalities and regions allowing
a redistribution of power as a result of a new state structure. But beyond
that, it would hardly have been logical to juxtapose the administration
of the autonomous regions and an exaggeratedly centralised state administration. The recourse to an effective decentralisation was thus imposed
and led to the recognition of the local character of certain affairs (territorial decentralisation), including the level of autonomous communities
about which line two of Article 150 makes clear that the State could
'transfer or delegate powers within the domains it heads',[16] or to confer
a degree of autonomy on specific public services by giving them legal
personality (decentralisation through services). From them, in the particular case of Spain, the recourse to the writing of these principles into
the Constitution is undoubtedly superfluous. It was correct to give great
emphasis to the principle, because previously this had appeared to be
devoid of·consistency and of interest. 'With the legislation of the previous
regime,' reminds M. Baena del Alcazar,[17] 'no effective powers were assigned
to the functions of public figures,' there was no real decentralisation but
only 'simple euphemisms masking a centralising political will.'

Another student of Spanish administration has demonstrated that the
incorporation into the Constitution of the principle of decentralisation
and the duty of the civil service to put it into practice will henceforth
lead to 'a system based on the notion of a closer link between the

administration and the administered through the transfer of functions to subordinate territorial units which will act with full decision-making capacity.'[18] This interpretation seems to be confirmed by the outline law which approved the bases of local administration. According to Article 3 of that text, the law, conforming to the decisions of Articles 137, 140 and 141 of the Constitution, 'recognises' the legal personality and the autonomy of the communes and of the provinces for the administration of their respective interests.' On the communes Article 18 of the law makes clear that for the administration of their own interests 'they will be able to promote any kinds of enterprise and to offer all the public services required to satisfy the needs and desires of the local community.' Moreover the principle put into Article 103 must also necessarily lead to a decentralisation through the services. This observation results from the relation that can hardly fail to be made between this and other diverse constitutional imperatives; notably those of Articles 128 and 129. The first establishes public initiative in economic activity, if necessary through the medium of 'enterprises', and thus eventually, of public industries. The second is particularly relevant, on the matter of social security, to the activity of public organisations whose function directly affects standards of living or the general welfare. These references to public organisations which have been given a legal personality should not be taken in isolation, but, believes Baena del Alcazar,[19] 'coupled with the decentralisation principle of Article 103, given its second sense of decentralisation through services.'

Co-ordination

The need to avoid any duplication and conflict of interests between organs at the same level of authority, is evidently not just a Spanish administrative concern. It would be convenient here, as elsewhere, to create between the organs a distribution of work which allows a rational and efficient functioning and, based on that, to harmonise this in a consistent way. For what concerns the central organs, is that there should be a rational division of labour between ministerial departments and that co-ordination of their activity should be enforced by governmental leadership (Article 97). If it was the only problem involved, the constitutional provision of a principle which is as elementary as that, and whose working is so necessary would seem to be superfluous. This is of undeniable importance when taken in the context of the special Spanish case: things threaten to become much more complex and difficult to resolve at the peripheral administration level (as stated above). It is known that Article 154 of the Constitution deals with the administration in relation to the autonomous communities. Alcazar, a specialist in these problems, believes that there is 'a constitutional will to reach a harmonised working, which is as desirable as it is difficult to achieve in practice.'[20] That is why the greater legal force given to the principle of co-ordination is undoubtedly pregnant with unseen consequences;[21] and those consequences are as much positive as they are negative. Depending on the way in which it is understood, it could certainly enable implicit difficulties of harmonization to be overcome rather better. It could also constitute a pressure point for a legislator desirous to empty the devolved regional authorities of real power by instituting powers to oversee them under the cover of rational co-ordination of the activities of devolved communities with those of the central state. In any event a satisfactory relation between the local and regional authorities and the government delegate, who must specifically (according to the terms of Article 154) co-ordinate their activities with those of the State, will doubtless not be reached without considerable difficulties.

Furthermore, use of their powers by these communities will, to some extent, cause a lessening of the extent of the interests of the peripheral administration and will thus benefit the devolved areas. But as the provincial branches of ministerial departments will continue to exist, co-ordination will be more difficult and the need to move towards a division of labour between the peripheral administrative authority and the local autonomous powers will become imperative. These diverse problems threaten to take on an even greater complexity and severity because (according to line two of Article 150) the State will retain the option to transfer or to delegate to the devolved autonomous localities 'facilities' coming initially from the group of what were state powers and which could henceforth be divided between two quite distinct authorities. With such potential cases it is not at all certain that the possibilities, opened by line two of Article 150, of establishing the transfer of some kinds of control from the State through an organic law, will facilitate co-ordination between communities who are jealous of their newly acquired autonomy. It must also be noted that the co-ordination between legally separate public personalities will sometimes give way to the unilateral control (i.e. subordination) of the State. Some of the conditions of Article 155 allow this institution to adopt measures capable of constraining an autonomous community which does not conform to obligations imposed on it by the Constitution or which work in a way which is against the interests of Spain. Finally there is an area where co-ordination could turn out to be particularly indispensible and difficult and that is in relations with the municipal authorities. That is a result of article 148(I–2e) which deals with the controls, such as they are, of municipal authorities and creates or allows a competition of authority, between the State and the devolved communities.

Citizen Participation in Administration[22]

Already in this chapter, when quoting Professor Baena del Alcazar, there has been occasion to note that the Francoist administration was, to an appreciable extent, domination by the minority entrenched behind the barricade of power. The Constituent Assembly of democratic Spain had to mark and signal change in this area as in many others. Its desire to bring together the administrators and the administered is clearly shown by Article 9(2), and therefore what concerns us here is that all public administration is obliged to facilitate that participation in political, economic, cultural and social life. It is an obligation cast in terms which are vast. According to Article 23 this participation must become effective, not only through the intermediary of freely elected representatives but through a direct participation in public affairs. It can therefore be noted that the dynamic of democracy (starting from the idea of representation which is only expressed more or less periodically through the act of election) leads to a participation implying an active citizenship role (individually or in association) in administration. The Constituent Assembly detailed the matter around this principle. The Assembly decided that the law will determine:

(a) the consultation of citizens, directly or through organisations and associations recognised by the law, in the process of elaborating administrative arrangements which concern them;

(b) the access of citizens to registered administrative archives except those about security and defence of the State, misdemeanours and people's private affairs;

(c) the procedure through which administrative decisions are taken guarantee, when needs be, the consultation of those concerned. Although still framed in a general form (since it leaves the settlement of detail to an ordinary law) and sometimes overtly insufficient, the Constitution declares itself on three series of questions of intrinsic interest since they touch on the intervention of the citizens in the decisions of administrative acts; the access of people to administrative documents; the legality of the administrative process including the consultation of those concerned.

The participation of citizens in the taking of administrative decisions

Noting the maladaption of administrative structures to the necessary transformation of their role in the contemporary world, Professor F. P. Benoît wrote, almost fifteen years ago: 'the future thus appears to lie within a lightening of vertical administrative structures and a direct participation of citizens in public affairs', that is 'in harmony with the democratic ideal', the purpose is not one 'of limiting the cooperation of individuals to a purely consultative role, but on the contrary help them to play an active role alongside the administrative authorities.'[23] Because in all evidence, these observations could well apply to today's Spanish administration, the way the 1978 Constituent Assembly dealt with the matter is all the more disappointing. In reducing participation to a phase of consultation integrated into the procedure of elaborating 'administrative arrangements' from, or of, citizens affected by it, the Constitutional rules added nothing to previous positive law. Article 130(4) of the Franco law on administrative procedure, still in application, determined that

> whenever it is possible and when the nature of the arrangements makes it desirable, the union organisations and other entities involved by the law in the representation or defence of general interests or corporate interests affected by the said law will be consulted and given the possibility to expound their point of view through a reasoned report in a period of ten days, including the deposition of the project, except when they are against public interests as duly outlined in draft project.

It can only be hoped, since the reference to union organisations should lead to the redundancy of these arrangements, that the new law will on this point extend Article 105 beyond the exclusive sectoral character of the system which has just been quoted and lead to an equality of treatment for all subjects of administration. It would be prudent to keep to Professor Garrido Falla's suggestion[24] that the legislature should not be limited to a system of strict consultation but retain the power to hold a public enquiry at a time when any interested party (without that term being defined with any real rigour) is duly informed, and would be able to make observations favourable or unfavourable to the project concerned.

Still on the problem of the first line of Article 105, it can be noted that the vagueness existing when the organisation and associations recognised by the laws are taken into account, leads to much uncertainty. In relation to the field of application on the regulatory texts, it can be asked what limits these are to territorial spheres of competence of these entities and associations. Besides it will perhaps be difficult to discover the most equitable representation when these organisations become too numerous which will certainly happen quite frequently. It would not be possible to exclude the resurgence of a corporate administrative power through this clause.

Access to administrative documents

Evidently a responsible participation by citizens requires access to appropriate information and the evolution of modern legislation is moving in that direction.[25] The Constituent Assembly took note of this when making it a fundamental right (Article 20–d) to 'freely communicate or receive truthful information through any means of diffusion' and guaranteeing 'access to registered and administrative archives'. Even so one may be sceptical about forthcoming legislative action, if one observes the restrictions which the declarations of principle have been subjected to since the very beginning of the Constitution-writing process. As Professor F. Carrido Falla has not failed to notice, 'the information developed by the administration, or that it obtains, for carrying out its functions (including in a co-operative manner as in the case of financial declarations) could constitute, if it is passed on, a danger to the security of the country or to the integrity and privacy of individuals'. Article 18 guarantees the 'right to integrity and to personal and family privacy', and as Article 20d (quoted above) is not limited to the sole right to communicate or freely receive information, but adds that the 'law will regulate, for the exercise of these liberties, the conscience clause and that of professional secrecy', Article 105–6 has quite naturally excluded anything which could affect the security and defence of the State and the constitution of offences against personal privacy from the right of access to administrative and registered archives.

Thus it is not surprising that the commentaries on that Article have often dealt with the extent and method of restrictions that the future law would place upon 'right of access' from the time that the legislature has a constitutional base from which to class as secret an enormous amorphous mass of documents. Apart from the legislation which guarantees the integrity and privacy of individuals and of the family, and professional secrecy (which is implied by Article 20 of the Constitution) Article 105–b announces, albeit implicity, a new law on official secrets which, it might be anticipated, will not be a simple updating of the previous law of September 1968. It is significant that in the space that the collective work *Comentarios a la constitucion* gives to this text, a large place is given, not to the right of access itself, but to the way in which the legislation will deal with it to guarantee such secrets and to the exact extent of limitations and prohibitions which in any case will be instituted (this, significantly, does not seem to be in doubt). Considering that the very spirit of the Constitution is one of great restriction, and that on this question it stands by the idea that even for 'non-secret information' there are always some inconveniences in communicating what bears on 'education, health, or the economy', it is not suggested here what the characterisation of such an ensemble of liberal permissive and reasonable law could have. Nevertheless there are questions about the time during which any document ought to remain secret, on the extent of the obligation of secrecy placed on civil servants, or on the problem of knowing whether the sanctions to which they are subject in this domain should be of a penal or disciplinary nature. It can be seen, without having to stress the point further, that the study of the Constitution does not lead Spanish students of administration to nurture great hopes.

Consultation of citizens and the process of elaborating individual administrative acts

Although it speaks of the citizens concerned, the first line of the Article deals with rule-making arrangements; the word 'interested party' is used in the singular showing that it is individual acts which are now under review. Effectively, the Constitution imposes on the legislator the task to determine 'the procedure through which the administrative acts will guarantee, when it is appropriate, the consultation of the interested party'. On this point, two observations can be made. In the first place, the relation which should be made between that line and Article 149 (1–18e) reveals that the importance of that guarantee of consultation should be understood as being very general. According to this last text, the powers of the State, as established by the constitution, touch notably on 'the bases of the legal regime of public administration which will guarantee under any circumstances a uniform treatment of those administered', or 'the common administrative procedure, without prejudice to the individualities which come from the autonomous communities' own organisations'. The result of these formulas, in particular from the reference to 'common administrative procedure', was an immediate follow-up to the guarantee of uniformity of treatment by public administrations without exception; the legislature is obliged to adopt a general text on the non-contentious administrative procedure which will guarantee for individual acts (conforming to Article 105) the consultation of the interested party. In our view the general nature of these constitutional formulas should signify that the law will not only concern all the state administration, but also those autonomous communities. (In this matter the reservation of individual characteristics from the organisation itself cannot be objected to validly.) As a matter of

fact, it is impossible to see to what extent the regional individual characteristics could create discriminations and lead to the legitimation of distor-
tions in the principle of equal treatment.

If it has just been said that the analysis of texts leads to the claim that
the right to consultation which has been discussed, was guaranteed 'under
all circumstances', that does not mean, however, that the subject concerned by any administrative act whatsoever, could demand to be consulted whatever the situation nor that the lack of consultation would
systematically constitute illegality. At first, the Congress of deputies
adopted a draft in which the guarantee of Article 105–c would work 'without being able to dispense with the hearing of the interested party in any
case.[26] In the definitive version of the text, as above, a restriction exists
because the consultation of the interested party should take place only
'when it is appropriate'. It is not being suggested that it is regrettable and
that an attenuation of the democratic inspiration is visible there. Case by
case, the formula could certainly lead to some difficulties of interpretation. That being so, the restriction is pertinent in so far as the principle
of consultation or of a hearing has meaning only under certain particular
circumstances, for example, when a right is in question or in certain
disciplinary cases, etc. It would doubtless not have conformed to the
requirements of a good administrative procedure to make it an absolute
rule imposed on the administration for all its decisions.

The Administration Effectively Subject to the Law

In all regimes a direct relationship between citizens and the administration is established as a result of which the citizens have rights which the
administration can consolidate or neglect depending upon the way in
which it chooses to use (or abuse) its powers. The results of this are
tension and conflicts which diverse forms of control are set up either to
control or regulate. Specific institutions and procedures tend to force
the administration to respect the rights of citizens. At the end of forty
years of dictatorship, there is in Spain an evident necessity expressed in
a distinctive way.

If they aim to guarantee rights by creating a respect for legality or
through the sanction of illegality, these controls do not have that single
result. 'They are intended to create at the same time the coherence of
administrative action and to contain it within the limits of an objective
legality. They do not separate the search for the general interest and
the protection of individual rights'. From administrative action to legal
decision, the forms are manifold; the subject projected for the second part

of this brief study already referred, in a way, to that because to enable citizens to intervene in the procedure of decree on issues which concern them, is to give them the practical possibility to directly control administrative action. None the less, *a posteriori* controls take on a special importance. The non-validity of the illegal act must necessarily be established by a public authority, 'the principle of legality only has real effectiveness if it is matched with a control of legality which has the object of implementing the establishment of its non-validity'. In Spain, as in many other countries, the control of administrative legality takes two possible forms; it can be either administrative or judicial. Without going into all the constitutional arrangements relevant to these controls, and without even attempting to be exhaustive on these two points, we will discuss here the particular form of non-judicial control which comes under Article 54 which institutes an 'Ombudsman'. In general terms, we shall see how the Constitution, essentially through Article 106(I), treats the problem of putting the administration under jurisdictional control.

A new form of non-legal control—the Defender of the People (Ombudsman)

In the words of Article 54 'an organic law will determine the rules about the institution of Defender of the People, High Commissioner of the Cortes, designated by it for the defence of the rights included under the present title [Title I—fundamental rights and duties], to that effect, he will supervise the work of the administration, and keep the General Cortes informed of it'. Through that formula, the Constitution has left the essentials of the setting up of the institution to an organic law. However, as F. Garrido Falla has appositely shown[27] it says enough on the institution to allow the determination, in comparison with foreign examples, of what will necessarily be the principal features of the Spanish version of the Ombudsman. In this respect, there is a key point on which there should be no doubt whatsoever. In contrast to the Ombudsman, the Defender of the People cannot get involved in the judicial process, contest, and even less revise, judicial decisions. The terms of Article 54 are quite clear; he can 'supervise the administration's activity'. But the control of the legality of an administrative action comes (according to Article 106(I) which will be analysed below) under the jurisdiction of administrative tribunals.

What then are the circumstances in which the Defender of the People can intervene? In the first place, when a private individual has been through the administrative authority without success. If, in this case, the legal action is unsuccessful as a result, not of explicit rejection, but because of administrative silence, the administration will not be able to plead that the recourse to the courts has not been made within the allotted time, to oppose the Defender's preclosure. Recourse for the defender will also be possible when the administrative juristic process involved by the interested party has not yet pronounced on the subject. The administration will only have grounds to oppose the move to the Ombudsman if the affair is being considered by the judicial process under Article 94 of the law on administrative procedure which allows, after the registration of a settled case, the consideration of the valid grounds of the petitioner. Finally, once a decision of the administrative law is prounounced favourable to the civil service, the authority of the court is imposed on the Defender of the People, although he could suggest reforms of the law. If something seems to come into the domain of the Defender of the People, it is necessary above all to question the efficacy of the new institution (even if this opens up a more or less uncertain perspective).

Some, following the lines set by Professor Martin-Retortillo, have already decided the matter by noting that this is an 'institution of a hybrid-type, so that one has no idea in which direction it will go, and which was conceived in such a muddled manner that it is, without any doubt, condemned to failure.'[28] Without being so profoundly pessimistic it is none the less permissable to retain doubts by remembering that certain original drafting errors were made in the Constituent Assembly. For example, two aspects of the institution will suffice to illustrate that belief. Having completed the investigations, the Defender of the People can only, by virtue of Article 54, report to the Cortes. What is likely to happen? Consistent with the arrangements under Articles 108(III) of the Constitution, they would be able either to demand through private bills (or questions) 'better information' from the government, from ministers, or from autonomous communities, something which would not always be completely effective; or they could call into question the political responsibility of the government, which, given the disproportion between the means and the ends sought, could only be used on very rare occasions.

Another grave imperfection in the system comes from the limitation of the role of Defender of the People by the Constitution to the protection of the rights recognised solely under Title I. It is true that Chapter 2 of the first Title constitutes a very long inventory of fundamental rights and of public liberties which should be given to all citizens in a truly democratic society. The restriction is none the less regrettable. It prevents any action by the Defender of the People as a general and complete controller of the likely range of administrative anomalies which are liable to harm the subject. Frequently the harm will not arise from an attack on a public freedom, but it is still a possibility and worthy of attention.

If the Constituent Assembly had judged it opportune to introduce the new institution into the arsenal of means of control available to the revived democracy, it was apparently in because it believed that the guarantees provided by the recourse to law or to the administrative courts needed to be supplemented, and did not suffice to completely remedy administrative arbitrariness. It is, then, illogical to have excluded this means of protection from spheres of action which are as important as, for example, the powers of town planning, which affect the citizen daily. More generally, it is particularly unfortunate that the bulk of public-servant activity was not made subject to control, as this, whilst not undermining any specific right, is often least accessible to those individuals whom it most affects. On the last hypotheses, the criticism of the constitutional restriction is all the more founded in that, in the absence of outright illegality, it is no longer possible to count on recourse to the administrative courts to which the Constituent Assembly also devoted a considerable body of deliberations.

The administration subject to control by judge

Article 9(I) 'citizens and the Public authorities are subject to the Constitution and moreover to judicial regulation'.[29] Concerning all public authority, this norm envisages, in the first place the administration which is thus obliged to respect all legal rules, including the constitution.[30] This is embodied in Article 106(I) which arranged that 'the tribunals control the rule-making authority and the legality of administrative action, as well as their submission to ends which justify them.' If the principle is clearly enunciated, the rapid way in which such an essential theme has been treated could seem strange.

In reality, observed F. Garrido Falla, 'The constitution was allowed the luxury of being laconic [and more explicitly] . . . because the law on administrative jurisdiction of 27 December, 1956, still constitutes (with the exception of certain necessary correctives) an adequate framework for the subordination of the administration to law.' That interpretation is effectively confirmed by the fact that the recent law of 26 December 1978, on the legal protection of fundamental individual rights continues to regard the 'recourse to administrative litigation' (like that organised by the text), as the legal remedy appropriate to the control 'of actions of the public administration which affect the fundamental rights of the individual' (Article 6(I)).[31]

The general nature of Article 106(I) is in itself positive because the legality of all administrative actions are brought under the courts.[32] 'The rule-making power' should therefore be understood in this way which, combined with the phrase on 'administrative action' permits the inclusion of any act, which the author chooses (administration in the strict sense, of from the government) since the Constitution sees this organ as being in reality the highest of the administration. It can then be verified that the already existing legal ordinance was consistent with the principle of the new Constitution because the already cited law of 27 December 1956 had established and organised the regulation of the submission to administrative courts of the work of all organs without exception. Article 39 of this law arranges that:

(i) the general measures enacted by the State administration or whatsoever entity or public corporation can be submitted directly to the administrative courts;
(ii) the actions taken under the general measures to apply them can also be brought before the courts;
(iii) notwithstanding the failure of a proceeding against a general measure, a new action may be taken against the preceding enabling act.

It therefore appears that the Constitutional laws and the legislative laws complement each other to the extent that in democratic Spain the use of the courts against excessive powers could be exercised as much against individual acts as against regulations and without needing to take account of their actual author.

The efficiency of control which results from that will once more be reinforced by the fact that, quite opportunely, Article 106(I) states that it is also for the judge to control the subordination of administrative acts 'to ends which justify it'. Administrative action should, of necessity, lead to an end which is in the public interest or public service, the use which is made of this goal as an essential element of action and of the indispensable component of administrative acts comes back in the last resort to the incorporation in the Constitution of the principle of discretionary control. In this way, Article 106(I) gives a concrete aspect to the principle of 'control of the arbitrary acts of public authorities' which figure in Article 9(3); the Constitution establishes, which goes without saying (but which is better said outright) that what is discretionary cannot become arbitrary.

Notes

1. M. Baena del Alcazar, 'Administration central y perifica', in *La administration en la constitucion*, Centro de estudios constitutionales, Madrid, 1980, p. 49.

2. cf. notably M. Baena del Alcazar, op. cit. F. Garrido Falla, in *Comentarios a la constitucion* (Civitas) 1980, Madrid. E. Linde Paniagua, *'La Coordinacion de las administraciones publicas'*, Servicio de publicaciones de ministerio de justicia, Madrid, 1981.

3. cf. notably F. Garrido Falla, 'La posicion constitucional en la administracion publica', in *La administracion en la constitution*, op. cit., p. 11.

4. Op. cit., p. 73.

5. Article 98 for the government and Article 103 for the administration.

6. *Traité de droit administratif*, Vol. I, Ed. L. G. D. J. Paris, 1980, p. 55.

7. *Curso de derecho administrativo*, Vol. I/2, ed. Tecnos, Madrid, 1981, p. 87.

8. Note that the presence in the government of one or several ministers is only optional, and that the constitution opens the possibility to the legislator to have members of the government, other than ministers, for example, Secretaries of State.

9. On 'peripheral administration' cf. R. Entreña Cuesta , op. cit., III et seq.

10. Consistent with the analysis above, the reference to public administration will, in this study, apply only to the central civil state administration.

11. Given what the Spanish administration has been until now, the constitutional authority was advised to refer to this principle and to complete it line 3 of the same Article (103), in detailing that the law which will create the statute of public administration will establish the necessary guarantees for the impartial exercise of this function. The enshrining in the constitution of this objectivity and impartiality reveals the justified desire to at last attain the political neutrality of administration.

12. In mentioning the two terms of law and right, the article signifies that Spanish administration comes under the ensemble of legal provisions whether it is a matter of written sources (which are not the sole ordinary or constitutional laws, but also those edicted by the administration itself) or un-written, such as the general principles of law.

13. cf. notably M. Baena del Alcazar, op. cit., p. 68.

14. *Commentarios a la constitucion*, op. cit., p. 1032.

15. No specific attention will be devoted to the decentralisation principle because, notwithstanding its elevation to the rank of the constitutional, it does not seem that things are really susceptible to change in the way it is used. The Spanish administration will doubtless continue to have recourse to it as in the past, notably through the 'peripheral' administrations mentioned above.

16. Although the concepts of autonomy and decentralisation are close it is important not to confuse them. The term 'autonomy' when it is used in the constitution about autonomous communities, has a particular meaning. It has a profound political significance in that it expresses the recognition of a historical personality. It also has a specific legal connotation: thus the autonomous communities are invested with an original legislative power; in the exercise of the self-government they have no overseeing authority, only a control of their legal jurisdiction.

17. M. Baena del Alcazar, op. cit., p. 63.

18. Rafael Entreña Cuesta, *Curso derecho administrativ*, Vol. I (2), p. 20.

19. M. Baena del Alcazar, op. cit., p. 66.

20. M. Baena del Alcazer, op. cit., p. 70.

21. The interest devoted to this theme by the Constituent Assembly appears all the more clear in the affirmation of the principle of Article 103, the preoccupation with co-ordination appears in numerous other articles, cf. E. Linge Panigua, op. cit., p. 18.

22. Comments which follow will often draw on the commentary on Article 105 of the Constitution by Professor Garrido Falla, op. cit.

23. F. P. Bénoît, *Le droit administratif français*, Ed. Dalloz, Paris, 1968, pp. 89, 137 and 231.
24. Garrido Falla, op. cit., p. 1055.
25. In this sense cf. the French Law 17 July 1978, bearing on the relations of the civil service to the public.
26. cf. *Commentarios a la constitucion* and Baena del Alcazar, 'La participacion de los cuidadanos . . . el acceso a los archivos y registros administrativos', in *Revista de administacion publica*.
27. BOC du 24 July 1978. Cortes Offical Record.
28. *Comentarios a la constitucion*, op. cit., p. 596.
29. *Diario de sesiones del Senado*, 31 August 1978, p. 2119.
30. Given that certain Constitutional provisions are for immediate application and are imposed directly on the administration and on the judge (for example, Articles A, 18 and 25) and that others (for example, Articles 39 and 40) have to be developed by the legislator such that Article 53 distinguishes between rights and liberties directly controlled by the tribunals and those which will be taken into account before them only 'according to the arrangement of laws which develop them'.
31. Law No. 62/1978, *BOE*, 3 January 1979. Cortes Records.
32. It must, however, be observed that a doubt remains about the legal immunity of government acts whose suppression perhaps implies a modification of Article 2(b) of the judicial law.

5 THE PEOPLES AND REGIONS OF SPAIN

MIKE NEWTON

Introduction

For centuries, according to Salvador de Madariaga, Spanish political life has oscillated between bouts of 'dictatorship' and 'separatism' which he equates with deep-seated and contrasting aspects of the Spanish character.[1] Applying this theory to the contemporary situation, Spain, after nearly forty years of the Franco dictatorship, is now once more experiencing a resurgence of the separatist phenomenon when the centrifugal forces of the country are in the process of liberating themselves from the centralist yoke under which they have laboured for so long.

Since the beginning of the nineteenth century there have been at least four periods when this pattern has reproduced itself, albeit under different political banners: (1) the *junta* movement, which erupted during the War of Independence or Peninsular War (1808–14) following the collapse of the Absolute Monarchy; (2) the *cantonalismo* phenomenon that bedevilled the attempt to establish a Federal Republic in 1873–4 after the overthow of Isabella II; (3) the 'nationalist' movements of the early twentieth century, partly provoked by the disintegration of the corrupt Restoration Regime and partly stimulated by the international promotion of the principle of national self-determination following World War I; (4) the democratic Republican movement which profited from the collapse of the monarchy of Alfonso XIII and which was accompanied by demands for regional autonomy. Expressed another way, Spanish politics have swung between two diametrically opposed traditions: the liberal democratic, pluralist tradition, best exemplified in the social and political development of Aragon and especially of Catalonia, and the unitary, centralist tradition, most recently epitomised in the Franco regime. In modern times, when the democratic tradition has come to the fore, it has always been accompanied by pressure for some form of regional autonomy; indeed, some form of devolution has been seen as an essential ingredient of that democracy.[2]

Two factors, however, would seem to distinguish the present movement for autonomy from previous experiments: firstly, the sheer scale and intensity of the present clamour among both the 'historical nationalities[3] and the other peoples and regions of Spain, and, secondly, the commitment of the political establishment (historically so reluctant to make such concessions) to an unprecedented degree of decentralisation—a commitment, albeit hedged around with ambiguities, that is enshrined in Article 2 and Section VIII of the 1978 Constitution.

In his analysis of twentieth-century nationalism A. D. S. Smith highlights three possible sources of pressure behind contemporary autonomy movements: economic, political and cultural.[4] With regard to economic factors, autonomists claim either that central government favours the more prosperous regions at the expense of the poorer outlying areas (like the Italian Mezzogiorno, the North-East of England, French Aquitaine, and the Andalusian and Galician regions of Spain) or that the government drains the resources away from the wealthy areas (like the north of Italy, the South-East of England, the Paris Basin and the Basque and Catalan regions of Spain) to support the poorer, more stagnant areas. This 'two-sided' theory of uneven development, developed by Tom Nairn in his study of Britain, is supported by Stanley Payne who convincingly applies the theory to the case of Spain.[5] Secondly, autonomists advance a set of political arguments against over-centralisation, claiming that the modern state has become too bureaucratised to meet man's social and political needs. Smith's analysis is applied basically to the contemporary resurgence of autonomy movements in well-established democratic states; how much more relevant this must be to Spain, a country prone to autocracy whose democratic experiments have been frustrated so often. Thirdly, using historico-cultural criteria, autonomists, especially in regions with a unique ethnic or linguistic identity (like the Welsh, Basques and Bretons), resist assimilation by what they consider an 'alien' culture that is usually allied to political centralism, and promote their own localised culture which they use as a powerful argument in favour of 'separate' treatment.

If one were to single out one of these areas of grievance as being responsible for the resurgence of this movement in present-day Spain, one would have to stress the resistance of her peoples and regions to the uncompromising political centralism imposed by Franco. Certainly it goes a long way towards explaining why, in this particular swing of the centrifugal pendulum, the 'historical nationalities' have been joined by numerous other regions in their clamour for self-government. However, this is inadequate as a total explanation, since, as is well known, certain autonomous movements like the Basque and Catalan, existed long before Franco. Indeed, to grasp fully the root causes of such developments, one must examine, however briefly, the Spanish experience of nation- and state-building.

Historical Background

To a large extent the so-called 'regional problem' in Spain is a problem of the State, which, since its tentative beginnings at the end of the fifteenth century, has not been fully able to integrate or assimilate the various ethnocultural and ethnolinguistic minorities of which it is composed. Of course, had the Spanish State long ago assumed and retained some form of federal structure that accommodated the interests of these peoples, this would not have been seen as a failure. Indeed, when modern Spain first emerged as a unified country after the union of the Monarchies of Castile and Aragón (1469) the capture of the last Moorish stronghold in Granada (1492) and the annexation of the Kingdom of Navarre (1512), it could be argued that Spain had already achieved a balanced kind of federal or consociational system. Charles I was not King of Spain, but King of Castile, León, Aragón, Navarre, etc. and on accession had to swear in the regional 'Cortes', to respect the administrative, legal, financial and cultural idiosyncracies of each kingdom or principality. This system of dualism or *'pactismo'*, closely analysed by Benjamín González Alonso, lasted more or less up to the end of the seventeenth century.[6] Thereafter the Bourbon Monarchy, in imitation of the policy of its French relations, attempted (forcibly when necessary) to unify the administration of the country. This involved the curtailing of many of the local rights or *'fueros'* enjoyed by former kingdoms—particularly Catalonia which had fought against Philip V in the War of Spanish Succession (1701–13). However, even in those times, the administration was organised according to the country's historical regions, based on former kingdoms or principalities. Unfortunately, after the War of Independence and the disintegration of the *ancien régime*, the liberals, supported by the Bourbon Monarchy, introduced a form of administration akin to the Napoleonic model, in which Spain was divided into fifty artificial provinces many of which cut across the lines of the former kingdoms. As the century progressed, the government further restricted the rights of the regional minorities. The theoretical justification for such policies was the liberal ideal that linked the equal distribution of the benefits of economic progress and social advances to the supremacy of a paternalistic, sovereign State.

As the nineteenth century advanced, old nation-states like France and Britain built increasingly stronger and more integrated nations, whose success lay more and more in the promotion of economic development, often linked to colonial aggrandisement. The end of the century also saw the emergence of new nation-states like Italy and Germany, which benefited even more than the older nations from a wave of romantic nationalism, whose highly emotional and cultural content helped to forge a deep sense of nationhood among all the component parts of the states concerned. As Linz and others have clearly demonstrated, Spain, unified as a State long before most other European nations and having long since passed through the imperial phase of development, failed to profit from this nationalist upsurge.[7] Indeed, paradoxically the fires of nationalism were kindled, not in favour of 'the Spanish nation', but, at local level, in favour of the ethnic minorities like the Basques, Catalans and Galicians, who at the turn of the century experienced a cultural revival, to be followed by the emergence of political nationalism.

However, the probable root cause of Spain's inability to weld together a more integrated nation was her failure to develop economically, which, in nineteenth century terms, meant failure to promote a nation-wide industrial (or even agricultural) revolution. One of the main reasons for this was undoubtedly the deep cleavages which, after the War of Independence, existed in Spain between the traditional Carlists (who favoured a return to the pre-industrial *'pactismo'* form of socio-political organisation) and the Liberals, the heirs of the French Revolution, who believed, at least in theory, in a constitutional Monarchy, centralised government and economic development. This cleavage resulted in the series of civil wars that plagued the nineteenth century, retarding material progress and exacerbating social and political divisions. The picture was also complicated at the end of the century when, also in response to the economic stagnation of the country and the failure to eradicate feudalism, Spain witnessed the emergence of powerful working-class movements, which added a further cleavage to an already deeply divided society. Paradoxically, in spite of its arguably laudable intentions, the working-class movement (itself deeply torn between Anarchists and Socialists) only served to further weaken the State and impede economic progress.

For historical reasons the mentality of the new liberal bourgeoisie (predominantly Castilian and Andalusian), having merged its interests with those of the landowning aristocracy, was uninterested in economic or commercial ventures. The economic development that did occur in Spain was promoted largely by the more progressive and more dynamic bourgeoisie of Catalonia (and, to a lesser extent, that of the Basque Country) which had for centuries developed more democratic forms of government and a more energetic commercial spirit. These were precisely the two regions whose peoples felt a strong sense of cultural separateness from the rest of Spain. Initially this was strengthened by the efforts of nineteenth century Liberals to curtail their *fueros* in defence of which most Basques and Catalans flocked to the Carlist cause. At the same time these peoples witnessed a flowering of their regional cultures. Later their sense of distinctiveness was fortified by their frustration with the inertia and interference of the Madrid bureaucracy in local political and economic affairs, coupled with a growing sense of superiority engendered by economic success. At the turn of the century this combination of factors led to the creation of the Basque and Catalan Nationalist parties, which, along with other regional movements, gathered momentum during the corrupt Restoration Era. The loss of Spain's colonies in 1898, at the very time when other countries were indulging in overseas territorial expansion, was their final confirmation of the incompetence of the Spanish State. Thus Spain entered the twentieth century economically retarded, socially divided and politically polarised.

Right up to the advent of the Second Republic (1931–6) this situation continued, indeed worsened, to the point where the economic, social and political differences between Spaniards became irreconcilable. There was no all-embracing loyalty to a superior national entity that could prevent the tragic polarisation that resulted in the Civil War. The well-intentioned but weakly supported liberal politicians of the Second Republic struggled hard against the odds to hold the ring between the opposing forces of fascism and socialism, liberalism and clericalism, centralism and regionalism, but failed in their bold efforts to implant democracy. This vision of democracy, envisaging substantial devolution to those regional minorities that desired it, had led to the granting of autonomy to Catalonia in 1932 and the three Basque Provinces in 1936. Had the Republic survived, almost certainly other regions like Andalusia, Galicia, Valencia and Aragon (where Statutes of Autonomy had been drafted) would have reached similar agreements with the Spanish State.

As is all too well known, the regime that was born out of the Civil War proved to be one of the most intolerant, regressive, anti-democratic and centralist dictatorships that the western world has ever known. And it was to be one of the most durable. After ruthlessly dismantling every single economic and political reform associated with the Republic, Franco was not content to impose rigid administrative, political and economic control over his people: he was determined to stamp out all cultural manifestations that did not conform to his narrow concept of traditional national (i.e. Castilian) and Catholic values. Thus the Caudillo not only swept aside Basque and Catalan autonomy but launched a ruthless and thoroughgoing persecution of their cultures, prohibiting the use of their languages at all levels of public life. Gispert and Prate express it in these terms:

To sum up not only the language but the culture, all cultural and folkloric manifestations of the different national communities were suppressed or distorted from the centre of the State. The existence of nationalities and authentic regional movements was ignored and replaced by a bastardised regionalism and a cheapened folklore that were totally lacking in content.[8]

Though some of the worst excesses of this policy were relaxed in the fifties and sixties, the regions continued to be subjected to the economic and political dominance of Madrid. Ironically, perhaps, in his clumsy and insensitive way, Franco was attempting to create, as well as a more effective State machine, a sense of loyalty to 'the Spanish nation', the National Movement being the intended vehicle for this process of conversion. What Franco forgot, however, while extolling the virtues of Isabella and Ferdinand and Spain's Golden Age of Empire, was that, during that period, there had been no attempt to *impose* legal, financial or administrative conformity on the regions of Spain. In the long run, far from suppressing the regional cultures, Franco only succeeded in revitalising them and converting the Basque Country and Catalonia (in particular) into the most determined centres of generalised opposition to his regime. Without any doubt, the birth of the Basque terrorist organisation ETA can be directly attributed to the repressive policies of the regime.

Regionalism in the Spain of Juan Carlos

Popular Movements

Though Spain made little, if any, political progress during the Franco era, the country bequeathed to Juan Carlos in 1975 was very different from the Spain of 1939. Such changes were largely of an economic nature, although they brought with them a whole range of social changes that the regime would neither have anticipated nor desired. After the stagnation of the years of autarchy (up to 1959) the country experienced, in overall terms, unprecedented economic growth which, in the space of less than two decades, transformed Spain from an underdeveloped to a developing economy with a rapidly expanding industrial sector. As she began to enjoy the material fruits of a consumer boom, the gap between Spain and her European neighbours narrowed. In social terms too Spain was becoming increasingly Europeanised as education, literacy levels and all aspects of communication improved and customs became more liberated. However, the price for this overall progress was very high. Far from narrowing the gap between the richer and poorer regions of the country, the regime's famous Development Plans, coupled with the discriminating effects of

foreign investment and tourism, only succeeded in widening it and generating a sense of grievance in poorer areas like Andalusia and Galicia, which
bore the brunt of high levels of emigration and unemployment. The granting of certain cultural concessions to the regional minorities failed to
reduce either their opposition to the regime or their determination to
continue the struggle for the recovery of their autonomy; indeed ETA
showed that a minority of Basques were even prepared to fight for total
independence from Spain. Such was the legacy of the regime and the new
context in which the struggle for autonomy would be fought out in the
post-Franco era.

A complex combination of factors, political, cultural, demographic and
economic can be seen as providing the impetus behind the resurgence of
the autonomy movement in post-Franco Spain. It can be partially viewed,
particularly in the case of the Basques and Catalans, as a re-assertion of
their cultural and linguistic distinctiveness and of their determination to
protect and promote it. In this sense the movement is a continuation of
the struggle initiated in the nineteenth century. Partly too one must take
into account the closely related and oft-reiterated demand of these peoples
for some form of self-government involving the restoration of political,
legal or administrative rights. Significantly, these regions which are the
most economically developed, are precisely those which have resisted most
energetically the Franco regime and pressed claims to political autonomy.

However, these factors alone cannot fully explain what Javier García
Fernández calls 'the blooming of demands for autonomy' which over the
last six years has spread right across the country.[9] To some extent this
broader development, involving nearly all the regions of Spain, can perhaps
be explained in terms of a wider malaise which, over the last twenty
years, has been affecting many developed countries of western Europe and
led to vigorous autonomy movements in Corsica, Greenland, South Tyrol,
Wales and Scotland. As was suggested earlier, various interpretations of
this malaise have been given, although one of the most convincing is that
which views it as a reaction to the remoteness and inefficiency of central
government. In Spain's case, this reaction has been particularly vehement
because the State under Franco was not merely highly centralised (as well
as highly inefficient), but autocratic. The civil rights which, in countries
like Britain and France, compensate to some extent for excessive centralism
were non-existent in Francoist Spain. Moreover, as we have already seen,
the price for Spain's overall rapid economic development has been
extremely high. The pre-war differences that existed between the developed
and underdeveloped regions have been exacerbated by the regime's post-
1959 economic policies. Spain's rapid transformation from a predominantly

industrial economy within less than twenty years brought with it severe depopulation of the central provinces and the rapid over-population of the industralised areas (now including Madrid) which have had to endure all the social problems associated with the influx of an 'immigrant' population. In the case of the Basque Country and Catalonia, where the indigenous populations have been striving to revitalise their local languages and cultures, this has led to considerable social tension. However, it is only in the more liberal, democratic atmosphere of post-Franco Spain that the regions which have lost, rather than gained, population have felt confident enough to add their autonomous demands to those with a longer tradition of regionalist protest.

The Official Response

Over the last six years it has to be recognised that the political establishment, whether for reasons of ideology or expediency, has taken unprecedented steps to respond to the popular pressures in favour of autonomy, which, to a greater or lesser extent, had been building up as part of the generalised opposition during the latter years of the Franco regime. Juan Carlos himself gave a mild boost to autonomous hopes in his inauguration speech of 22 November 1975 when he stated: 'A just order, equal for everyone, makes it possible to recognise, within the unity of the Kingdom and the State, the regional peculiarities which are the expression of the diversity of peoples that make up the sacred reality of Spain'.[10] Prior to this, the monarch had issued a decree aimed at the protection of the regional languages. In the early months of his reign Juan Carlos made it possible for many exiles, including numerous Basques and Catalans, who had settled in Europe and Latin America, to return to Spain. In September 1976 the Suárez government permitted the public use of the Basque and other regional flags, which was a gesture with great symbolic value for those concerned. In the same month the Premier issued his Political Reform Law which was to pave the way for the restoration of democracy in Spain; significantly this contained a reference to the need to make concessions to the regions. In their manifestos, published prior to the 1977 elections, all the major parties committed themselves to some degree of political devolution. It should be stressed however that there was considerable variety in interpretation, from the administrative decentralisation recommended by the right-wing Popular Alliance and the more or less federal solutions advocated by the Socialists and Communists. The solution favoured by Suárez's Union of the Democratic Centre (UCD) (which won a convincing victory in the elections) was basically an extension of the formula adopted by the Second Republic, involving the re-structuring of the State along autonomy statute lines and the free election of regional assemblies. A particular feature of the UCD proposals, and indeed of the formula eventually agreed in the Constitution, is that the final form of the State was left an open question and, at least in the early stages, the initiative for autonomy was left in the hands of the regions themselves.

This *laissez-faire* approach also applied to the 'pre-autonomy' process which, without prejudicing the content of the Constitution, was encouraged by the government in the wake of the 1977 elections. Between the autumn of 1977 and the end of 1978 the Minister for the Regions, Manuel Clavero, negotiated provisional autonomy arrangements, first with the three historical nationalities, then with all the other regions. In each case, the regions were represented by their Parliamentarians. At the culmination of each process, a regional body (part-executive and part-legislature, but with very limited powers) was constituted from a combination of Parliamentarians and provincial representatives. This lengthy process was clearly designed by the government to take the steam out of a situation of mounting popular pressure, in the knowledge that to have made no conciliatory moves during the eighteen-month-long constitutional process would have aggravated the existing central–regional tensions.

The conversion of these provisional bodies into fully autonomous organs had to await the promulgation of the new Constitution in December 1978. The sections of the documents dealing with the structure of the State and the status of the regions (by far the longest) were easily the most controversial. Somehow a balance had to be struck between the fears of the Centre and Right that reference to the nationalities of Spain was a threat to the national unity of the country and the obvious preference of the Left for a federal-type solution which would involve a fundamental shift of power from Madrid to the regions. Local Parliamentarians were equally concerned that autonomy might be a mere disguise for administrative decentralisation, in which the central government would still take the important decisions on regional affairs. The Basques, represented by the Basque Nationalist Party (PNV), complained that the Constitution did not go far enough to recognise their historic rights; at one point they withdrew their Deputies from the Cortes and subsequently advocated abstention in the Constitutional referendum to the Basque electorate. The Andalusian and other regionalists (though not represented in the Cortes) were very unhappy about the distinction drawn in Article 2 between the nationalities and the regions of Spain. The argument over this point in fact reflected the fundamental dilemma facing the drafters of the new Constitution, that is between the need to satisfy the aspirations of the

Basques and Catalans with longstanding claims to autonomy, and the fear that, in favouring the latter, they would be laying themselves open to charges of discrimination from other regions.

In fact the 'two-tier' concept seems to have prevailed. According to Transitional Provision No. 2, those regions which had in the past voted in a referendum in favour of autonomy would be permitted to proceed by a relatively simple process towards full autonomy: the Assembly of Parliamentarians would draw up and approve a draft statute which, following scrutiny by the Constitutional Commission, would be submitted to a regional referendum (approval requiring a majority of affirmative votes in each province of the region concerned) prior to final ratification by both Houses of Parliament. By this procedure the Basque Country, Catalonia (both in 1980) and Galicia (1981) were able to accede to full autonomy. For the other regions the Constitution envisaged that the 'normal' procedure enshrined in Article 143, would involve an initial process of popular consultation whereby an autonomous initiative could only proceed with the prior backing of all the Provincial Councils concerned as well as two-thirds of the Municipal Councils. Subsequently, a Statute would be drawn up by an Assembly (comprising members of the Provincial Councils—at that time still unreorganised) and the Parliamentarians of those provinces; this text would then be passed to the Cortes for approval as an ordinary law; when approved the region would be able to assume competence over a limited area of decision-making (Article 148). Only after a further five years could a region proceed towards the full range of competences envisaged in Article 149.

The disadvantages of this route, highlighted by Clavero himself, include the non-specification of the organs of government of the new Autonomous Community, the non-compulsory nature of the transfer from partial to full autonomy and the fact that the Statute is approved without prior negotiation or referendum, with the attendant risk that a Statute could be imposed by a majority in the Congress and Senate whose political colouring was very different from that of the regional Assembly.[11] Evidently these two-tier arrangements made no provision for a region which, while not fulfilling the requirements of Transitional Article 2 (i.e. it was not regarded as an historical nationality), could still claim mass backing for full autonomy. As a 'bridge' solution Clavero suggested an alternative procedure (Article 151.1) whereby such a region could, under certain conditions, take a short-cut to full autonomy. These conditions included the need for the initiative to be supported by three-quarters of the Municipal Councils, as well as all the Provincial Councils of a given region and, to back the initiative, a popular referendum which would require an affirmative vote by an absolute majority of the electoral roll in each province; only when these steps had been taken could the region follow the procedures of Article 151.2 (outlined above), including a *second* referendum on the actual text of the Statute. This was the tortuous route which Andalusia was to demand in its struggle for autonomy.

In order to understand fully the issues which these popular and official moves towards autonomy have thrown up in recent years, it would seem appropriate to examine, in some detail, the evolution of the autonomy movements in various regions from the Franco regime to the present day. As well as situating each within the economic, social and political context of the region concerned, an attempt will be made to highlight the similarities and differences which each movement exhibits in terms of origins, composition, aims and success, as measured both by electoral achievements and the content of the Statutes of Autonomy that have been granted. In a recent essay José Pérez Vilariño argued that, given a minimal level of collective identify (likely to be based on a common culture, history and language), the factor most likely to determine the intensity of autonomous demands is the region's level of economic development.[12] If this is the case we should find that the Basque Country and Catalonia far exceed Galicia and Andalusia in the vigour of their autonomous movements and in the success achieved.

Catalonia

Catalonia rests her case for autonomy on the historical existence of the separate principality of that name, on the survival of its separate political, financial and legal traditions as an autonomous part of the Kingdom of Aragon and on the preservation of a distinct culture and language. At the turn of the century modern Catalan nationalism grew up partly out of the attempt to recover the *fueros* lost in the eighteenth century and partly out of the frustration of the industrial bourgeoisie with Madrid's bureaucratic interference in the region's economic affairs. In 1901 this frustration led to the foundation of the socially conservative Lliga Regionalista which, at both national and local level, successfully contested seats on the basis of a broad interclass electoral appeal and in 1914 secured the establishment of the Manocomunitat composed of the merger of four regional councils. However, when the capitalist system that it represented came under increasing pressure (especially from 1917) from the Anarchist-dominated labour movement, the Lliga threw in its lot with Madrid authoritarianism and was thenceforth doomed as a regional political force. Its place was taken by the more radical Esquerra Republicana de Catalunya

(ERC), founded by Francesc Macià which appealed to intellectuals, petit bourgeois and rural workers. This party was dedicated to the establishment of a Catalan Republic within a Federal Spain. Emerging as the dominant force in Catalonia after the 1931 elections, the Esquerra (under Luis Companys) pressed for, and in 1932 achieved, political autonomy for the region, embodied in the restored Generalitat. Under the Statute of Autonomy, Catalonia became an autonomous region within the Spanish State and the Generalitat's powers embraced most areas except foreign and ecclesiastical affairs, customs, tariffs, etc. Catalonia was to prove to be the only autonomous region of the peacetime Second Republic and as thus provided a bastion of democracy and Republicanism.

Following the fall of Catalonia (which had given full support to the Republic) Franco annulled the Statute, outlawed all her autonomous institutions and thereafter pursued a ruthless policy of economic discrimination, political repression and cultural alienation. As in other regions, however, Franco's policy failed utterly and indeed produced results diametrically opposed to those intended. Not only did Catalonia preserve (and even strengthen) her separate identity and will to self-government, but the repression united her people in widespread opposition to a hated, centralist regime. However, the complexion of forces that made up the opposition, combined with changes in the economic and social structure of the region, was such that in the post-Franco era the political panorama and the nature of the nationalist movement were bound to be very different from the pre-war situation.

The internal struggle against the regime was conducted, on the one hand, by Socialists and Communists who for the first time began to play a significant role in Catalan politics, and, on the other, by new Christian and Social Democrat groups like Jordi Pujol's Convergència Democrática de Catalunya (CDC) which combined economic and academic interests to promote Catalan culture, especially its language. The growth of the Catalan Socialist Party (PSC) can probably be attributed to a variety of factors: the need to fill the enormous vacuum left by the evaporation of the Anarchist movement, the national image of competence and modernity projected by Felipe González's mainstream PSOE and the impact of the Castilian-speaking immigrants, employed mainly in the large urban centres.

Following the inter-party dissension of the early Franco years, the opposition movement assumed an increasing unity by the late sixties, which, in 1971, crystallised in the creation of a loose but effective organisation, the Assamblea de Catalunya, that embraced Communists, Socialists, Christian and Social Democrats, as well as several non-political groups. In addition to amnesty and basic political rights, the Assamblea demanded the re-establishment of the 1932 Statute.

As political parties emerged from illegality in the spring of 1977 it was clear that the dominant Catalanist parties (now occupying the centre of the political spectrum) would face tough opposition from Socialists and Communists who, through clandestine political and syndical cells, had borne the brunt of the struggle against Franco and consolidated their position. Indeed, the historic elections of June 1977 gave a conclusive victory to the PSC headed by Joan Reventós with 15 seats and 28 per cent of the vote; this compared with the 11 seats and 17 per cent for the CDC, 9 and 17 per cent for the UCD and 8 and 18 per cent for the Communist PSUC. However, the overall victory of the Left (most convincing in terms of votes) should not lead us to conclude that this was an anti-Catalan vote since all parties, with the exception of the far Right, had campaigned in favour of some form of regional autonomy.

The Esquerra had done very badly (one seat) in these elections, but its leader (and former Premier of Republican Catalonia), Josep Tarradellas, was destined to play a key role during the establishment of provisional autonomy. Premier Suárez, in order to circumvent anticipated criticism of his proposals by the Catalan political parties, decided to go right over their heads and take the one step that would unite them all and the Catalan populace at large, i.e. the return of Tarradellas as interim President of a restored Generalitat. This was an astute move that satisfied Catalan desires for a symbolic link with their past legality as an autonomous nation. The manoeuvre was crowned with success on 29 September when the Generalitat was formally re-established by Royal Decree.

The body entrusted with the drafting of the new Statute of Autonomy in Sau was the Assembly of Parliamentarians of the region. The fact that its dominant components were the centrist nationalists and the national parties of the Left (currently content to play consensus politics with the ruling UCD) may explain why, ultimately, it granted less power to the Generalitat than its predecessor of 1932. As Norman Jones has shown, along with certain powers that amount to full autonomy with legislative authority (and this covers the all-important control over educational and cultural matters) and devolved powers (involving local execution of central government policy), there are certain elements that amount to mere administrative decentralisation.[13] Possibly a certain disillusionment with the terms of the Statute was reflected in the 40 per cent abstention rate in the regional referendum held on 25 October 1979, although 89 per cent of voters did register their approval.

Following the general and municipal elections of March and April 1979 (when the Left again demonstrated majority support), it was widely assumed that the PSC would triumph in the elections to the Catalan Parliament held on 20 March 1980 which would place the final seal of approval on Catalonia's passage to full formal autonomy. In the event, Jordi Pujol's reformed coalition, Convergència i Unió (CiU), with 43 out of the 135 seats, emerged victorious—the PSC having secured only 33, the PSUC 25, and the UCD 18 and, perhaps surprisingly, the ERC 14. Reflecting the generally moderate nature of the Catalan electorate, neither the far Right nor far (nationalist) Left gained a single seat. On the other hand, the achievement of the Socialist Party of Andalusia (PSA) (representing the interests of the majority of immigrants) in winning two seats was a dramatic warning to both Catalanist and national parties that here was an issue not to be ignored. But for the animosity between Socialists and Communists, it is very possible that a Popular Front-type government might have emerged. Eventually, however, after making an offer of a coalition with the PSC (which was rejected), Pujol accepted the support of the UCD and Esquerra to enable him to form the first Catalan government of the post-Franco era. Pujol was duly sworn in as the 115th President of the Generalitat.

A 1979 survey on the 'national' identities of party voters showed that the percentage of voters who felt more Catalan than Spanish was 29.1 and 28.6 for the ERC and CiU respectively compared to the 10.2 and 10.1 for the PSC and PSUC respectively, while for those who felt as much Spanish as Catalan the figures were ERC: 25.1; CiU: 51.2; PSC: 36.7; PSUC: 34.6.[14] So far perhaps the figures are predictable. However, the most interesting statistics indicate that, for those who consider themselves purely and simply Catalan, the percentages are ERC: 25.7; CiU: 8.0; PSC: 18.4; PSUC: 28.3. This would seem to suggest that there has been a two-way merging of identities, with many Socialists and Communists considering themselves Catalan (and this section must include many immigrant workers), while very few of the voters for the region's major nationalist party consider themselves exclusively Catalan. Such a degree of integration plus the electorate's rejection of extremism would seem to bode well for the stability of Catalan democracy. Many problems, however, remain to be solved, including the question of the full assimilation of the Catalan-speaking immigrants; a longer-term problem could be presented by the cultural movement, Los Paisos Catalans which demands the re-unification of the Catalan-speaking peoples, that is French and Spanish Catalonia, Valencia, Andorra and the Balearics.

The Basque Country

The Basques rest their claim to autonomy not so much on the prior existence of a separate political entity so much as on their ethnic, cultural and, above all, linguistic distinctiveness. As a political movement Basque nationalism largely grew out of Carlism which had stoutly defended both regional *fueros* and the Catholic Church, both threatened by nineteenth century Spanish Liberalism. Unlike the Catalan Lliga, the Basque Nationalist Party (PNV), founded in 1894 by Sabino de Arana, was not supported by the Madrid-linked bourgeoisie, but by the urban middle-classes (professionals, intellectuals), the intensely Catholic peasantry and the clergy. Up to the thirties the PNV was electorally less successful than either the Lliga or the Esquerra, but its social composition enabled it to survive the class struggle traumas of the early twentieth century and it remained the only political expression of Basque aspirations down to, and well beyond, the Civil War. During the life of the Republic it was torn between defence of its Catholic interests, when it tended to support the Right, and the struggle for autonomy, when it favoured the parties of the Republican Left. In their attempts to secure regional autonomy, the Basques were markedly less successful than the Catalans; the government was able to exploit the considerable intra-regional differences reflected in various autonomy referenda to stall all efforts to implement a Statute. In fact the region had to wait until October 1936, well after the outbreak of war, before autonomy was granted in the artificial circumstances created by its geographical separation from the rest of Republican Spain.

Nowhere was the Basque 'religion/autonomy' dilemma more graphically illustrated than in their agonising choice in July 1936 between supporting a Catholic but centralist Franco and a pro-autonomy but anti-clerical Republic. In the end the profound desire to control their own affairs won the day except in Carlist-dominated Navarre, which felt betrayed by the Republic's generally anti-Catholic line and which threw in its lot with Franco.

Following the collapse of the north in the summer of 1937, Franco annulled all Republican legislation in that part of Spain, including the Statute of Autonomy. As with Catalonia, he was not content merely to re-impose political centralism but was determined to eradicate all manifestations of Basque culture, in particular their language. However, the Basques reacted to such repression with as much, if not more, vigour than the Catalans and, during the course of the Franco dictatorship, the region became a hot-bed of generalised opposition to a system which did more to alienate Basques from Madrid than any other previous centralist regime. Restricted in their speech and movements and harassed by the non-Basque security forces, the Basques felt justified in feeling that they were living under an army of occupation. As a result, potentially hostile groups united in a widespread active and passive struggle against the regime, which stood opposed not only by the major part of the Basque clergy, the urban middle-class and the peasantry, but a broad spectrum of urban workers and even by certain sections of the industrial oligarchy. This does not mean, of course, that all such groups were nationalist in their sympathies; it does suggest, however, that, in spite of Franco's restoration of the supremacy of the Catholic Church, the great majority of Basques opposed his regime.

From the 1960s onwards this united hostility, combined with demographic changes, produced two significant new changes in Basque politics: firstly, a generally leftward trend among both national and nationalist groups and, secondly, a proliferation of groups claiming to speak for the nationalist cause. Undoubtedly, one of the most important events of the Franco era was the foundation in 1959 (as a splinter group from the PNV) of the Basque terrorist organisation ETA, dedicated to the establishment of a separate Basque Republic, Euzkadi, comprising the four Spanish and three French provinces. In its affirmation of revolutionary Marxism and of radical working-class nationalism, ETA combines two once irreconcilable ideologies, Catholic nationalism and Socialism. The organisation owes its 'success' not only to its tightly-knit, cell-like structure and the dedication of its members, but also to widespread passive support from ordinary Basque citizens, who have come to view the *etarras* as freedom fighters. Police torture of Basque political prisoners, the bogus trial of Burgos in 1970 and the execution of two ETA members in 1975 only served to consolidate this myth.

The political panorama that emerged in the post-Franco era was much more complex and more fragmented·than that of Catalonia. Of the national parties clearly the dominant ones would be the Socialists and Communists who, especially through their respective trade unions, had demonstrated great capacity for the mobilisation of opposition to Franco. In the latter years of the regime, as the PNV's influence began to wane, such political options also became increasingly attractive to sections of the middle class, especially the new strata of middle management, technicians, etc. On the nationalist side the PNV could no longer claim to be the sole standard-bearer of the Basque cause: it now faced a challenge from a whole range of *abertzale* or nationalist groups from Social Democrats to Revolutionary Communists.

In the June 1977 elections it was the Socialists who emerged victorious with 25 per cent of the vote and 9 seats, closely followed by the PNV with 24.4 per cent of the vote and 8 seats. However, in a sense this did not mean a drop in the overall nationalist vote, which (compared with the elections of 1936) rose from 28 to 35.6 per cent. However, the PNV could not deny that this 'shared' nationalist vote had moved significantly to the Left since the 1930s, when it would have been inconceivable for a radical Left party like Euskadiko Ezkerra to win one seat in the Madrid Cortes. Taking into account the increased Socialist share of the vote the overall shift to the Left of the Basque electorate was very marked.

After Catalonia, Euzkadi was the first region to accede (in December 1977) to pre-autonomous status, with the establishment of the Basque General Council (CGV) comprising representatives from Vizcaya, Guipúzcoa and Alava, but not Navarre. Clavero's comments on the great difficulties which he faced in these negotiations testify to the complexity of the Basque problem.[15] As during the subsequent constitutional debate the key issues were the Basque demand for the restoration of the economic agreements (*conciertos económicos*) granted in 1876, the PNV struggle for recognition in the Constitution of the Basques' historical rights and the intractable problem of Navarre, divided between a UCD committed to a separate region which maintained strong links with Madrid and the PNV and PSOE which both favoured integration with the CGV.

Once the Constitution was approved, the Basque Deputies lost no time in presenting their Statute of Autonomy to the Cortes. However, continued wrangling, particularly over the question of the *conciertos económicos* and the establishment of a Basque police force, delayed its final approval until July 1979 and it was to be October of that year before a regional referendum was held. There is no doubt, however, that, because of its often intransigent attitude, reinforced by the extra bargaining power that escalating ETA violence afforded it, the PNV was ultimately able to extract concessions from Madrid that would not otherwise have been possible. The Statute of Guernica may not have given the Basques quite the degree of autonomy granted in 1936, but still confers considerable powers upon their local institutions: the *conciertos económicos* have been restored and the CGV has the right to levy and collect its own taxes, it has exclusive control over education and culture, a major say in overall economic policy and responsibility for the newly-created Basque Police Force.

In view of all these autonomous successes, it might be thought that the traditionally poor relations between Madrid and Euzkadi would have improved and that at least some popular support for ETA would have evaporated. However, this has not been the case: ETA violence has continued unabated, labour unrest has been considerable and political disillusion, as reflected in increasingly high abstention rates in elections and referenda, has deepened. The reason for this is probably a combination of factors: Madrid's failure to treat the amnesty question (of such special interest to Basques) with sufficient urgency; the provocative behaviour of the security forces in handling demonstrations (like the one in Vitoria in March 1976 when police shot down five demonstrators); the tactless and often insensitive way in which the whole constitutional and autonomy question has been handled. Yet it also has to be said that Madrid's willingness to co-operate has often been undermined by the internal divisions among the Basques themselves—divisions which reflect the age-old clash between ethnicity and class.

The general and municipal elections of March and April 1979 served to confirm two developments in Basque politics: firstly, the left-wing and nationalist trend (as reflected in the spectacular success of the pro-ETA coalition Herri Batasuna in sending 3 deputies to the Madrid Cortes) and, secondly, the steady rise in the abstention rate, evenly spread across the four provinces. Given the success of the PSOE (albeit predominantly in Vizcaya and Guipúzcoa), it was predicted by many that they would be successful in the regional elections of March 1980. This, however, was not to be. Without any question the victors were the PNV, whose leader, Carlos Garaicoechea, became the Chief Executive of the CGV and the President of the new autonomous community of Euzkadi. The big surprise of the election, however, was the performance of Herri Batasuna which came overall second to the PNV both in terms of seats (11 to 25) and of percentage of votes (16 to 38). The PSOE had been relegated to third place with 9 seats and 14 per cent of the vote, while the ruling UCD was, at least in terms of votes, humiliatingly beaten into fifth place by Euskadiko Ezkerra. Thus, out of the 60 seats in the Parliament, no less than 42 had been secured by Nationalists and, out of those, 17 were won by candidates of the far Left; moreover, if these 17 are added to the 9 seats of the PSOE and the one Communist seat, the predominance of the Left in general becomes abundantly clear.

From the point of view of political stability, however, perhaps the most significant statistic is the fact that six parties obtained 6 per cent or more of the popular vote, suggesting a level of fragmentation far higher than in Catalonia or indeed anywhere else in Spain. Polarisation would also seem to be a feature of the Basque political scene, since, while the extreme Left HB captured 16 per cent of the vote, the far Right Popular Alliance (AP) secured 5 per cent. When one adds to this the even more disturbing fact that, in terms of national identification, 25 per cent of all voters who consider themselves to be Basques pure and simply are to be found in the pre-independence party, Herri Batasuna (compared to the 4 per cent in the equivalent Catalan party, BEAN)[16] the enormous difference between the political complexions of the two regions becomes most apparent.

Galicia

With Andalusia Galicia shares the dubious distinction of being among the poorest regions of Spain. Geographical isolation and poor communications have been partly responsible for an economic backwardness that is reflected in the existence of a predominantly rural population engaged mainly in farming (often at subsistence level) and fishing; it has also encouraged the preservation of a weak but distinct Celtic culture based on a separate language used by over 70 per cent of the population. Socially, with a predominance of small farmers and only a small percentage of urban workers, it has tended to be very conservative and political movements advocating looser ties with Madrid have not usually generated much interest, except among the small intellectual and professional classes. The vast majority of Galicians seem to have been generally content to accept centralist control from Madrid, in spite of the legacy of neglect and underdevelopment that this has meant for them.

Although the Galician autonomous movement can be traced back to the middle of the nineteenth century, when autonomous demands were linked to Federal Republican ideas and accompanied by a cultural '*Rexurdimento*', it bore little political fruit until the days of the Second Republic. The Autonomous Galician Republican Organisation (ORGA) founded in 1929 was represented by its leader Casares Quiroga in the Pact of San Sebastián more because of its association with Azaña's Republican Action than because of its concern with autonomy. It was the more locally orientated Partido Galleguista (PG) which pioneered the Statute of Autonomy approved in a regional referendum in December 1932. This was presented to the Madrid Cortes three days before Civil War broke out in July 1936; as with the case of Andalusia (see next section) the considerable lapse of time reflected the lack of a strong popular movement in favour of autonomy as well as internal political squabbles.[17]

During the Franco era Galicia suffered from economic neglect and cultural repression epitomised by the endemic emigration which continued unabated and whose root case (the division of the land into highly inefficient *minifundios*) was only partially eradicated. Industrial development was negligible; over half the labour force of the region, the highest percentage in Spain, is employed in the primary sector. Following attempts in the fifties by small intellectual groups to launch a cultural revival, two significant nationalist groups emerged in the next decade; the Galician Socialist Party (PSG), which favours autonomy, and the more radical Union of the Galician People (UPG), which advocates independence for the region. The latter, which significantly has links with ETA, attempted, unsuccessfully, in 1975 to launch an armed struggle against the regime, but has since restricted itself to political activities.

The political spectrum that has emerged in the post-Franco era in Galicia is wide and complex; indeed, there is a strong tendency to fragmentation and polarisation, which would be more dangerous but for the apparently apathetic, apolitical nature of much of the electorate. The Left includes national parties like the Communist PCG and the PSOE and nationalist groups like the UPG, the PSG, and the extreme-Left MCG, while the Right is defended by the far-Right Popular Alliance (AP) and the UCD. As in Andalusia there is no right-wing or centre-wing party linked to a strong bourgeoisie to fly the banner of autonomy, and the disparate groups of the Left are ideologically divided with differing views on Galicia's future role within the Spanish State. Significantly, in the confused period prior to the elections, the inability of these groups to forge any permanent alliance (there were five attempts in two years) only served to confirm the instability of Galician politics.

In the 1977 elections Suárez's UCD, with 20 out of the 27 seats contested in the region, won a clear victory over their nearest rivals, the AP (4 seats) and the PSOE (1 seat). However, it must be emphasised that this represented only one-fifth of all the voters in the region because of the high abstention rate (40.64 per cent). This alarming but traditional trend had already manifested itself in the referendum on the Political Reform Law (31 per cent) and was to worsen during subsequent Galician polls. Significantly the nationalists, divided as they were, gained not a single seat. This meant that they had no voice on the *Xunta de Galiza*, restored under the pre-autonomous arrangements of March 1978 and they only had a minority say in the draft Statute that was drawn up by the Assembly of Parliamentarians, dominated, of course, by the UCD.

Although the draft document was formally presented to the Cortes for scrutiny in June 1979, it was not destined to be approved until October of the following year. The main reason for this long delay was the blatant attempt by the ruling party to impose on Galicia a Statute which, hedged around in many articles by references to the overall authority of the Spanish State, fell far short of the degree of autonomy attained by Basques or Catalans.[18] The original draft was opposed not only by the nationalist and left-wing parties of the region but by the regional branch of the UCD. After much heated debate and controversy, an amended document had to be re-submitted to the Assembly of Parliamentarians before being finally approved in the Cortes. During this process it was clear that the government, having made considerable concessions to the Basques and Catalans, was determined to use its parliamentary majority in Galicia to impose a more restricted Statute.

This manoeuvre was denounced by nearly all the nationalist parties in the region which urged the electorate to abstain in the subsequent referendum on the Statute held in December 1980. No doubt the endemic tendency to abstain in Galicia was a significant factor, but it could by no means account for the alarmingly high rate (71 per cent) recorded, which must be, to a large extent, related to general public disillusion with the way in which the autonomy process has been handled. Although 73 per cent of voters voted in favour of the Statute, as a percentage of the electoral poll, this represented little more than 20 per cent; thus the Statute is dangerously lacking in public support.

As in Euzkadi and Catalonia neither the 1977 nor the 1979 general elections proved a reliable indicator of voting intention in the elections to the Galician Parliament in October 1981. While it was the Right which emerged triumphant, the laurels of victory did not go to the UCD (24 seats) but to the far Right AP (26 seats) vigorously led by Franco's ex-Minister of Information, Manuel Fraga; the PSOE was able to garner 17 seats, while the remaining four seats were shared by the nationalist parties. In the sense that national parties had won a clear victory (with an AP–UCD coalition government emerging in the Xunta) these results provide a marked contrast to those of Euzkadi and Catalonia, but to the extent that the UCD's share of the votes fell dramatically, they fitted in with a strong national trend—later to be repeated in Andalusia. Since the AP has consistently argued in favour of a regional rather than an autonomy solution for Spain, it is very unlikely that a vigorous effort will be made to ensure that real power and substantial resources are transferred to the Xunta. Yet the ruling coalition cannot afford to be complacent: the consistently high abstention rates cannot be entirely attributed to apathy and disillusion; the massive demonstrations in favour of autonomy on 4 December 1978 testify to the existence of a growing sense of regional identity, which, given more moderation and unity among the nationalists and a failure by the Xunta to tackle the deep-seated socio-economic problems of the region, could be channelled in other political directions.

Andalusia

The present autonomy movement in Andalusia may well be predominantly a reaction to the political centralisation and economic neglect of the Franco era. However, its origins can partly be traced to the *junta* and Federal-Republican movements of the nineteenth century and, more recently (in the early twentieth century), to the activities of a small group of *andalucistas* led by the lawyer, Blas Infante. Economically Infante, who shared with the Anarchists a profound concern for the plight of the *jornaleros*, was strongly influenced by the ideas of the American economist, Henry George with his theories on the abolition of private property and the socialisation of land via a single tax on all urban and rural property. Politically he was very sympathetic to the ideas of the Federal Republicans (led by Pi y Margall), advocating an autonomous Andalusia within a Federal Spain and believing, like the regenerationalists of the period, that only the economic and political revitalisation of the regions could lead to the regeneration of Spain. However, Infante stressed that none of this could be achieved without a cultural renaissance involving a re-awakening of the Andalusian sense of identity based partly on the assimilation of their Moorish past.

The Regionalist Assemblies which he and his followers of the Andalusian Centres organised in 1918 and 1919 may be seen as a conscious attempt to involve a wide range of political and other organisations in this broader process of cultural revival. Certainly it could be argued that his reluctance to found (or for a long time even to join) a political party related to his conviction that this wider purpose could not be achieved from within such narrow confines.

In terms of political achievement the movement was hardly successful. Standing as part of mixed regional-national candidatures in 1918 and 1919 and as a Federal-Republican in 1931 Infante failed to get elected. The petitions for autonomy which were sent to Madrid in 1916 and 1919 were ignored. To a large extent this was predictable, given the fact that the *andalucistas* constituted a small section of a minority social class, i.e. the petit bourgeoisie, squeezed between the landowning aristocracy tied to Madrid centralism and the Anarchist-dominated working-class.

Under the Second Republic, the Juntas Liberalistas created by Infante spearheaded a more hopeful campaign for regional autonomy. This culminated in the Assembly of Córdoba in 1933, involving delegates from all the region's provinces and political and cultural organisations. Although the text of a Statute of Autonomy was agreed, little subsequent progress was made to translate aspiration into tangible reality. Apart from the anticipated hostility of the Centre-Right government, at bottom even the national parties of the Left had little enthusiasm for autonomy, concerned as they were with the wider issues of the class struggle. Moreover, provincial rivalries, epitomised by the Granada delegation's suggestion of an autonomous Eastern Andalusia based on that city, impeded progress. However, the main reason, apart from the low level of regional consciousness was undoubtedly the lack of a purely Andalusian party committed above all else to the attainment of political autonomy. This was the major lesson to be learnt by the *andalucistas* of the post-Franco era.[19]

Over the last six years all the major parties in the regions have, to a greater or lesser extent, accepted the need for regional autonomy as a means of combating the underlying economic and social ills that over the centuries have made Andalusia one of the poorest areas of Spain. However, there is little doubt that the pioneer of autonomy has been the PSA led by Alejandro Rojas-Marcos. Originally this party, founded clandestinely as a publishing group in the University of Seville in 1965, was just one more embryonic political party, vaguely committed to Marxist ideals, and involved in the stuggle against the regime. Only later, as the Socialist Alliance of Andalusia (ASA) did its regionalist nature become apparent. Even at its First Congress in 1976, when it became the PSA, its ideas on decentralised socialism (*Socialismo autogestionario*) seemed to take precedence over the regional question. After its poor showing in the 1977 elections (and having already in 1978 welcomed into its ranks surviving members of Infante's movement) the PSA modified its stance, claiming to be the nationalist party of Andalusia. As in the days of Infante, however, Andalusian 'nationalism' was not to be confused with the 'right-wing' and 'bourgeois' parties of Euskadi and Catalonia but was to be regarded as left-wing and working-class. Rojas-Marcos and party theoreticians like José Aumente were at pains to stress that the party represented a coherent integration of socialism and left-wing nationalism and not simply a loose coalition of regionalists and socialists.

Whether this modification was based on expediency or ideology, it proved very successful electorally. In the general elections of March 1979 the PSA returned five deputies to the Madrid Cortes and in the ensuing local elections secured over 250 councillors in all eight provinces of the region. Up to this point the national parties of the Left had not seriously faced the autonomy question; henceforth they could not afford to ignore it, nor the challenge of the PSA.

The PSA had been the first party, in 1973, to press for regional autonomy (not, it should be stressed, independence); similarly it was the first party, in 1976, to draw up the Blueprint of a State of Autonomy. In the latter, following the lead of the historical *andalucistas*, it demanded that agrarian reform be included among the areas of competence exclusively reserved for the Junta de Andalucía. The PSA was also prominent in the historic *Día de Andalucía* on 4 December 1977, when over a million *andaluces* all over the region demonstrated in favour of autonomy; this constituted the first popular expression of *andalucismo* since the 1930s.

During this time (1976–79) of course, the PSA had no political power; having won no seats in the 1977 elections, it had no representatives on the pre-Autonomous *Junta de Andalucía* that was established by Royal Decree in April 1978 and dominated by the Socialists who had emerged clear victors in those elections. However, this may well have worked to the advantage of the PSA which, working as an extra-parliamentary pressure group criticising the Left's 'collaboration' with Madrid, was able to present an image of dynamism and commitment to local needs. Naturally, the PSA's position changed after the 1979 elections, when it was allocated one seat in the regional government, and in the summer of that year it was able to play its part in the drafting of the Statute of Carmona.

It would be a mistake, however, to underestimate the role of the other parties in the autonomy process. As early as 1979, eleven political parties in the region had signed the Autonomy Part of Antequera agreeing to secure autonomy for the region by the speediest route, i.e. via Article 151. Given the dangers of abstention and the number of provinces in the region (8) the demands of the referendum process (outlined above) clearly posed serious obstacles. However, when, for reasons that are still difficult to fathom, Suárez and the UCD decided to recommend abstention to the Andalusian electorate, the chances of victory seemed even more remote. Thus, when it transpired that the autonomy initiative of 28 February 1980 had failed only in the province of Almería (with 42 per cent), all the parties of the Left hailed it as a moral victory. The credibility of Suárez and the UCD, already shaken in Andalusia, was severely impaired.

In succeeding months the Premier tried to placate the outraged Andalusians, who were now united as never before, by promising that the region would soon see her autonomous institutions functioning, though only on the basis of partial autonomy (Article 143). However, the parties of the Left, with the full support of the great majority of Andalusians, would now settle for nothing less than full, immediate autonomy. The PSA deputies used their new position in the Madrid Congress to denounce Suárez's 'deception'.[20] Eventually a compromise was reached that would enable Andalusia to accede to full autonomy pending approval in a second regional referendum of an amended Statute. In this second ballot the hurdle was less steep: provided that over 50 per cent of voters *across the whole region* voted in the affirmative, autonomy was assured. And indeed, although the abstention rate was higher than in 1980 (47 per cent compared with 37 per cent), on 20 October 1981 the Andalusians voted overwhelmingly in favour of autonomy. Indeed, ironically, both in national and regional elections and referenda they have turned out in far greater numbers than the Basques, Catalans or Galicians.

In May 1982 the people of Andalusia voted in the first-ever elections to a regional Parliament. As was widely predicted, the Socialists, who had triumphed in the 1979 general and local elections, emerged clear victors. Subsequently, the Socialist leader, Rafael Escuredo, for four years provisional Head of the Junta, was elected as the first President of the Autonomous Community of Andalusia. With 66 out of the total of 109 seats in the Junta, Escuredo was able to form a majority PSOE government, the first ever to be formed on Spanish soil. Apart from the extent of the Socialist victory, the two other surprises of these elections were the 17 seats secured by AP (compared with the UCD's 15) and the very poor showing of the PSA, reduced to a mere 3 seats. The AP's success can no doubt be attributed to the widespread dissatisfaction with the UCD (which has also affected right-wing voters) but the complete humiliation of the region's only significant regionalist party is less easy to explain. Though part of the explanation undoubtedly lies in the lack of resources available to a small non-bourgeois regionalist party, the serious rift in the party which in December 1980 led to the expulsion of seven members of the Executive Committee, allied to the authoritarian-style leadership of Rojas-Marcos, must have played a major part in alienating public sympathy.[21]

Looked at objectively does the revised Statute of Carmona give Andalusia genuine potential for self-government? There is no doubt that, when the appropriate transfers have been made, the document potentially gives the region the opportunity to proceed towards a substantial degree of self-determination within the framework of a democratic Spain. She will have considerable say over the way revenue is raised and spent; the Andalusian Parliament will be able to pass a law establishing the way in which the Junta will integrate and co-ordinate the activities of the Provincial Councils; the region will have its own police force; she will have exclusive control over cultural and educational matters. However, in several ways the Statute has been watered down from its original form by debate in the Cortes and certainly does not satisfy many of the demands of the PSA. The latter's farmer spokesman in the Congress, Miguel-Angel Arredonda, has drawn attention to the fact that agrarian reform is not included within the areas of exclusive competence of the Junta (albeit being listed as a basic objective), that the idea of a *concierto económico* was rejected and that many areas of competence are circumscribed by references to the role of the State.[22] This explains why in the October referendum campaign the slogan of the PSA was ' "Yes" to the Statute, in order to improve it in the Andalusian Parliament'. There is no doubt that, while it represents the best opportunity the Andalusians have ever had to shape their own destiny, it does not bear close comparison with the Statutes of Sau and Guernica.

Thus the Andalusians now have their own autonomous government. Unlike its counterparts in Euzkadi and Catalonia, however, it is not a nationalist but a Socialist government. PSA leaders like Miguel-Angel Arredonda have argued that this situation is a contradiction in terms and that a party, whose orientation is nationwide, cannot truly fight for the interests of the region.[23] On the other hand, it may be argued that, now that a Socialist government has been installed in Madrid, the lines of communication between Madrid and Seville will be considerably better than those between Madrid, Barcelona and Vitoria. Certainly the Andalusians under the Socialists would seem to have a better chance of seeing their autonomy functioning efficiently than the Galicians.

* * *

In the four (and only four) territories that have been granted full autonomy under Article 151, there would seem to be a close correlation between the strength of the nationalist movement (especially the strength of a nationalist party) and the degree of autonomy attained. Although neither the PNV nor the CiU were actually the dominant parties in the pre-autonomous bodies of those regions, they were powerful enough to exert a considerable influence over the nature of the Statutes finally agreed. On the other hand, in Galicia and Andalusia, whose Statutes are more restricted, the nationalist parties are politically weak and/or divided and the autonomy process, particularly in its later stages, has been controlled by national parties, the UCD and the PSOE. Moreover, there is also a substantial degree of correlation, as Pérez Vilarino has suggested, between the extent of autonomy attained and the level of economic development of a given region, which is closely related to the existence of a local bourgeoisie to spearhead that development. Historically, and even today, the bourgeoisies of Galicia and Andalusia have been tied economically, socially and politically to Madrid and have little interest in encouraging, let alone financing, the growth of nationalist parties committed to a much greater degree of independence from the centre. None the less while the prospects for Galician autonomy seem bleak, there is a little more hope that the Socialist government in Andalusia will seize its unique opportunity to embark on a radical programme of socio-economic transformation.

Autonomy and the New Structure of the Spanish State

The granting of autonomy to these four regions is only part of a wider process that involves the complex and conscious restructuring of the Spanish State in a way that has never before been attempted in Spanish history. Yet what that new structure will ultimately be has at no stage been clearly defined; even the Constitution, with its 22 articles devoted to 'The Territorial Organisation of the State', leaves this fundamental problem largely unanswered, although Article 145(I) which prohibits the federation of Autonomous Communities, would seem to exclude the possibility of a federal structure.[24] Following the 1977 elections the victorious UCD, whether for political reasons or out of a genuine desire not to impose any rigid pattern, preferred to let the situation evolve, leaving the initiative squarely with the regions themselves. In practice this meant leaving the important decisions to the elites of the dominant party or parties in any given area. This flexible approach has had both advantages and disadvantages. On the credit side, local politicians have been given *carte blanche* to decide whether and how to launch an autonomy initiative and also on what territorial base, and by which route to do so; they have been able to participate democratically in vital decisions affecting the new shape of the Spanish State. However, on the debit side, the government has left the impression that the whole process lacks any sense of direction and ultimate purpose. It has also led to a number of anomalies. For example, as Anselmo Carretero has pointed out, the intended Autonomous Communities of Castile-León and Castile-La Mancha bear little relation to any cultural or political entities either past or present; historical reality would seem to demand the creation of three autonomous regions based on the three former Kingdoms of León, Castile and Toledo.[25] A consequence of the merger of León and Castile has been the successful attempt by the provinces of Logroño and Santander to 'secede' and request the formation of the uni-provincial Autonomous Communities of Rioja and Cantabria; though it can be argued that these areas form distinct geographical and economic units, historically both have been closely associated with Castile (though not with León).

The existence of these and other uni-provincial communities like Asturias, Madrid, Murcia and (thus far) Navarre, whose provincial councils will eventually merge with the regional governments concerned, underlines further the inevitably heterogeneous nature of the new Spanish State, which, as Professor Gonzalo Saenz de Buruaga has pointed out, can be neither federal nor regional but is destined to consist of a great variety of different relationships with the central government.[26] In one sense, as Linz has shown, this pattern would simply be the reflection of the very diversity of the country; from an administrative point of view, however, the establishment of relationships with Autonomous Communities as economically, demographically socially and culturally diverse as, for example, Andalusia and Asturias or the Canaries and Valencia is bound to create numerous problems.[27] The ultimate shape of the new Spanish State matters less, of course, than its efficiency. However, given the traditional shortcomings of Spanish bureaucracy, the addition (except in the uni-provincial areas) of an extra tier of government, plus the fact that regional deputies are unable to earn a salary, would not seem to bode well in this respect. One of the major tests of the efficiency of the system will be its ability to tackle the serious economic problems faced by regions like Andalusia, Galicia, Extremadura and Castile, while not alienating the richer areas like the Basque Country, Catalonia, Asturias and Cantabria which will be obliged to contribute to their development through the Interterritorial Compensation Fund set up under the terms of the 1978 Constitution. On the one hand (perhaps paradoxically) a strong initiative must be taken by the State to set in motion the re-distributive process; on the other, the newly created Autonomous Communities must feel that they are active participants in the process of change.

This whole issue in fact highlights the basic dilemma of Spain's autonomy legislators: the extent to which substantial powers can be given to the 'region-based' communities without giving offense to the 'nation-based' communities who feel that they merit preferential status and the extent to which such a status can be granted to the latter without arousing resentment and a feeling of discrimination among the former. While, particularly in the wake of the attempted coup of February 1981, one can understand the motivation behind the UCD–PSOE pact to 'harmonise' an autonomy process which, at least to all appearances, had been allowed to drift, the parties concerned will have to make a monumental propaganda effort to convince those regions on whom the slow route has now been imposed that, in the short term, closer ties with Madrid could work to their advantage.[28] In theory, even in five years' time, the major parties could 'conspire' to frustrate the progress of such regions to full autonomy; however, given the fact that, to a large extent, the government is responsible for having stimulated regionalist activity in areas where formerly it was dormant or non-existent, it would be well-advised to allow the constitutional process to run its course, whatever the administrative difficulties involved.[29] The lesson of Andalusia should not be forgotten.

Conclusion

This study has concentrated on the nature, context and role of regional nationalisms in Spain and their relationship to the Spanish State. This concentration should not, however, lead us to assume that there is no substance to the concept of 'the Spanish nation'. In all the regions, albeit with varying emphasis, there is a substantial degree of consciousness of belonging to such a community, in addition to belonging to the regional community. Indeed, in certain regions, particularly in the geographical centre of Spain, the level of 'national' is undoubtedly greater than that of 'regional' awareness. In his study of Basque Nationalism Pedro González Blasco rightly points out that, compared to, say, the multi-national empires of Europe prior to 1918 or the new Third-World nations that have sprung up in Africa and Asia since the early sixties, Spain has probably achieved a greater degree of integration based on a common history.[30] In spite of the social, political and regional cleavages which continued to divide Spain during the nineteenth and early twentieth centuries, and which culminated in the Civil War of 1936–39, this 'state' nationalism has by no means evaporated. Indeed it can be argued that even the Franco regime contributed to this process; this was achieved not so much by the regime's conformist, centralising influences and its determination to stamp out political and cultural pluralism, but came about as a result of increased economic prosperity, greatly improved communications and higher levels of education and literacy. On certain issues the Spanish can unite as well as the British or the French. For example it has been demonstrated time and again in history that an external threat to Spain as a whole can expect a surprisingly united front of opposition. After the Napoleonic occupation of 1808 large numbers of hitherto supporters of the French Enlightenment and opponents of Spanish absolutism flocked to the 'national' cause. In more recent times, at the end of the Second World War, when the Allies decreed their diplomatic and economic blockade, Franco was able to rouse considerable patriotic support. Stretching back many generations, Spanish political leaders, albeit for their own purposes, have found an echo in the majority of Spanish hearts when they have reiterated the Spanish claim to Gibraltar. It can be argued, of course, that such outbursts are rare, of an emotional and ephemeral nature and often the result of political manipulation; on the other hand, is the emotional response not the key test of any nationalism and can such outbursts be anything but ephemeral responses to particular challenges and crises? In any case, for all its contradictions and variety, does not Spanish political and cultural life, both past and present, demonstrate the existence of countless underlying characteristics common to all Spaniards whether Basque, Catalan or Andalusian? Ironically, argues Madariaga, one of these characteristics is precisely their tendency to 'separatism':

> Much of the uncompromising and intransigent character of these home-rule problems, their tendency to separatism, far from being justified by their more or less solid arguments as 'differences', turn out to be the outcome of an identity of character between Catalans, Basques and other Spaniards. The more separatist a Catalan or a Basque is the more Spanish he reveals himself to be.[31]

It is to be hoped that, when the pendulum of national consciousness has swung back to a more intermediate position between loyalty to the *patria grande* and the *patria chica*, all the peoples and regions of the country will work in solidarity to protect the still fragile and finely-balanced web of political structures that together they have begun to create. In the long run only a deepening loyalty to the wider entity can ensure the survival and consolidation of the smaller units for which so much enthusiasm has recently been generated. This is what Adolfo Suárez was pleading for in his famous televised speech when he stated: 'The new State that emerges requires the same emotional warmth as the new Communities'.[32] For this warmth to be created, many old prejudices will have to be buried, many new bridges will have to be built and many hard sacrifices will have to be made. In 1973 Juan Linz hinted at the kind of sacrifice that will have to be made when he wrote:

> Castilian-speaking Spaniards will have to give up the idea of a Spanish nation created largely by them and accept a more decentralised, largely multi-lingual State. The periphery, while enjoying a new sense of nationhood, will have to combine it with loyalty to the multinational State, a loyalty expressed in an active participation in the central politics and government and in a willingness to share in the burdens of common history of centuries and the symbols of the State.[33]

This message is still relevant today.

Postscript

Compared with the elections of 1 March 1979, those of 28 October 1982 have shown a general trend away from regional parties; compared with the election of June 1977, however, the results are remarkably similar in this respect.[34] The overall fall in the regional vote has not affected the performance of the major nationalist parties, the Catalan CiU and the Basque PNV which (albeit marginally) have actually improved their position both in terms of votes and of seats in the Madrid Congress. This increase in support could be interpreted as approval of the policy of pressurising Madrid to abandon or drastically modify the notorious LOAPA which, as we have seen, seeks to strengthen the government's hand in controlling the devolution process; on the other hand, it is more likely that it is explicable simply in terms of the electorates' general approval of the way in which these parties have been running their respective regional governments, coupled with the traditionally higher level of regional consciousness in those regions. As far as the smaller regional parties are concerned the results probably seem very disappointing and will no doubt be followed by much internal recrimination and self-analysis. This applies particularly to the PSA which has lost all 5 of its deputies and hence its power base in Madrid. On the other hand, it can be argued that, if the PSA's historical role was to pressurise Madrid into conceding autonomy via Article 151, this has been achieved and the party, like other small parties in the newly Autonomous Communities, can concentrate on making an impact in the regional forum.

In the long term this move away from the regional parties, at least in national elections, should not necessarily be seen as retrograde; indeed, it could be interpreted as a mildly encouraging sign that, thanks (among other things) to the largely successful creation of Autonomous Communities (most of which are now functioning in some form or other) the real or perceived dangers of national disintegration are now receding. In these elections it would seem that Spaniards have tended to vote predominantly along party lines rather than along a regional-national axis, and that national issues have dominated in the election campaign. The Spanish people, indeed, seem to have demonstrated a remarkable degree of unity in favour of moderate but definite change, as offered by the PSOE of Felipe González.

How are the regions likely to fare under the new Socialist Government? Regionalist hopes should not be pinned too high and it should be remembered that the PSOE was a co-signatory of the 1981 Autonomous Agreements (*Acuerdos Autonomicos*), including the controversial LOAPA. In spite of theoretical sympathy for federalism and electoral assertions of support for the full implementation of the autonomy programme, the Socialists are likely to retain a tight grip over the course of events. However, the PSOE must always remind itself of the important part which the regional question played in the downfall of the UCD. It should remind itself too that, in spite of its substantial majority in the Congress and the Senate, that it cannot always automatically count on the parliamentary support of the Socialist parties in, for example, the Basque Country and Catalonia, which are firmly committed to wide-ranging autonomy for these regions.

If the next round of national elections (theoretically scheduled for 1986) produces a confirmation of these voting patterns, the Socialists will be able to take credit for having successfully negotiated the complex labyrinth of transferring economic and fiscal powers to the new Autonomous Communities. However, a strongly regionalist swing along the lines of the 1979 elections—a swing that involved a revival in the fortunes of the minor regionalist parties—would suggest disillusion with that process. The implications in four years' time of a strong resurgence of anti-Madrid centrifugalism could be disastrous for the stability of Spanish democracy.

Notes

1. S. de Madariaga, *Spain, A Modern History*, Jonathan Cape, London, 1961, pp. 22–3.
2. J-M. de los Santos, *Andalucía en la revolución nacionalista*, Aljibe, Granada, 1979, p. 118.
3. This has come to mean the Basque Country, Catalonia and Galicia.
4. A. D. S. Smith, *Nationalism in the 20th Century*, Martin Robertson, Oxford, 1979, pp. 150–65.
5. T. Nairn, *The Break-up of Britain: Crisis and Neo-Nationalism*, NLB, London, 1977. S. G. Payne, 'Regional Nationalism: the Basques and Catalans' in W. T. Salisbury and J. D. Therberge (eds), *Spain in the 1970s*, Praeger, New York, 1976, pp. 76–102.
6. B. González Alonso, 'Reflexiones históricas sobre el Estado y la autonomía regional en España' in *Revista de Estudios Regionales*, Extraordinario Vol. II (1980), pp. 21–43.
7. J. J. Linz, 'Early State-Building and Late Peripheral Nationalisms against the State: The Case of Spain' in S. N. Eisenstadt and S. Rokkan (eds), *Building States and Nations*, Vol. II, Sage Publications, Beverly Hills/London, 1973, pp. 32–116. See also P. González Blasco, 'Modern Nationalism in Old Nations as a Consequence of Early State-Building: The Case of Spain' in W. Bell and W. E. Freeman (eds), *Ethnicity and Nation-Building*, Sage Publications, Beverly Hills/London, 1974, pp. 341–73.
8. C. Gispert and J. M. Prats, *España: un estado plurinacional*, Editorial Blume, Barcelona, 1978, p. 299.
9. J. García Fernández, 'Crónica de la descentralización: el panorama descentralizador al acabar' 1980 (I), in *Revista de Estudios Políticos*, No. 11 (1981), p. 175.
10. J. C. Borbón y Borbón, *Primer Mensaje del Rey*, Madrid, 1975.
11. M. Arévalo Clavero, *Forjar Andalucía*, Argantonio, Seville, 1980, p. 134.
12. J. Pérez Vilariño, 'La demanda de las autonomías en España', in *Información Comercial Española*, No. 571 (March 1981), pp. 141–51.

13. N. L. Jones, 'Catalunya triomfant: three years of nominal autonomy', in *Proceedings of the Third Conference of Hispanists in Polytechnics and Other Colleges*, C. Cobb (ed.), Bristol Polytechnic, 1980, pp. 180–204.

14. J. J. Linz, 'La crisis de un Estado unitario . . .', in *La España de las Autonomías* Vol. 11, Espasa-Calpe, Madrid, 1980, pp. 651–752.

15. Clavero, op. cit., pp. 105–8.

16. BEAN: 'Bloc d'Alliberament Nacional' (Left-wing Block for National Freedom).

17. The Galician question is briefly touched upon in Madariaga, op. cit., pp. 235–6 and pp. 404–5 and in J. J. Linz, op. cit., pp. 90–2. A detailed but polemical study worth reading is S. Alvarez, *Galicia, Nacionalidad Histórica*, Editorial Ayuso, Madrid, 1980.

18. For details and comment see J. L. Meilán Gil, 'El Estatuto de Autonomía para Galicia', in *La España de las Autonomías*, op. cit., pp. 513–63. See also Pérez Vilariño, op. cit., pp. 150–1.

19. See J. A. Lacomba, 'Las provincias andaluzas y el problema de la autonomía: 1931–33' in *Homenaje a Antonio Domínguez Ortiz*, Ministerio de Educación y Ciencia (Madrid), 1978, pp. 727–43. Consult also by the same author 'La Segunda República española y las autonomías: el caso andaluz' in *Revista de Estudios Regionales*, Extraordinario Vol. II (1980), pp. 71–99.

20. For their troubles, in the summer of 1981 Suárez almost succeeded in a move to eliminate the *andalucistas* as a separate parliamentary group. See *Andalucía Libre*, No. 37 (June 1981), pp. 6–7.

21. In September 1981 this was an option frequently expressed to the author not only by members of the *sector crítico* of the party but also by certain members of the party hierarchy. The evident disaffection of the former is expressed in two unpublished documents (i) *Manifiesto candidatura crítica*, dated 14 December 1980 and (ii) *Manifiesto de Montilla* dated 11 January 1981. After the regional election Rojas-Marcos resigned as leader of the party; he was replaced by the Mayor of Seville and PSA deputy for that city, Luis Uruñuela.

22. M. A. Arredonda, 'No hay autonomías sin partidos nacionalistas' in *Andalucía Libre*, No. 40 (Seville), pp. 6–7. Arredonda was, in June 1982, replaced as spokesman of the party by the PSA deputy for Seville, Juan Carlos Aguilar.

23. Arredonda, idem.

24. See G. Arino Ortiz, 'El Estado de las Autonomías: Realidad política, interpretación jurídica', in *La España de las Autonomías*, op. cit., pp. 11–117.

25. A. Carretero, 'Embrollos en torno a Castilla' in *El País*, 17 September 1981. See also by the same author, *Los pueblos de España*, Escuela Nacional de Estudios Profesionales, Mexico City, 1980, pp. 29–260.

26. 'A federal solution for Iberia?', paper given at the Conference of the Iberian Social Studies Association, University of Keele, April 1979 (as yet unpublished).

27. J. Linz, op. cit., pp. 701–3.

28. This pact is enshrined in four agreements, including the notorious Law on the Harmonisation of the Autonomy Process (LOAPA), published as *Acuerdos Autonómicos*, Servicio Central de Publicaciones de la Presidencia del Gobierno (Madrid), September 1981. One of the major provisions is to ensure that, following Andalusia's successful challenge to the government, all subsequent petitions for autonomy are to be channelled via Article 143, thus obliging the regions concerned to wait a further five years before applying for full autonomy.

29. L. Lopéz Rodó, *Las Autonomías, encrucijada de España*, Aguilar, Madrid, 1980, p. 24.

30. González Blasco, op. cit., p. 346.

31. Madariaga, op. cit., p. 238.

32. Quoted in *El País*, 21 May 1980.

33. J. Linz, 'early State-Building . . .', op. cit., pp. 105–6. See also the opinions of Carretero, *Los pueblos de España*, op. cit., pp. 229–60.

34. J. Sánchez, 'Las elecciones de I de Marzo 1979: un éxito regionalista', in *Revista de Estudios Regionales*, Vol. 3 (1979).

6 THE 1982 ELECTIONS AND THE DEMOCRATIC TRANSITION IN SPAIN

BRUCE YOUNG*

Introduction

The results of the 28 October 1982 general elections had no precedent in Spanish history. For the first time the Spanish Socialist Party (PSOE) emerged from democratic elections with an absolute majority of seats in parliament. Indeed, it was the first time that any Spanish political party had emerged from such elections with an absolute majority of seats. Even more, it would be difficult to find a historical precedent anywhere in the world for these elections. The outgoing governing party, the Democratic Centre Union (UCD), not only lost the elections but was almost reduced to the status of a parliamentary rump. The outgoing prime minister not only lost power, but lost even his parliamentary seat, as did his entire cabinet of ministers with one solitary exception.

This was no ordinary electoral switch; such unusual results clearly call for an unusual explanation for which I shall try to offer some of the basic elements. For reasons of space, however, I shall have to confine myself to what seem to me the most important elements, excluding matters of detail, even when these are in fact of considerable significance. I shall concentrate on the causes for the changes of fortune of the four main parties which operate throughout the national territory, that is, the Socialist Party (PSOE), the Democratic Centre Union (UCD), the right-wing People's Alliance (AP) and the Communist Party (PCE). About the regional parties, and the other national parties, I shall have much less to say.

Before discussing the causes for the dramatic changes manifested in the 1982 general election results, one must analyse more closely the results themselves.

A Brief Analysis of the 1982 Election Results

 A comparison of the 1982 results with those of the previous general elections of 1979 and 1977 reveals a spectacular advance, between 1979

*For Dolores and Fernando, and for their children and grandchildren.

and 1982, of the Socialist PSOE and of the right-wing AP, at the expense both of the main Centre party, the UCD, and of the Communist Party, the PCE.

Let us look first of all at the seats obtained by those parties in the Congress of Deputies (see Table 6.1). Congress is the lower chamber of the Spanish Parliament, and of much greater importance than the Senate, which is the upper chamber. In Congress, which has a total of 350 seats, the PSOE increased its representation from 121 in 1979 to 202 in 1982. Meanwhile, the AP shot up from 9 to 106 in the same period. It is interesting to note the contrast between the AP's spectacular advance in 1982 and the significant reverse it suffered in 1979. On the other hand, the UCD crashed down from 168 seats in 1979 to only 12 in 1982. In 1979, its 168 seats made it the biggest single party, and even though it lacked an absolute majority of seats in Congress its position as the party of government was thereby assured. But in 1982, it not only lost the contest with the PSOE but had to cede the position of the main party of opposition to the AP. Finally the PCE, which in 1979 had registered a modest advance, suffered a humiliating defeat in 1982, obtaining only 4 seats as compared to 22 in 1979.

Table 6.1   Congress seats obtained in 1977, 1979 and 1982

	PSOE	AP	UCD	PCE
1977*	118	16	165	19
1979*	121	9	168	22
1982†	202	106	12	4

Cambio 16, 1 November 1982.
†*Radio Nacional de España*, 12 November 1982 (*Junta Electoral Central*).
Note: includes main national parties only.

These changes in the pattern of distribution of Congress seats reflect corresponding changes in the distribution of votes, although it should be noted that the Spanish electoral system is so constructed as to allocate disproportionately fewer seats for fewer votes (see Table 6.2).

A more detailed breakdown of the 1982 election results is to be found in the Appendix. This appendix includes data for the Senate as well as Congress. More important, it details the results obtained by parties other than the four already mentioned but which also achieved representation in parliament. Of those other parties, one—the Democratic and Social

Table 6.2   Percentage of votes obtained in 1977, 1979 and 1982

	Participa-tion	PSOE	AP	UCD	PCE
1977*	77.9	29.5	8.3	34.7	9.2
.1979*	68.1	30.5	5.9	34.9	10.6
1982†	79.6	46.1	25.4	7.3	3.9

Cambio 16, 1 November 1982.
†*El País*, 31 October 1982.

Centre (CDS)—operates throughout the national territory, whilst the rest are regional parties whose base is in either Catalonia or in the Basque Country only.

The CDS was set up by former UCD Prime Minister Adolfo Suárez as an 'alternative' centre party to the UCD. Suárez was replaced as UCD Prime Minister in February 1981 by Leopoldo Calvo Sotelo, but remained in the UCD until the breakdown of his negotiations with the new UCD leadership at the end of July 1982. The founding Congress of his new party, the CDS, did not take place until the beginning of October 1982, on the very eve of the official election campaign. In the campaign itself, Suárez presented the CDS as a party of the progressive centre, situating it somewhat to the left of the UCD. Even taking into account the obvious difficulties posed by the task of setting up the machinery of a new party in the very midst of an election campaign, the results achieved by the CDS were modest, and clearly disappointed its founder, who seems to have expected that his own charisma would suffice to achieve something just a little better than 2 seats in Congress and 2.89 per cent of the total vote.

The performance of the regionalist ('nationalist') parties in Catalonia and the Basque Country was much better. In Catalonia, the centre-right Catalan nationalists of Convergència i Unió (CiU) increased both their percentage of the vote and their representation in parliament. But the smaller Esquerra Republicana de Catalunya (ERC), which represents the moderate Left of Catalan nationalism, did less well: its percentage of the vote dropped slightly, although it retained its single seat in Congress.

In the Basque Country, the main regionalist party, the Basque Nationalist Party (PNV), which is the moderate centre-right mainstream of Basque nationalism, consolidated its position and indeed advanced slightly. Euskadiko Ezkerra (EE), which represents the radical but non-violent Left of Basque nationalism, experienced a very slight decline in its portion of the vote but kept its single seat in Congress. Finally, the coalition Herri Batasuna (HB), which gives political support to the military wing of the Basque terrorist organisation ETA, increased its portion of the vote very slightly but lost one of the three seats it had won in the 1979 Congress, as a side-effect of the higher level of participation in 1982 (this loss will presumably not bother them very much if they maintain their traditional stance of refusing to send their elected representatives to the 'parliament of Madrid'). Table 6.3 gives further comparative data on the Congress results for the Basque Country in 1982, 1979 and 1977: one further important feature which deserves mention is the recovery by the PSOE in 1982 of ground lost in 1979, with the result that it now holds the same number of Congress seats for that region as the PNV. In Catalonia, the PSOE now holds 25 Congress seats as compared to 12 for CiU. These facts should be kept in mind, since they qualify to a greater or lesser extent the 'consolidation' achieved by the CiU and PNV respectively.

Table 6.3 Congress seats for the Basque Country, 1977, 1979 and 1982

	PSOE	PNV	HB	UCD	EE
1977	7	8	—	4	1
1979	5	7	3	5	1
1982	8	8	2	1	1

Cambio 16, 1 November 1982.

In contrast to Catalonia and the Basque Country, regionalist parties elsewhere experienced total defeat. The most important of them, the Andalusian Socialist Party (PSA), which won 5 seats in the 1979 Congress, was unable to win a single one in 1982. There are now no regionalist parties outside Catalonia and the Basque Country with representation in the national parliament.

A few words should be added about the fortunes of the various groups of the far Left and far Right. The decline and fall of the far Left, long evident, was fully confirmed by the 1982 results. As for the ultra-Right, Blas Piñar, the leader of the biggest fascist group, Fuerza Nueva (FN), lost his seat in Congress, leaving parliament free of fascist representation. Fuerza Nueva's no less fascist rival, Solidaridad Española (SE), which campaigned to get the rebel Civil Guard Lt. Colonel Tejero elected under the thought-provoking slogan 'storm into Congress with Tejero', not only failed to achieve this objective but could only manage to scrape up some 25,000 votes in the whole national territory. The total fascist vote barely topped 100,000, out of more than 21 million votes cast. Less than a month after the elections, on the 20 November, the seventh anniversary of Franco's death, Blas Piñar announced the dissolution of Fuerza Nueva.

The Crisis of the Centre

The Socialists' triumph was facilitated, to put it mildly, by the collapse of the UCD and the crisis of the Centre in general. It is to this phenomenon —the crisis of the Centre, which had guided the country through the first years of the transition to democracy—that I should like to turn now.

The UCD's defeat was not exactly unexpected. It followed a long period of internal struggle which first became publicly damaging in 1980 although in fact it had begun much earlier, and which culminated in the years 1981–82 in a series of splits in the UCD, with the departure of numerous deputies to form or join new parties. First (November 1981), former UCD Justice Minister, Francisco Fernández Ordóñez left and set up the social-democratic Partido de Acción Democrática (PAD), which in October 1982 entered some of its members as independents in the electoral lists of the PSOE; then the Partido Demócrata Popular (PDP) of ex-UCD Christian Democrat, Oscar Alzaga, which ended up in a fully-fledged electoral coalition with the conservative AP (in the interests of 'liberalism', as its theorist Herrero de Miñón was later to explain in *Diario 16* and elsewhere); again the Partido Demócrata Liberal (PDL) led by Antonio Garrigues which, holding a different view of 'liberalism', tried and failed to make an electoral coalition with what was left of the UCD, the latter now under the leadership of Landelino Lavilla, one-time Speaker of Congress; finally the CDS of former UCD Prime Minister Suárez, which gave up the UCD as a bad job and presented itself independently to the electorate.

This 'alphabet soup', not surprisingly, was not at all to the taste of any section of the electorate. The credibility, and the capacity to govern, of both the UCD and its leaders were seriously damaged. The whole process seemed to many to confirm the theory, assiduously spread about by the Socialists and others, according to which the UCD was a coalition of forces without any coherent political basis of unity, formed out of an alliance of convenience between groups and individuals with quite different political orientations or in many cases without any definite political orientation of any kind, brought together only by a common desire to retain the power they had acquired or inherited from the former regime.

This impression was reinforced by unseemly events on the very eve of the election, for instance the quarrel that broke out toward the end of September between the UCD and the PDL over the distribution of places in the electoral lists between these two formations, which were at that time supposed to have agreed upon an electoral coalition. The coalition, which had been agreed between the UCD leader, Landelino Lavilla and Antonio Garrigues Walker for the PDL, broke up due to the refusal of the UCD's provincial chiefs to accept places on the lists which would have facilitated the election of PDL members: they were afraid that they themselves would be pushed out. This quarrel was universally understood as a fight over 'cutting up the bacon' and its bitterness as a reflection of the scarcity of bacon available for cutting.

In my view, however, for an adequate explanation of the Centre's crisis it is necessary to delve somewhat deeper. The UCD was the party in power in the early years of Spain's transition to democracy, and was in a sense the chief political architect of that transition; for an adequate explanation of its rise and fall we must turn to the nature of that transition itself and of its problems.

Before Franco's death, the democratic opposition thought that Spain's transition to democracy would have to be preceded by what was then known as a 'rupture', that is, they thought that the transition would have to be initiated outside Francoist institutions and legality, and to be forced through in the course of a frontal attack directed against them. In point of fact, however, these institutions legislated their own disappearance, which took place within and not against the then-prevailing forms of legality. There was a 'rupture' with Francoism, certainly, but so to speak *from within* instead of *from outside*. No doubt the 'rupture' would not have taken place at all had it not been for the pressure exerted by the Spanish people, but the fact remains that it took a different form and course than had been expected by the democratic opposition.

That opposition was politically disoriented by this process, and the disorientation persisted for some time; even now it has, perhaps, not been overcome. For years, not just Communists and Socialists, but many other sectors of the democratic opposition vacillated between two (as it seems to me) equally erroneous interpretations of the situation. According to the first of these misinterpretations, either no change had taken place at all or else the change was merely superficial. This view was (and is) particularly characteristic of the far Left, but it has also been influential in much wider circles. Thus, as late as 1980 we find no less distinguished a figure than Juan Luis Cebrián (editor of the internationally-respected independent Madrid daily *El País*) writing in his book, *La España que bosteza* that 'what is being contrived is a structural perpetuation of the Francoist power system, and its democratic legitimation', and that 'the famous "rupture from above" (*"ruptura desde el poder"*) has been formally rather than really democratic'.[1] I would not contest for a moment the need to criticise, and to criticise very sharply, the very many and very grave failures and insufficiencies of Spain's democratic transition, as well as the extremely serious dangers which to this day still threaten what has been achieved so far. But I would contest this particular way of exercising that criticism, this particular manner of conceptualising these failures, insufficiencies and dangers. The philosopher and sociologist Aranguren wrote as far back as 1968, quoting Duverger, 'it is very easy to change the so-called formal freedoms into real ones: all you need to do is to suppress them. We realise their value precisely when we lose them'.[2] Millions of Spaniards felt the truth of these words during the attempted coup of 23 February 1981; as one of the deputies put it when he emerged from the Cortes after his liberation: 'now all of us know what freedom is and why we must not lose it'. A democracy with failures and insufficiencies is still a democracy, and it does not cease to be real because it is endangered. The notion, then, that Spanish democracy is somehow 'not real', or is 'merely formal', should be dismissed; that democracy has many problems, but this is a misinterpretation of their nature, a misinterpretation which, incidentally, seems to me to owe some part of its currency in Spain itself to a certain tendency in that country to romanticise the older western European democracies and exaggerate their virtues.

But a second (as it seems to me) misinterpretation of the transition has also been influential. According to this, the famous 'rupture' had actually taken place, but it had been 'negotiated'. This second error led to a tendency to overestimate the successes of the democratisation process. For instance, in the early years of transition the PSOE presented itself as a governmental 'alternative' in such a way as to appear to suggest that Spain was already a consolidated democracy.

Very frequently, both these erroneous interpretations of the transition co-existed within the same political group or even the same individual. In addition, attitudes inherited from the past remained persistently influential in circumstances which were increasingly rendering them inappropriate if not downright dangerous. Thus, the Left took years to recognise the anti-democratic nature of ETA terrorism, continuing, even if semiconsciously, to regard ETA as heroes of the anti-fascist struggle instead of as murderers and enemies of democracy in no way superior to, even though different from, military and civilian coup conspirators, Even today. the process of the demystification of ETA is not complete.

What, then, are we to say of Spain's transition? We would do well, I think, to start by giving up altogether the attempt to interpret it in terms of 'rupture', regardless of the precise manner—for there are many possible variants—in which such an interpretation might be worked out. The whole idea of a 'rupture' is misleading, in so far as, first, it inevitably suggests a sudden, once-and-for-all event instead of a long-term process. But second, the idea of 'rupture' makes it difficult, if not impossible, to take account of that complex interplay between changes initiated 'from within' Francoist institutions and changes imposed 'from outside' which is precisely characteristic of the Spanish transition process. To be sure, transition from Francoism to democracy requires profound, and not superficial, changes, and no doubt a desire to emphasise this is one motive for those who use the idea of 'rupture'; but the radical nature of the changes required can be specified in other terms which are free of the misleading associations of the expression 'rupture'.

Looking, then, at the transition as a long-term process involving a complex interplay of changes initiated 'from inside' Francoist institutions and changes imposed 'from outside', of changes 'from above' and changes 'from below', we can distinguish, up to 1982, at least three distinct phases in the transition. First is the phase of the political reform, leading up to the general elections of 1977. Next comes the phase of the Constitution, from 1977 to 1979; this phase was marked by 'consensus' between the country's main political parties in the elaboration of the Constitution. The third phase begins with the UCD's victory in the 1979 elections; during this phase, the general 'disenchantment' which had begun in the previous phase becomes deeper, the internal crisis of the UCD emerges publicly and leads eventually to its fragmentation, the government becomes increasingly ineffective and the country's problems intensify. This phase comes to an end with the PSOE's victory in the 1982 elections and the initiation of a new phase whose first moments are marked by a resurgence of hope, albeit a hope very different in kind from that of the heady days of 1977.

The rise and fall of the UCD, and the crisis of the Centre in general, has I think to be understood in relation to the different characteristics and tasks corresponding to the different phases of the transition process. The UCD was first formed as a coalition between politically diverse groups and individuals such as ex-Falangists, Christian Democrats, Liberals, Social Democrats, technocrats and others with no distinctive political or ideological profile whatsoever, many of whom had held positions of power under the former regime but who accepted the need to give up the 'immobilism' practised by Arias Navarro, the first post-Franco Prime

Minister, and to introduce a democracy along western European lines. In other words, the formation and early role of the UCD corresponded to the fact that the democratic transition was *initiated* from within the Francoist institutions but *culminated* in their replacement. The difficulties, mentioned above, experienced by the democratic opposition outside the UCD, and the Left in particular, in first acknowledging even the existence of this unexpected development and later in adjusting to it, facilitated the UCD's consolidation and its 1977 election victory. During the next phase, the UCD could claim with much justice to have guided the country through the period of the Constitution, even though the document was elaborated under conditions of 'consensus'. In the circumstances, the UCD's 1979 election victory was hardly surprising. But with the period of the Constitution's elaboration over and done with, the UCD's troubles began in earnest. Oversimplifying somewhat, we might say that these troubles began precisely when it became necessary to move on from the tasks of *elaborating* the Constitution to those of *applying* it. A Constitution is a set of fundamental laws; obviously there is a very considerable difference between the proclamation of such laws, important though that is, and their application, and between their application in general terms and their application to specific, concrete problems. In other words, the rights and duties proclaimed by the Constitution on the legal plane require practical translation on the social plane, that is, they require to be developed through the implementation of those social reforms which are needed to embody them and to guarantee their practical efficacy. For instance, it is not enough, though it is important, to proclaim the right of all to education, health care, and to work, as does the Spanish Constitution; it is also necessary to ensure that society is so organised as to facilitate the realisation of these rights, and it is obvious that in the Spain inherited from Francoism this requires far-reaching social reforms. Or, to take another example, the Constitution proclaims it to be the duty of the Spanish authorities to promote the removal of social obstacles which hamper equality of access by individuals belonging to different social classes to the opportunities offered by society (Article 9.2). This potentially very radical provision clearly requires very radical social reforms to give effect to it. Now, it was precisely when, after 1979, it became necessary to work out such a set of detailed social reforms, that is when it became necessary to move from general legal-political *principles* to concrete political *policies*, that the political incoherence of, and the political differences within, the UCD came to the fore; and indeed they had to do so. The controversies which arose within and which eventually fragmented the UCD in the period 1979–82 were generated precisely through the operation of the kind of dynamic just described; they concerned issues such as tax reform, divorce, the autonomy process, educational reform, and so on. Whilst the different factions of the UCD fought interminably between themselves over these and other issues, the great problems of the country, unemployment, terrorism, coup conspiracies, went unsolved and even untackled; long-overdue reforms were either not implemented at all, or else were implemented at half-cock, or else were pushed through at the cost of intensifying the UCD's internal tensions; the government's effectiveness and authority steadily diminished; and the impression was given to the country of a party made up of quarrelsome mini-Machiavellis interested only in personal power-seeking and self-enrichment.

To sum up: the same factors which gave the UCD its hegemony in the early years of the transition brought about its fragmentation and defeat in later years. The tasks of the later phases of the transition demanded another political formula than that which had worked so well in an earlier period. On 28 October 1982, the electorate made their choice of this new formula with an unprecedented majority; future years will show to what extent the PSOE deserved that confidence.

As for the UCD, its merits in the initial phases of the transition deserve the fullest recognition. However, whilst it may be that the Centre will rise again, it is more than unlikely that it will do so in the form of the old-style UCD. That formula is, I think, dead, and should be allowed to rest in peace.

The Crisis of the PCE

Apart from the UCD, the other big loser in the 1982 elections was the Communist Party, the PCE. As in the case of the UCD, its defeat followed a bitter internal struggle. But this matter will be dealt with much more briefly than the crisis of the UCD.

Under its General Secretary, Santiago Carrillo, the PCE had vowed allegiance to what he termed 'Eurocommunism'. In other words, to put it simply, it rejected the Soviet model of Socialism and accepted democracy. In the course of 1980, a grouping within the PCE, alarmed at its decreasing levels of activity and membership, began a campaign to renovate the Party. These 'renovators', as they were known, called in effect for the application of Eurocommunism to the PCE itself: in other words, they campaigned for its internal democratisation.

The response of Carrillo and his supporters was not long in coming: in November 1981, the renovators, whose ranks included prominent PCE leaders and a group of influential Madrid councillors, were expelled from the PCE. The damage to the PCE and to its credibility was considerable. It is difficult, after all, to place much trust in a party which preaches democracy but which refuses to apply it within its own ranks. After the election defeat, Carrillo resigned as General Secretary. However, his replacement, Gerardo Iglesias, is known to support the Carrillo line, and Carrillo himself will remain the PCE's chief spokesman in parliament. It therefore seems likely that the PCE's crisis will continue.

The Rise of AP

As a result of the elections, the People's Alliance (AP) of Manuel Fraga Iribarne has become the main party of the opposition. Its rise is a very important phenomenon; unfortunately for lack of space I will be unable to explore the issues involved fully. AP is a conservative (some would say a very conservative) formation. Its leader, Manuel Fraga, was a minister under Franco and, even more important, in the first post-Franco government of Arias Navarro, where he held charge of the Ministry of the Interior. In this latter position he established a reputation for authoritarianism which he has never managed to shake off. Fraga, and the AP, have explicitly stated their support of and loyalty to the 1978 Constitution. Indeed, on occasion don Manuel has shown himself capable of valiant actions in defence of the Constitution; his conduct during, and immediately after, the attempted coup of 23 February 1981 impressed many.

For all that, the AP's attitude to the Constitution is not free of ambiguity. It has often criticised particularly sensitive sections, in particular the section on autonomies and the article abolishing the death penalty. Nor is its attitude to coup conspiracies entirely clear. After the discovery of the coup intended for 27 October 1982, Fraga unpleasantly surprised his parliamentary colleagues by calling for 'understanding' for the conspirators. The manner in which these ambiguities will be resolved is one of the major question marks hanging over the new legislature. Whilst no-one could plausibly compare the AP with the fascists, it might be claimed that it is not free of residual authoritarianism.

What is certainly true is that the AP's election campaign succeeded in attracting many of the votes which formerly went to Blas Piñar's fascist *Fuerza Nueva* (FN). In fact, a noteworthy feature of FN's own campaign was the ferocity with which it attacked Fraga and the AP. AP, for its part, made quite explicit efforts to attract the fascist vote by, for example, distributing leaflets bearing the legend 'don't waste your anti-Marxist vote: vote for AP'. This must qualify, to some extent, the optimism generated by the sharp decline in the fascist vote. On the other hand, the transference of these votes to AP might be understood as a means of redirecting them through democratic and constitutional channels.

But let us turn now to the main victor of these elections: the PSOE.

The Socialist Programme

The programme on which the PSOE won the 1982 elections was widely characterised both in Spain and abroad as 'moderate'. The label is accurate if by 'moderation' is meant the absence of sweeping nationalisations, readiness to co-operate with political and social forces outside the PSOE, and so forth. But 'moderation' is a relative term. The apparently modest reforms envisaged by the PSOE would, in fact, under Spanish conditions amount to a revolution of a kind—a peaceful revolution, to be sure, and one aiming not at socialism but at the effective modernisation and democratic consolidation of the country.

Some of the more important measures proposed by the PSOE may be summarised as follows.

Economic policy

The PSOE aims to create 800,000 new jobs net over its four years mandate, through a combination of measures: using a modest level of public investment to stimulate growth in the private sector, whose primacy in the creation of new jobs is recognised; lowering the retirement age to 64 in its first year of office and then by 6 month stages per each succeeding year of office; shortening the working week, to a maximum of 40 hours in the first instance; and by setting up a jobs creation fund. The PSOE is also pledged to improve the scanty provisions for unemployment benefit, establish a sliding scale for pensions, linking them with the cost of living, and set up certain selective price controls.

Promotion of social equality

The PSOE's programme concentrates on education and, to a lesser extent, women's rights. The present schools law, which the PSOE considers biased in favour of the private sector, will be repealed. A new law will be put into effect under which all schools in receipt of public funds (which include many private and church schools) will be run with the full participation of teachers, parents and pupils, in line with the Constitution. Pre-school education is to be provided for all 4- and 5-year-olds, as well as school places for all up to the age of 16. A law guaranteeing university autonomy will be passed and provision for student grants improved.

Discrimination against women in various fields will be fought, with special emphasis on education and work. Discrimination between the sexes, presently practised in certain school subjects, will be abolished. A watch-dog body will be set up to get rid of sexism from school texts and to combat discrimination against women in vocational education and the selection of careers. A special programme will be set up to get rid of illiteracy amongst adult women. New legislation will be drafted to pro-mote equal rights for, and the protection of, women in employment. The law penalising abortion will be relaxed, but not abolished. Impor-tant reforms will also be undertaken in housing, social security and health provision.

Civic liberties and public order

The penal code will be reformed, protection against illegal detention reinforced, and the right to legal aid guaranteed. A jury system will be established in line with the Constitution. The military justice code will be replaced. In future civilians will in no circumstances be tried by military courts. Spain's still-chaotic systems of police and state security will be rationalised, and the Civil Guard placed more firmly under the control of the Ministry of the Interior. The trade-union rights of members of the police will be reinforced, short of recognising the right to strike. The freedom of expression will be clarified and reinforced, whilst at the same time the right of reply in the media will be guaranteed. The right of conscientious objection will be recognised. Terrorists and military con-spirators will be fought with equal vigour.

Reform of public administration

A series of reforms will rationalise and democratise public and state administration both in its mode of operation and in its methods of recruit-ment and promotion. Corruption and patronage will be fought with the aim of making public servants more accountable to that public whom they are supposed to serve. An end will be put to the practice whereby the same person may hold several posts in the public administration whilst doing little or no work in any of them.

Foreign policy

Spain's integration into the EEC will be pursued. As regards NATO, the PSOE proposes to hold a national referendum on the question of Spain's membership. In this connection, it should be noted that the PSOE's public statements on NATO have tended to become increasingly less firm in their opposition to Spain's presence in the alliance.

The implementation of these proposals will require a great deal of political intelligence and determination. Powerful forces in Spanish society will resist, for instance, the education reforms, modest though they may appear. Naturally those officials whose interests are threatened by the reforms of public administration can hardly be expected to co-operate with enthusiasm in the elimination of their own privileges. As for the proposed military reforms, which in addition to those listed above include reforms in the system of military education, it seems clear that these cannot be expected to yield fruit in terms of changes in the attitudes of the officer corps for a number of years. The problem of how to handle military affairs in the meanwhile therefore remains, and there is no formula for solving it. To some extent the PSOE's room for manoeuvre in this respect will be conditioned by its success or lack of it in other fields. Finally, there are, it seems to me, some notable obscurities in the PSOE's programme; one of these is the autonomy process. During the previous legislature, the PSOE co-operated with the UCD in drawing up the so-called LOAPA (law for the harmonisation of the autonomy process).[3] The ostensible purpose of the LOAPA was to introduce some order into Spain's autonomy process, which in different regions has taken very different forms. This, no doubt, is a desirable and necessary objective. However, both the PNV and CiU saw the LOAPA in quite a different light: in their view it represented an attempt retrospectively to claw back important parts of the previously granted autonomy rights. Some compromise over this matter would appear to be both possible and necessary, amongst other things to prevent exploitation of the issue by the terrorists of ETA.

The 1982 Elections and the Democratic Transition

The election campaign was punctuated, on the one hand, by acts of violence staged by ETA and other terrorist groups, and on the other by the uncovering, at the beginning of October, of yet another coup conspiracy. This one was meant to take place on 27 October, the day before the elections themselves, and was planned to be extremely violent, as the conspirators' own documents revealed. Once again, terrorists and conspirators, from their different positions, were pursuing through similar methods an identical immediate objective: the destruction of Spanish democracy.

On the 28 of October the Spanish people went to the polls; there was not a single serious incident in the whole national territory. The level of participation was the highest ever: 79.6 per cent. Voting took place in what I can only describe as an atmosphere of dignity and gaiety. In the early hours of the following morning, the Socialist leader Felipe González, by this time Prime Minister elect with a massive parliamentary majority, appeared on television: 'these elections have been won, not so much by a particular party, as by democracy and by the Spanish people'.

I have the impression that many people in Britain still view Spain in terms of the Civil War, or rather of a certain romanticisation of the Civil War. But in point of fact the situation in Spain today is utterly different from that prevailing before the Civil War. Today there are no churches burning, no plans for collectivisation, and no Popular Front. There is still, to be sure, a danger of a military coup. But such a coup, today, would be unable to conceal itself successfully under the cloak of anti-Communism. Most important of all, there has been a collective effort to overcome what might be called the 'civil war mentality', to replace it with the conviction that the country's problems can be solved only on the basis of mutual respect, and to make this conviction a practical reality in political, social and everyday life. This is what might be called the ethical component of the Spanish democratic transition—and its human significance. It is this, above all, which has been stressed time and again by the Head of State, King Juan Carlos I. I should like to end this article by quoting his words, from a speech delivered in Cologne on 20 May 1982: 'Without ruptures or discord, without exclusions or vengeance, we have established, in the briefest period of time, an order based on freedom, co-existence and dialogue. Without threatening the peace which we value above all things, for we have felt in our own flesh the pain of discord and of war, we have overcome the temptation of immobilism and have begun to move forward toward great objectives . . . Spain today holds no rancour, no desires for revenge, no envy, and no ambition other than its own perfection through the efforts of its men and women.'

It is upon the PSOE, as the party of government, that the main responsibility now rests to give political direction to this ethical impulse, to convert it, on the basis of increasing popular participation, into the directing force of the country's democratic renovation. Upon the PSOE's success or failure in this depends the immediate future of Spain's democratic transition.

Notes

1. Juan Luis Cebrián, *La España que bosteza*, Taurus, Madrid, 1980, pp. 22 and 25.
2. J. J. L. Aranguren, *etica y política*, Guadarrama, Madrid, 1968, p. 161.
3. *LOAPA: Ley Orgánica de Armonización del Proceso Autonómico*. See Chapter 5 on this law.

7 SPAIN: THE ARMY AND THE TRANSITION

PEDRO VILANOVA

Introduction

The analysis of civil–military relations in contemporary Spain, is at the same time, a complex and contradictory task. It is evident that Spain is a country in which, as is well known, the Army is of primary importance, as much in what happens as in what does not happen. It is also well known that until now the transition to democracy has been largely possible thanks to the restraint of the larger part of the Army, although it could very well disagree with future trends.

The theme developed here could be viewed from many angles: a purely historical analysis of the history of the Spanish Army, the sociology of its structure, a formal description of its organisation and of its officers, analysis of its military doctrine, etc. All of these are practical, possible and necessarily included. But the characteristic of this work, is that a distinctive focus has been preferred. I take the theme to be that of the delimitation of Army intervention, as an institution, in the process of the construction of contemporary Spain, and, in this particular case, in the process of transition from the Franco dictatorship to democracy: a weak, not particularly effective, democracy, but a democracy nevertheless.

From this perspective, the methodological problem is principally that of how to describe a series of facts and of symptoms which enable an understanding of the mood of an institution which is hermetically sealed. For example, in strictly legal terms, the Army, as an institution, as part of the State, has followed the pattern of the transition. Though only a few officers created incidents, these are signals that something is happening inside the institution of the Army. From this point of view, the trial of the accused in the *coup d'état* of 23 February runs against the grain of many forecasts. This was so although there ought to have been many more in the dock (according to the statements of the accused themselves), although the trial at times took on an uncommon and sometimes torpid aspect (with open justifications of coups which the Tribunal did not feel it opportune to silence), although the movement in support of the coup leaders found sympathy in numerous units and regiments, although the government gave proof of a notable lack of energy, appropriate to all executive power, although the trial lasted over three months, and although the sentences, still unconfirmed, disappointed a large sector of public opinion, including the Prime Minister, Calvo Sotelo. Apart from the sentencing of Tejero and Milans del Bosch to thirty years, the rest of the sentences were light, about six years internment: only one-third of the condemned men were excluded from a further military career and the rest have remained in the Army. Nobody should forget that the two hundred civil guards who participated in the coup had been sent back to their posts some time before the trial. Given these conditions, to cover the subject of the Army in a vague manner would not appear to be useful. It is difficult (not to say impossible) to make forecasts and time is needed to bring to light data on and analysis of a subject about which every body knows, or believes they know, something, but upon which nobody can pretend to know everything.

Some Thoughts on the Past

To understand certain aspects of the Spanish Army's behaviour an examination of the past is indispensable. The Spanish Army has a long tradition of intervention in political life above all during the first two-thirds of the nineteenth century. Between the War of Independence and the Restoration (that is to say between 1805 and 1875) there were some twenty or so *pronunciamientos* (military coups of the palace revolution kind). Surprisingly, active intervention of soldiers in political life, almost always through the *pronunciamiento*, was mostly liberal; that is anti-absolutist and in favour of a constitution. The presence of officers in the first Cadiz Cortez in 1812 made possible the adoption of the most progressive measures, like freedom of the press, for example. The reason for this liberal attitude amongst the leaders of the Army is complex, but it is possible that the War of Independence against the French invader, which caused a total collapse of all Spanish institutions (including the Army) from the *ancien régime*, played a decisive role: the wholesale incorporation of guerrilla units and middle-class people into a 'democratic' Army (into the officer corps) is important because this was once the exclusive domain of the aristocracy. On the other hand, at the end of the war, the prisoners of the French returned amongst whom there were several thousand Spanish officers who had absorbed many elements of the liberal ideology from the events of the French Revolution.

The frequent intervention of the Army, the most effective force amongst Spanish institutions, corresponded for the most part of the nineteenth century to the long era of institutional weakness: the monarch was characteristically entrenched, the bourgeoisie, too feeble—politically and economically—to be able to raise its standard with an essential revolution at all levels, and the Army occupied a privileged position. It must be understood that none of the intervention of the Army, through *pronunciamientos*, led to a specifically *military dictatorship* before the General Primo de Rivera installed himself in power in 1923. For the rest, the absence of any political programme in itself implied that the military leadership tended to shape its particular inheritance out of the diverse political currents which already existed: liberals, conservatives, etc. Put another way, the political parties were obliged to try to propagate their ideas organically within the diverse groups of opinion which existed inside the Army. This happened to the extent that within the Army, until well into the twentieth century, there were many opinion newsheets, which accurately reflected the discussion of the general political situation, but from 1875, a dynamic of Army development moved it towards the more conservative part of the political spectrum—towards the Right. Why was this? Numerous reasons could be suggested which are persuasive explanations of the Army's actions during the first decades of the twentieth century.

In the first place, with the 1875 Restoration of the Monarchy (following a conservative *pronunciamiento*) a sort of *institutional consolidation* started in Spain, the ascendancy of a political regime which, with ups and downs, lasted until 1931 when the Second Republic was proclaimed. During this period, the Army withdrew increasingly from the political scene and, progressively assumed other functions. In the second place, the appearance, especially after 1860, of social movements which were increasingly combative, in consequence of the nascent development of the working class and of the endemic pervasiveness of peasant uprisings, led the Army to progressively take up the defence of 'public order'. This reached its zenith in the great strikes which started the twentieth century, for example, the 'tragic week' of 1909 in Barcelona, the general strike of 1919, and above all the repression in Asturias in 1934. In the third place, the colonial wars played a decisive role: to the first defeats of the second half of the nineteenth century (above all in the Latin American colonies) must be added the colonial disaster of 1898 (with the loss of Cuba and the Philippines) and then the Moroccan disaster of 1921. The Moroccan colonial war, whose final phase lasted from 1907 to 1927, decisively marked an entire generation of Spanish officers: these were then known as the 'Africans' (amongst whom it is possible to distinguish Franco and the leaders of the July 1936 uprising).

The Army was unable to achieve a break-through when it was used as the tool for the colonial adventures: it was incapable of analysing the political causes of its military defeats, and it was indignant when the 'politicians' channelled the annoyance of public opinion exclusively against the Army. From this grew the active hostility to the political parties in general and to everything stained with anti-militarism in particular. In the fourth place, the problems presented by the Civil War were not new for the Spanish Army, which had been consolidated as an institution in the second half of the nineteenth century, in part thanks to the successive Carlist wars against the dissident dynastic pretenders of some northern regions. After several 'Carlist wars' which were in reality civil wars, the Army discovered in the development of Catalan and Basque nationalism (principally after the turn of the twentieth century) a new menace which was described as 'separatist'. Their incomprehension of the national phenomenon, which included regionalism, led the Army to take up centralist positions of various different sorts which have persisted until today.

Primo de Rivera's dictatorship from 1923 to 1929 was not only the logical culmination of the move towards the Right whose final destination would be a brutal repression of the political, but this time it was on its own account (as has been said, for the *first* time), and showed several characteristics which partially presaged the features of what was to become Francoism. From the standpoint of the collective memory of the Spanish Army, the most important feature of the Primo de Rivera dictatorship was that its implantation was only possible because of the acquiescence of the higher Army leadership, and its fall was for the same reason; additionally, this implied the definitive crisis in the main commanding institution, that is, the Bourbon monarchy. In its own time, the Republic had overwhelming popular support, *but* it should not be forgotten that the withdrawal of the King, the holding of elections and, through the result, the installation of the Republic was possible thanks to non-obstruction by the majority of the Army command. This was not because they were fervent Republicans, but because of a general political situation in which the dominant political classes were obliged to abandon their system of traditional domination, particularly after the final disgrace of the Primo de Rivera dictatorship, and they appeared resigned to playing the new card of parliamentarianism. The defeat of the conservative classes in this domain was the fundamental reason for the military uprising of July 1936.

The Civil War

Above all, the experience of the Republic was reflected in the Army, partly from the Army's professional point of view (with the reform attempts by Azaña in 1931), partly political (creating political organisations inside the officer corps: UMRA, Union de Militares Republicanes Antifascistas, and UME, Unión Militar Española (the last being clearly right-wing and coup-oriented)). The *coup d'état* of 1936, after the attempted insurrection of Sanjurjo in 1932, was not the work of the entire Army, but that of a disaffected third or so of the active officer corps. This is not the place for a digression on the military policies of the Republic after 1936, on which several books could be written, but it is useful to underline that the Republican government was not capable of imposing an Army policy which could deal with the dangerous military situation right away, that is, one capable of taking utmost advantage of all the officers and units of the Army which were not actively compromised in the rebellion. Amongst other reasons (weakness of external support, etc.), this was because the militarisation and transformation of militias into a centralised popular army was adopted with tragic tardiness.

On the rebel side the situation was very clear; material assistance (by the fascist governments of Italy and Germany) was effective and massive from the outset; the most efficient Spanish Army units—the legion and the African regulars—were with the uprising from the very beginning; and the militarisation of the occupied zones by incorporation of conscripts into the new Army was done on the basis of an implacable fascist-style discipline, which had tangible military results. But the fundamental factor was that a part of the Army was actively engaged in a political conspiracy and played the main role from the start.

In reality, behind the uprising were the most conservative forces of Spanish society: the landed aristocracy, the financial oligarchy (banking and industrial), the Church, and a variety of right-wing political groups: absolutist monarchists, Carlists, fascists, (Falange and JONS) etc. As established in the plans of General Mola, the brains of the conspiracy, the movement would be a simple *pronunciamiento* from which would result a dissolution of the Cortes and the Constitution, and which would set underway a 'military directorate'. The ambiguity of the project, the suppression of any constitutional reference whatsoever, lead to the observation that the model was the repetition of the Primo de Rivera dictatorship. Nobody amongst the coup conspirators, foresaw a Civil War of three years duration. They envisaged only a simple military coup.

Fundamental, for future consequences, was the initial political ambiguity of the uprising's putting the Army into a privileged position; otherwise, it is accepted that the arrival of Franco in power was possible thanks to a series of manoeuvres and the need for a compromise formula. This enabled the use of the Army to move to the dissolving of the *political* diversity of the right-wing forces and the creation of the *national bloc*, and the fusion of all the groups into the so-called 'Movement' (for which purpose it was necessary to repress the orthodoxies of Carlism and falangism) and the constitution of a 'new order' in which the only *coherent and real political force* was the Army. For several decades, the Franco regime was placed above the Army as the New State structure. For its part, the Army was *always* the real political base of the entire system of Franco's domination.

The Army under Franco's Regime

Already before the end of the Civil War and specifically after 1937, Franco had consolidated the new order based on the construction of the State, with all its bureaucratic, legislative and constitutional implications. The State was, during the first phase, *the Army holding political power*. In the final stage before the death of Carrero Blanco, the presence of the Army in government was limited practically to the three branches (Army, Navy and Air Force) and the Prime Minister himself. What happened in between? Schematically, it could be said that the economic development of the Franco regime implied a parallel evolution of its political organs towards increasing *institutionalisation*, that is to say a consolidation of the institutions which were at the same time capable of legitimising the system, and to perpetuating its mechanisms to secure its *continuation*.

It can be noted that in the general history of the Franco regime, the presence of the Army in the State apparatus (in the successive government teams) progressively decreased as a function of the aforementioned attempts at institutionalisation (successive laws and referendums of 1946, 1947 and 1966) and the advent of political necessities of various sorts which appeared and which were represented (this last point was a direct function of the development and consolidation of monopoly capitalism and Spanish social development): Christian Democracy of the 1950s, Opus Dei and Technocrats of the 1960s, etc. Despite the gradual disappearance of the Army from important political posts, the presence of the Army was decisive: between 1939 and 1969, of the ninety ministers whom Franco appointed, more than thirty were military. From that it must be made clear that Franco always had as Number Two a soldier of the purest Franco stamp: the most obvious cases were Muñoz Grandes and Carrero Blanco.

The presence, or identification, 'in the first instance' of the Army and the State diminished in proportion to the apparent consolidation of Franco's institutions; the Army was pushed onto a secondary level in the last period of Franco's rule, becoming only a 'guarantor of the system'; yet none of this prevented the appearance and development of a series of new problems which showed that none the less the crises of Franco's system had, in fact, extended into its final support.

What were these problems or crises in the Army? It is impossible to speak of the evolution of the Army under Franco without bringing in the problem of repression. In the Spanish case, in 1936 the dominant classes decided to abandon once more both Republican legality and parliamentarianism and to turn to a military coup to impose an authoritarian regime. It was clear from the first, that the central objective of the operation was to destroy politically and physically the adversary and its trade-union and political instruments (left-wing parties and workers' unions) and, at the same time, to change the type of institution (the Republic), which, without being revolutionary, allowed the forces mentioned to develop. After ending the war, the Army took up the continuity of repression at a massive level. With the resurgence of guerrilla war after the end of the Second World War, repression was maintained on a significant scale until the beginning of the 1950s. Although declining numerically it was qualitatively transformed—amongst other reasons, through the need of the Franco regime gradually to integrate itself into the international scene especially at the time of the Treaties with the United States in 1953 and admission into the UN in 1955.

Moreover, the repression of political activities fell into the hands of the Army during the entire second phase, which ended in 1963 when the *Tribunal de Orden Publico* (TOP) started to work and took over part of this repression. (In that year the anarchists Delgado and Granados and the Communist Grimau were condemned and executed by military tribunals.) The third stage, during which political repression passed into the hands of the civil authorities (by means of exceptional jurisdiction), imposed on the Army responsibility for the repression of exceptional political crimes (stated by the regime to be 'terrorism', 'banditary', etc.). In practice, this meant that the Army was burdened with the most unpopular political tasks by the Franco regime and pitted against mass-mobilisations by the democratic anti-Franco movement after the end of the war: Burgos in December 1970, Puig Antich, 1974, and above all judgments leading to the executions of 27 December 1975. This third phase is the most important for the internal consequences that it had for the Army. During the Burgos trials in 1970, the tensions between the most extreme faction of the Army (the Generals Garcia Rebull, Iniesta Cano, etc.) and the groups which had reached *professional* positions appeared under the light of publicity. After the executions of the anti-Franco FRAP and ETA in September 1975, it is known that there were a series of incidents between officers: military lawyers retired from the trials, democratic statements by certain units, etc.

It must be remembered that, despite the special jurisdiction (military tribunals, summary trials) in the hands of the Army, most of the Army units were not involved in the Civil War; in any case, what has determined the path of the Army over the last fifteen years is a series of problems stemming from the technical and military conditions of the Army and its relations with other armies (above all, with the American and the French, as much through contacts as in joint manoeuvres): in a word, the problems of any army in an industrial society.

Lastly, one of the most important factors in the crises, tied to the problem of repression, is the connection with and responsibility of some members of the officer corps in the special repressive branch of the Franco police. As far as is known, and without taking into consideration the political police, there were inside the Army the *servicio de investigacion militar* (SIM) known by the number of *Segunda bis*, and the *servicio de inteligencia del ejercito* (SIE), joined directly or indirectly to the Prime Minister's Information Service a form of 'police of police' directly responsible to the Prime Minister and administered by high military authority (under Carrero Blanco, the head was Colonel San Martin, who was moved by Arias Navarro when he arrived in power). These services intervened inside the Army and *against* officers in a number of grave cases: at passing out in 1975 over 2,000 officials signed their names to a petition for total amnesty for political prisoners and political exiles; at the end of 1975, came the incident of the officers Julve and Busquets and above all, the detention of twenty or so officers in July 1975, during the investigations into the clandestine military organisation UMD. The larger part of the officer corps resented the existence of the multitude of parallel police organisations as much for their activities as for the fact that they entirely escaped the control of regular military hierarchy.

In addition to the factors of the crises, there are also the professional difficulties which are typical of all modern armies; these can be resolved into two principal areas: the problems arising from the professional and social situation of officers (low pay, the need for several jobs) and the problems of their technical and material education (low intellectual level, disciplinary problems) and on the other side a deficiency of equipment used, and the extreme dependency of the Spanish Army on the USA and on France, in arms procurement.

Finally it is necessary to consider another factor which can be called the 'international question'. The Spanish Army in 1975 faced a series of problems whose political importance largely surpassed the cadre of the institution itself and affected the entire country: on the one hand, the problem of the western Sahara was strongly felt in the Army, which did not understand the path that the colonial history of Africa had taken. It obliged them to act as the police against the people of the Sahara and their stronger and most combative organisation—the Polisario Front. The Front obliged them to withdraw from the frontier with an acute war psychosis to face Moroccan ambitions and finally, to withdraw from the colony after the political 'arrangement' between Rabat and Madrid which opened the door to the Moroccan Army and to unanswerable accusations from the Saharan people of treachery and abandonment. The French Army knows this colonial situation very well.

On the other hand, Spain's place within the strategic set-up of the western world was debated. Until then, Spain had formed a part of the Atlantic forces through its bilateral and dependent relation with the United States, but they did not belong to NATO for internal political reasons. A large section of the officers considered that to be a preliminary to the European Armies' 'evolution towards democratic system' that is to say, the re-establishment of a democratic regime.

The Army and the Transition

When Franco died in November of 1975, there was a general recognition that the attempt to democratise the regime would need the approval, although not explicitly, of the Army. The analysis of the transition and its principal features has always got to include the incidence of this 'factor X' which in contemporary Spain is the Army. With the arrival to the Head of State of King Juan Carlos, the situation developed in the following way (at risk of over-simplifying inherent in a work like this one):

(a) The succession of Juan Carlos had been produced using the institutional mechanisms of Franco's system. That meant that there was no 'democratic break' and that explains some of the ambiguities in the first phase of transition, such as the reticence of the democratic opposition in the first months of 1976.

(b) It should not be forgotten either that the promulgation of the

Constitution in December 1978, was only three years after Franco's death, and the institutional edifice of the State, its system of organisations and institutions, descended for the most part directly from Franco, was dismantled. Only in a few cases, were laws passed to bring about partial reforms, but those were limited, in the expectation of a new Constitution.

(c) In this general framework, the Army was the institution which was at the same time tied by its nature and structure most closely to the previous regime, and the one having the greatest reservations when confronted with the democratic change, and which, in sum, held greatest power, i.e., the monopoly of arms, to move the balance one way or the other.

The immediate post-Franco period

This was characterised by the first two governments of the Monarchy. In December 1975, a few days after the death of Franco, the King nominated a first government, presided over by Arias Navarro, Franco's last Prime Minister. This was a clear attempt to maintain continuity and resulted from the pressure of the most extreme right-wing sectors. This experiment, which lasted six months, had an evident sympathy from the military hierarchy, well represented in the government through its three military ministries (Air Force, Navy and Army). However, the political blockage led this first government to delay on the contemporary imperatives, forcing the King to allow a government crisis which led to the government of Adolfo Suárez. Although the Head of Government was an unknown, Suárez presented a programme which was greeted with great hopes by the democratic opposition.

Suárez met the military hierarchy in September 1976, and negotiated the details of transition, with the promise, it would appear, to exclude the Communist Party from legalisation of political parties. This promise was in any case not kept since Suárez, in June 1977, reached the first democratic elections with *all* the parties and unions legalised, thus producing tense reactions in several sections of the officer corps. General De Santiago and Admiral Pita de Veiga, resigned their commissions as a protest against the legislation of the Communist Party and the trade unions.

The period of the Constituent Assembly

With the holding of the first elections in June 1977 the period of the Constitutional Assembly was opened. The first Cortes (parliament) was held with the task of drawing up the first Constitution, a task which was concluded on the 29 December 1978, with the ratification of the Constitution. At this time the armed forces confronted a triple problem: in the first place the military reform pushed by the government through the medium of General Guitierrez Mellado, whose central object was an efficient, technical and professional army on the European model, and a general diminution of political temptations; in the second place, terrorism, which, since 1977, was taking an increasing number of human lives (using the Gardia Civil and other State security organisations as targets), was moving against officers (nine generals were assassinated in a year and a half); in the third place, the Army faced the implantation of a political system which included two elements they considered unacceptable; the legalisation of 'Communism' and the creation of devolved regional governments, which in a certain Spanish military tradition was tantamount to separatism and a desire to destroy Spanish unity.

Yet the constituent period came under the rubric of the so-called 'consensus', that is, of a policy of seeking out the main agreements amongst all the political and social forces in turn on the great issues of the time. The Constitution itself and the Moncloa pact (signed as a series of general social/economic agreements between parties, unions and employers and the government) were, at the end of 1978, the great events of policies which appeared to be at the confluence of the majority's desires but which could have been discouraged at any time by a few impatient officers.

Provisional Democracy

It cannot be said that, with the promulgation of the Constitution in December 1978, the situation had a tendency to normalize. The great problems of the country, for example, terrorism, unemployment, the economic crises, the weakness of the institutions increased rather than diminished. With them ended the consensus, above all for the anticipated elections of March 1979, a time from which a strong polarisation in the system of parties was created as well as a crisis which latterly caused the gradual disintegration of the UCD, the motive force of the transition.

It was during this period that the confrontations were worst, or at the least the incidents between military and civil authorities. Between 1979 and 1982, several cases occurred which illustrate better than others the symptoms of the secular confrontation that took place between civilians and the military. The Atarés case, to take an example, of November 1978: just before the promulgation of the Constitution, General Guitierrez Mellado went to Valencia where (to a group of officers) he explained, as Lieutenant General and as the Minister of Defence, what the Constitution was. General Atarés of the Guardia Civil, interrupted him and insulted him: he was called a 'traitor and a pig'. Guiterrez Mellado ordered his arrest. Months later, in May 1979, a military tribunal absolved General Atarés, and the sentence was ratified by the Captain General of Valencia, Milans del Bosch.

More serious was the *'Operación Galaxia'*. The trial of two officers (one of whom was Tejero, who invaded the Cortes on 23 February 1981) showed that in November 1978, several officials had met to prepare a coup against the government. Handed down in 1980, the judgment came as a scandal, for Tejero and Ynestrillas (the only two accused of a plot which was in all probability much wider) were given seven months and six months respectively. Ynestrillas was, in addition, a captain and was promoted to commander two days after being given his liberty.

Besides the judicial case, like the scandal of the Lockheed bribery, which led to a sentence of six years for Colonel Grandal, and of a Lieutenant Colonel, inculpated for having fabricated illegal 'pencil-guns' (which can fire a bullet) and given seven years, the tribunal itself asked the government for the sentence to be extended beyond one year 'given the gravity of the alleged events'.

Again in January 1982, a curious judgment against two officers happened. One of them, Colonel Graino, of democratic persuasion, was given two months' close arrest for having written a Madrid newspaper article in which he stated that there were Army Officers of extreme right-wing views. This was simply an opinion. In the same military court, Captain Juan Milans del Bosch, son of the Captain General of Valencia implicated in the February 23 1981, coup, was judged. This captain publicly insulted the King in a bar calling him a 'useless pig'; he was given one month's arrest 'for the misdemeanour of slight insult'.

All these events, with many others, show that the tendency observed, in civil–military relations from 1976, was a negative one. Although there have since been some flutuations there has been no deterministic process. This is as true for the reforms of the Army structure (the rejuvenation of conscription, better recruits, accelerated promotion of the better trained officers, the preparation of NATO needs of which Spain formed a part after 1982), as for the attempts at internal democratic reform. Essentially the results remain insufficient for Spanish democracy.

Besides these incidents discussed, there have been many others that have never gone to the tribunals. Incidents which have concerned the government have increased because of lack of energy, while the opposition has been wary of awakening 'factual power'. It might be surmised that the resignation of Suárez, in January 1981, and the first moves in the

23 February coup, were directly due to the military pressure. The circulation of illegal petitions in the barracks, the right-wing incidents, the lack of reference to the Constitution in military speeches, have also been signs of this general tendency. It was against this background that the 23 February 1981 coup was produced, which was the most severe attempt against Spanish democracy, and it has enabled the highlighting of the tensions and limits which exist in Spain today.

Spain: an Uncertain Future

The attempted *coup d'état* on the night of 23 February 1981 within Spain, gave a mixed impression to the world outside, and particularly in Europe and the United States there is no clear understanding about what happened, not even in democratic and progressive sectors which are acquainted with Spanish society and with the process of democratic transition since the death of Franco. It appears that the perception of many sectors of democratic opinion in Europe and the United States is not able to set aside a dramatically inexact and simplified vision of reality.

Contemporary Spain has not been subjected to an uncountable number of military coups. For example, between 1816 and 1936, Spain underwent forty-nine *pronunciamentos*, some successful and others not. From 1875 to 1936, the average went down, but the brutality of the attempts which succeeded balanced this factor: a dictatorship of six years from 1923 to 1929, and a tragic civil war from 1936 to 1939. Put another way, political life in contemporary Spain (while Europe constructed a model of the State which is more or less democratic and liberal) has been squarely under the authority of a military institution. The military apparatus strengthened and entrenched itself under the Franco regime to such an extent that some of the central control remained unmodified during the transition. It escaped reform while the government concentrated on maintaining a balance between opposing groups, i.e., between Left and Right, between peripheral nationalities (Catalonia and the Basque country) and the centre, between workers and employers organisations. In this way, although the current Spanish democratic regime benefits from the support of the great majority of the political forces (excepting the extreme Right and Basque terrorism) all the social forces find themselves on a sort of probational liberty. What happened in the evening and on the night of 23 February?

On the one hand, there is what is known: 6.22 p.m. a group of almost three hundred *Guardias Civiles* (a paramilitary force which has public order functions similar to the *carabineros* in Chile or the *carabinieri* in

Italy) entered the Assembly of Deputies (the Cortes) and took the entire government and the deputies prisoner. Television pictures recording the incident were more eloquent than any declaration, and it is not worth emphasising it here. Perhaps the date was technically well chosen, because the voting for a new Prime Minister was taking place (vacant after the resignation of Adolfo Suárez a few weeks before), and this was the only day in a long time when it would have been possible to capture *in a single act*, the legislature and the executive. Thus an important power vacuum was created, one of the coup's objectives.

Afterwards came the tension of that night, the freeing of the deputies in the morning of 24 February, the reactions at a national and international level, and the recovery of a situation of normality with a clear understanding of the fragility of democracy.

But it remains true that the coup was the subject for speculation in the media and the subject of endless questions. For example, it was known that in reality there were at least *two* projected *coups d'état* under way at the end of January 1980. The first headed by Tejero, the Lieutenant Colonel who took the Cortes, and by General Milans del Bosch, can be defined as a coup in the Chilean manner, or, in keeping with the Spanish tradition, as a repetition of the July 1936 coup which opened the way to civil war. The second, more complex one, has remained considerably obscure. It was headed by General Armada, who for twenty years was the confidential aide to the King and was military head on 23 February. His plan was the option called a 'Turkish coup' in Spain: that is, a low-key coup, without extensive manoeuvres, with few apparently repressive aspects, and which would suppose an agreement with some of the parties, limited in time and to return to 'democratic normality', but with the central objective of fighting terrorism. But in Turkey, there are today 32,000 political prisoners and the 'low-key' aspect has given way to a much sterner reality.

Numerous plans intersected by chance, and it is supposed that at the end of 1980, in the course of pre-coup meetings, many officials across Spain were involved. Because they were known to each other, numerous projects were brought together. What is known is that the initial idea was to carry out a coup after 21 March or, perhaps, 2 May through the operation *'florecen los almendros'*, but it was brought forward for security reasons, and because of Suárez' resignation in January, which was something not directly foreseen by the coup conspirators. Things did not go as envisaged, to say the least this time, and the coup was a failure. This failure was due to political and technical causes.

According to observers, the coup was technically well prepared: it envisaged the occupation of the Congress of deputies, as the means of neutralising executive legislative powers, it envisaged the occupation of the television centre (in Spain the system is a state one, and in consequence, it was enough to occupy the central office in Madrid) and the main Madrid radio stations; the occupation of the strategic places in Madrid with units of the Brunete armoured division was planned (the most important and operational of the Spanish army, with bases around Madrid, with some 10,000 soldiers and armoured cars and tanks) and it was imagined that, faced with a *fait accompli*, the King would accept the facts and the political parties would accept the inevitable.

The first and main political error proved to be the King's reaction. Not only did he refuse to give in to the coup, especially the 'Turkish coup' version, but he headed the anti-coup reaction, particularly within the Armed forces, with the *neutralisation* of those temptations to accept the coup in military sections not previously connected with the coup.

Elsewhere technical errors prevented the coup 'taking off' as planned: various radio transmitters were never occupied; control of television was cnly short-lived (from 7 p.m. until 9 p.m. in the evening); other military regions (Spain is divided into nine military regions, each one of which included various provinces) failed to join forces with the coup and those meant to extend support obviously vacillated. Significantly, it has been difficult to substantiate the claim that the coup was supported in regions other than Valencia. There may have been other factors, amongst them the fact that the general at the head of the Brunete Armoured Division did not fall in behind the coup, and although he was to be found 300 kilometers from Madrid on 23 February, he was able to return in time to stop the mobilisation of the most important units in this Division. Without that, occupation of Madrid would have taken a mere three hours.

Nevertheless the apportioning of blame to only thirty officers, the determination of the military authorities (including the most constitutionalist, like the joint chiefs of staff) not to allow a complete purge to take place, and the limitation of punishment, make the current outlook pessimistic enough.

The King himself said, on the day following the coup, to the main political leaders: 'It was stopped this time, but I will not be able to do it again.' Put in other terms, if on 23 February, some generals used the King's name to convince the undecided, the next time he will be the first target. The next coup will be against the King. The King also said, and this opinion coincides with that of the best observers, that 80 per cent of the officers believed the coup conspirators to be 'patriots and men of honour', who perhaps were mistaken in the time and in the method. But the percentage of officers hostile to democracy, for fascist or authoritarian reasons (a minority), is paradoxically greater today than it was in 1975, on the death of Franco, when many soldiers accepted the idea of peaceful, gradual change, and under the King's direction. The combined effects of terrorism (with nine generals killed in two years), economic crises, unemployment, and the revolution in lifestyle has made the military's attitude to Spanish society much more hostile today than it was five or six years ago.

Unless there is some resolution of this attitude within the short or medium term, the future of the democratic regime remains tenuous. This view leads one to an analysis of a situation which has not been understood outside Spain. It is generally thought (including in several sectors in Spain) that a *coup d'état* is not possible, that the failure of 23 February shows that the coup had no social base, that it lacks international economic and political support and that the regime's future is ensured by Spain's greater involvement in Europe, i.e., NATO, and her membership of the Common Market. A more pessimistic view can be taken. Spain has lived these last one hundred and eighty years under authoritarian and not democratic government, except for the turbulence of the second Republic and the last five years. Moreover, the democratic regime is not only fragile, but constitutes an exception. In the case of a military coup which succeeds, there can be few illusions, since from the weight of the initial protests (more on a political level), it is evident that the new situation will tend to create its own social base, its own economic support (national and international) and it is not credible to think, for example, that the multinationals would get involved in a 'boycott to the death' of the new regime. It is necessary to become accustomed to the idea that in certain parts of the west, in Europe and in the United States, the idea of a northern conservative Europe supported by two authoritarian regimes of the south (Turkey and Spain), with guarantees offered to Greece and Portugal, is perfectly acceptable. In this way the argument that the entry of Spain into NATO will democratise its Army is groundless. Portugal was a member of NATO from the beginning without the dictatorship of Salazar and Caetano being in the least affected. The coups in Greece, in 1967, and in Turkey, a few months ago, took place with the complicit silence of NATO and of the member countries starting with the United States. Nobody in Spain has forgotten the declaration by Alexander Haig at 2 a.m. on 27 February: 'What happens in Spain is an internal affair'. No comment.

Postscript

Between the writing of this chapter and its printing several important events have occurred in Spain which bear directly on this theme.

The first, and most important, was the completion of the general elections of 28 October. On this, two observations can be made: the first is that these were unexpected elections. The legislative term was not due to end before March 1983, but Prime Minister Calvo Sotelo believed its opportune to bring the date forward in order to prevent the erosion of his party and to hinder the Socialist advance. It is well known that neither of these objectives was achieved because the UCD was reduced to a tiny minority force and the Socialist victory was a crushing one.

The second observation has to be seen in the context of our theme. The new Socialist government will have to face, amongst other crucial security problems, those of national defence and the power of the armed forces. It is not just the classical situation of the transfer of powers, within the institutional alternance of democratic societies. For Spain it is the first time since the Civil War of 1936–9 that the Left has taken command of the Government and in consequence of the administration of defence and security. There is much speculation on the attitude of the Army to Socialist military police although everything indicates that the Socialists will be particularly moderate in this domain.

On this issue, the immediate future must raise some uncertainties: what will be the real attitude of the Socialists on the NATO issue? Spain has formally been a member of the Atlantic Alliance for a few months, but its effective military integration has not yet been achieved. Given these conditions everything appears to point to the PSOE not withdrawing from the Atlantic Alliance although (going by the speeches of some of its leaders) it is possible that a re-negotiation of the Spanish military contribution to the NATO set-up could be attempted. Similarly the Socialist leaders have made clear their desire to redefine current bilateral relations with the United States; the most recent friendship and co-operation treaty, signed in 1976, ended in September 1981. Since then bilateral negotiations were shelved, with mutual agreement, to give priority to the negotiations which were then taking place between the Spanish government and the Atlantic Alliance. For the PSOE, whatever the final result, the Atlantic commitment of Spain cannot be called into question, although they are looking for a new formula in this relationship.

Finally, on governmental matters, the PSOE will have to take into account the needs of the Armed Forces for new arms and material. The new government will have to decide in the next few months whether the negotiations started by the government to buy the new F-18 fighters to modernise the Air Force will proceed.

However, the most serious of recent occurrences was the discovery of a new attempt to stage a *coup d'état* and the resurgence of terrorism with the killing of General Lago Román, head of the Brunete Armoured division (some of whose officers were involved in the attempted coup of 23 February 1981). Some other events centred on the elections. The recent *coup d'état*, discovered a few days before the election, was envisaged for the 27 October, that is to say, a few days before the elections. Technically, in so far as can be discerned, it would have been much firmer and more effective than that of the 23 February 1981. It envisaged, for example, an attack by artillery units on the King's Palace, the Government, the central administration and the occupation of press, radio and television communications centres. Once again the attempt appeared to be centred on Madrid, with the hope that other outlying military regions would support the action or at the very least accept the action taken as a *fait accompli*. It is disturbing that the reactions of the outgoing UCD government were limited to the detention and prosecution of three officials (Colonels and Lieutenant Colonels), a change of post for some twenty suspected officers, and a series of prudent declarations of limited credibility intended to appease public opinion. Once more, the Government's policy appeared to be to accept a compromise with the military hierarchy, in that the investigations were not pressed beyond the absolute minimum possible, and to leave the non-judicial disciplinary measures in the hands of the Army.

A period of uncertainty is opening, and it is difficult to predict in these circumstances, but it appears certain that whatever coup attempt is carried out will be against the King and all the institutions, and in the case of a success the resulting coup will be violent and bloody. This possibility cannot be excluded, although neither must one fall into a sort of negative fatalism, because for any coup to succeed it would have to overcome a considerable number of technical and political obstacles.

8   SPAIN AND THE EEC

PETER HOLMES

Introduction

The election of the new Socialist government in Spain can be viewed as a historic turning point in the history of the country. Alternatively it can be seen as simply one further step on the path towards political modernisation that has occurred since the death of Franco, a process which is gradually (not so gradually in the eyes of some, perhaps) bringing Spain closer to the main community of European nations.

When Spain emerged from the cocoon of forty years of Francoist dictatorship the country's ruling elite had to decide fairly rapidly on what shape the new Spain should have. Fortunately the King and Prime Minister Suárez boldly determined that the government should be democratic and it turned out that the bulk of the technicians of the civil administration, if not the army, had been quietly anxious for such a move for years and eagerly co-operated.[1] The question remained what position Spain should occupy in the international stage. Should it try to build up its traditional links with Latin America or the Arab world?[2] Should it remain a member of the non-aligned movement (as it briefly was) or join NATO? Spain has in fact just joined NATO but its presence in the military alliance is not fully accepted by everyone in Spain. On the other hand there has been no serious opposition within any part of the mainstream of Spanish politics, including the Communists to the idea that Spain's political and economic future lay with the rest of western Europe and in particular the EEC.

Spain's desire to join the EEC can be traced back to her emergence from the Franco dictatorship in both its political and economic aspects. Until the mid-1950s Spain's ostracism by the international community, and the inclination to *dirigisme* of a fascist economic system combined with the dictator's distrust of the outside world to produce a policy that was officially described as 'autarky'.[3] In 1959 the regime decided to launch a programme of economic liberalisation, and, under the influence of various international agencies such as the World Bank, GATT and the OECD, began a new phase in Spain's economic development based on a modern pattern of industrialisation, and a full participation in the world economy. Franco tried to establish closer links with the EEC as part of this process but was rebuffed. In 1970 Spain signed a 'Commercial Agreement' with the EEC but this is the loosest type of preferential trade agreement that the EEC can offer, and Spain was left to understand that any further integration could only follow democratisation. The paradox is that whereas in the 1960s Spanish leaders saw economic benefits of closer links with the EEC without any kind of political harmonisation, the current situation is that membership is being sought primarily for political reasons even though it is widely recognised that economic integration would create some difficulties. Now that Spain is an acceptable candidate, her prospective entry would involve a leap-frog jump over Israel, Turkey and the Maghreb from being one of the countries whose degree of trade preference has been among the loosest to being a full member. The 1970 agreement did not require Spain to do more in the way of tariff reduction than to give the EEC a preferential reduction on industrial goods of 25 per cent for most items, leaving the basic level of tariffs in Spain one of the highest in Europe against 7–10 per cent for the EEC.[4] The EEC, on the other hand, agreed to lower its tariffs by a minimum of 60 per cent against Spain. A move towards completely free trade between Spain and the EEC would involve much more dislocation on both sides than was the case when Britain joined the EEC. It is common to think of Spain as a mainly agricultural country and to focus on the agricultural side of her relations with the EEC but this is very misleading. Over the years Spain has industrialised heavily and acquired an economic structure that is far closer to that of modern Italy. Nevertheless her economy still reflects the inheritance of the Franco era.

The Structure of the Spanish Economy

The overall structure[5]

Spain's level of economic development puts her in a class somewhere closer to Italy than to her fellow Mediterranean partners Portugal and Greece. GDP per capita in 1979 is reported by the OECD as $5,300 in Spain against $5,700 in Italy and $4,100 in Greece. Such figures do not mean a lot especially in view of regional disparities but there are certainly whole regions of Spain whose average income levels are higher than some whole regions in France.

Agriculture only accounted for 19 per cent of the work-force and about half that proportion of GDP in 1979, against 36 per cent of the work-force in industry and 44 per cent in the tertiary sector. Other social indicators such as number of cars, TV sets and telephones per 1,000 population put

Spain some way back down the economic league table, as do social services and education. But the high levels of industrial output and the establishment of a democratic system mean that she is likely to display a more even pattern of socio-economic development by the time she is (if ever) a full member of the EEC.

Spain's trade is less important to her than is the case for other western European economies. Exports were 9 per cent of GDP in 1979, against 22 per cent in Italy. Traditionally, Spain has always run a large deficit on her 'visible trade' (i.e. exports and imports of goods). The EEC always sells more to Spain than she buys from her (though not in the field of food and agricultural goods). Spain is a consistent net importer of food and agricultural products, mainly cereals from the USA for animal feed.

The deficit on goods is largely offset by a surplus on services, mostly tourism and the remittances from emigrants in the EEC. Both Spain's employment and balance of payments position have been badly hit by the return of migrants from Europe. A new outflow of 20–75,000 workers per year in 1969–73 turned into a net inflow of 30–90,000 in 1973–77.[6] Membership under current economic conditions does not seem likely to be able to offset this.

Spain does not in fact need to have a balance in its current account in order to keep its international payments in order, since it has been the recipient in recent years of large amounts of direct foreign investment, which has kept up as domestic investment has stagnated. Much of this was originally just to get round Spain's high tariff barriers but multinationals have begun to use Spain as a base for sales to the rest of Europe as well.

The State has always been involved in the management of the economy. A fascist economic system is inherently *dirigiste*, and while recent years have seen moves towards liberalisation there has also been a growth of intervention in the field of social security, and tax reform designed to preserve the multi-party support for the new constitutional system.

Macro-economic developments[7]

When the democratic regime took over Spain there were considerable fears that an inflationary bonanza might create economic instability that would undermine the country's political stability, much as in neighbouring Portugal the running down of the foreign exchange reserves built up under Salazar eventually necessitated the controversial intervention of the IMF. In fact this has not happened, and from the point of view of being a prospective macro-economic partner for the EEC, Spain's record makes her no less attractive a prospect than, say, Italy.

In the first two years after the oil price-rise the Franco regime (not wholly without justification), continued what was already expansionary economic policy to offset the deflationary impact of the diversion of expenditures to OPEC and the slump in Spain's export markets. Although unemployment stayed below 6 per cent till 1977 the balance of payments worsened and the inflation rate went over 20 per cent. One of the first tasks of the new government was to introduce stabilisation measures and to reduce the rapid rate of monetary expansion in Franco's later years. At the core of their programme was the Moncloa Pact of October 1977.[8] This provided for a major series of economic and social reforms in exchange for which the newly legalised trade unions gave a general undertaking to restrain wage demands. Among the reforms promised were an overhaul of the tax system, including the introduction of a wealth tax (intended to be one of the heaviest in Europe) and of the social security system. On the whole this programme must be judged something of a success. The inflation rate, which had been accelerating began to fall, and although Spain still has a slightly higher rate than the average for the OECD (and the EEC) in the low teens, slow progress is being maintained. The OECD in their 1981 survey of Spain remark that there are certain contradictions in that while monetary policy has been fairly tight, fiscal policy has continued to be rather expansionary, and there has been no formal incomes policy. On the other hand, they observe that democratisation has led to generally better industrial relations which makes macro-economic management easier, not harder. This, if true, is important for Spain's potential as a member of the EEC.

In fact there have been a series of national wage-agreements during the course of 1981. The government, the employers and the unions signed an '*Acuerdo Nacional de Empleo*' proposing further wage restraint in exchange for attempts to keep up the level of employment by the government. Figures published in mid-1982 suggest that the inflation rate continued to creep down during the course of 1981, but the rise in unemployment seemed to be inexorable and will be one of the main concerns of the new government.

Unemployment has been rising continuously since 1970 when the rate was under 2 per cent until 1981 when it was around 15 per cent. The new government will not have a lot of freedom of manoeuvre. We have already observed that the OECD categorised the macro-economic policy of the late 1970s as already fairly expansionary. This is in contrast to the situation inherited by Mitterrand in France whose predecessor had tried to run a budget surplus thus leaving considerable freedom to borrow more without seeming to go 'too far'. In Spain the government would have to run a deficit that would be a substantially higher fraction of GDP than is proposed in France if it were to try and reflate, which would weaken the peseta, the value of which has fluctuated against other currencies since the mid-1970s, though by early 1982 it was roughly on a par with its 1977 rate. The new government devalued sharply. The Socialist programme aims to increase state spending using additional public investment to create extra jobs. They are wary of financial over-commitment, hoping (perhaps too optimistically) to raise extra funds for expansionary purposes by rationalisation of the existing state sector. There appears to be little anxiety in business circles about the prospective impact of a Socialist government, perhaps because of the party's express commitment to a negotiated incomes policy.

Spain's Economy and the EEC

Trade[9]

In the years since the signature of the 1970 commercial agreement Spanish trade with the community has grown very fast. The fact that the EEC reduced her (already lower) tariffs by more than Spain reduced hers has led to some resentment within the community. Whereas in 1970 Spanish exports to the EEC were only 57 per cent of her imports, the coverage had risen to 98 per cent in 1980. It is argued by Spanish analysts that this simply reflects the continuing strength of the Spanish econnomy, since over the same period the overall ratio of exports to non-oil imports rose from 56 to 90 per cent. Exports to the EEC rose by 940 per cent over the period 1970-81, while overall exports rose by slightly more, 1,030 per cent. The share of Spain's exports going to the EEC therefore remained somewhere between 40 and 50 per cent over the period. On the other hand her share of the EEC import market rose from 0.95 per cent in 1970 to 1.41 per cent in 1981.

Industry[10]

Spanish industry still bears the marks of the mildly anti-capitalist Franco era. Independent entrepreneurial capitalism has not got off the ground. Of the 30 largest corporations, 29 are controlled either by the state holding-company INI or by foreign multinationals. Many of the largest private firms are in alcoholic beverages, but there does not seem to be any powerful local food-processing firms (like Unilever or Nestlé).

The dualism of the agricultural sector is reflected in industry in the large number of very small firms. Part of the reason for this may be the domination of the credit market by a few very large banks which do not give access to small firms wanting to grow. The OECD have criticised this aspect of Spanish industrial development (OECD Surveys, 1980 and 1981).

After the very rapid growth of the 1960s industry has been in the doldrums for some years. The world economic crisis hit Spain rather badly in the 1970s, partly as a result of her inheritance from the previous decade. The pattern of industrialisation appears to have had two rather unfortunate features. Firstly the emphasis on heavy industry left Spain with a high energy dependence and on the other hand the sectoral structure of Spanish industry is disproportionately biased in the direction of areas that have been worst hit by the general economic recession and the impact of newly industrialising countries, i.e. steel, ships, and 'textiles-clothing-and-leather'.[11]

These are all areas where Spain has in recent years moved over from being a low-cost producer like Brazil or Taiwan to being more like a western European high-cost producer, though she remains strongly competitive in certain parts of the textile industry. Her wage costs have risen considerably in recent years. Estimates of costs in Spanish shipbuilding put Spain on a par with the rest of the EEC. As an EEC member Spain would probably be an eager participant in the EEC's protectionist and market-sharing arrangements in these sectors rather than being eager for a free market free-for-all.

The government is worried about the prospects for industry in general and has asked for a long transition period before elimination of all tariffs. The high and selective pattern of protection that Spain has been able to maintain even since the 1970 agreement means that her industry is going to have to undergo a major process of adaptation and possible restructuring in order to align itself with the pattern of relative prices and costs prevailing in the EEC where in principle tariffs have been virtually eliminated *vis-à-vis* the outside world.

This could for example affect the Spanish motor industry. This sector has grown strikingly in recent years (in 1978 Spanish output was 1.0m cars against the UK's 1.2m). But certain parts of the industry are much healthier than others. Ford has a thriving operation in Valencia integrated into its world-wide operations and with high levels of pay and productivity. Other car makers have been constrained by government policy to use much higher shares of Spanish made components than is the case with Ford. Liberalisation of the car component trade will force a change in the operations of the car manufacturers but give them a great opportunity. At the same time the car component manufacturers will suffer.

The car industry gives an interesting idea of some of the effects protectionism has had on Spanish industry. Five multinationals control the industry, having been led to invest in Spain as an alternative to being able to import, but the protectionism given to them led to structural weaknesses, proliferation of models, and inability to exploit economies of scale in the small Spanish market. Government regulations forcing the use of 90 per cent Spanish components, created a protected market for the manufacturers of those. A special law of 1979 allowed Ford to use only 50 per cent Spanish parts provided it concentrated on the export market. It is presumably this carrot and stick that has made the Ford operation the most efficient and successful in the country. This is in marked contrast to SEAT which was established long ago by the state and FIAT but which, because of financial troubles, had to be taken over completely by FIAT in 1981 at the government's request.

The car industry is not entirely typical but it displays many of the characteristics of Spanish industry in the face of the EEC: control of key sectors of multinationals (often EEC-based), distinct potential strength but structural weaknesses requiring considerable adaptation in the face of the prospect of free trade.

In addition to the high levels of protection the Spanish tax system has been a point of controversy in negotiations with the EEC: the EEC has insisted on the adoption by Spain of VAT. All countries give rebates of indirect taxes already paid on goods subsequently exported, but the EEC has claimed the Spanish system gave more scope for unfair subsidies than the complex but 'transparent' VAT. Spain has agreed to this.

Agriculture[12]

Spanish agriculture provided 10 per cent of GDP in 1979. Spain is in fact a major net agricultural importer (like the UK and Portugal; unlike the whole EEC-9 and Greece). She exports fruit and vegetable products to the EEC and imports mainly cereals from the US as animal fodder. Her agricultural production is largely oriented towards domestic consumption. Apart from citrus fruit the share of her fruit and vegetable output exported is rather low, but this may change after entry to the EEC. Total output has just kept pace with consumption in recent years. For most products the increase in output has come about from an increase in the area under cultivation not from growth in productivity, except for crops grown on irrigated land. The technology used in the past for irrigation has required a lot of capital and water. Estimates have suggested that Spain faces a shortage of water that would restrict the prospects for irrigation.[13] She is also losing her best irrigated land to urbanisation along the Mediterranean coast. Her low levels of output per man and per acre considerably offset the low levels of wages in agriculture, though the cost of labour is a difficult concept in the case of small family farms.

There is enormous geographical diversity. Mediterranean fruit and vegetable products are largely grown in favourable conditions along the coast of that name. The arid centre grows cereals; the wet but poorly organised north, dairy and other temperate items. Olives come from Andalusia. In general each individual product is overwhelmingly grown in one or two provinces or regions (e.g. 50 per cent of oranges in Valencia, 30 per cent of apples in Lerida). There is also a striking dualism in farm size. In the north of Spain tiny farms of a few acres are predominant and often further subdivided into a dozen or more strips as was the case in the middle ages. In the south such *minifundios* exist side by side with gigantic estates of thousands of acres which take up most of the land in Andalusia. Income levels vary a lot between the different types of agriculture. Low productivity is caused by poor land, but in the wet north-western region of Galicia structure and organisation are significant factors. In virtually all products Spanish land yields are way below those in the EEC-9.[14] It is sometimes difficult to tell how far this is the inevitable result of adverse geography, poor land, lack of water, etc., or of bad management. These low yields have led many to think there is a vast potential to be unleashed when Spain does join the community and perhaps receives higher prices. In fact for products other than fruit, vegetables, olive oil and wine, Spain has maintained a price support scheme based on the Common Agricultural Policy (CAP) which gave price levels very close to CAP levels. For fruit and vegetables the EEC system of 'reference' prices as a trade barrier meant that farms oriented towards the export market have been more or less obtaining CAP prices for some time. As we have noted, demand has been rising in the fruit and vegetable sector in Spain at a rate that has kept pace with the growth of supply. Spain has not done all that well in many fruit and vegetable products. There have been complaints about imports of apples and her peach and tomato exports are weak compared with Greece.

There is no doubt that in certain fruit and vegetable products Spain may be able to expand, but the main determinant of the potential is going to be whether she can introduce new types of irrigation using drip and sprinkler technology that use complex networks of pipes and valves to feed water directly to the plants instead of washing it across fields, wasting most in the process (and incidentally leaching the soil badly).

If indeed there were a major expansion of fruit and vegetable production what would be the effect on the CAP? For many fruit and vegetable products Spanish prices are below EEC levels and free competition could bring down earnings of French and Italian producers. The CAP at present protects fruit and vegetables by import restrictions rather than internal market intervention, which has led the French and Italians to call for an extension of the CAP mechanisms in this sector before Spain joins, so that stock-piles can be used to hold up prices.

The cost would be immense and unlikely to be accepted by other member-states of the EEC who could veto it. The 'northern' members of the EEC have an interest in cheap fruit and vegetable prices (apart from glass-house tomato growers, who are in fact competing in a wholly different segment of the market). As a strong producer Spain has indicated that it will not seek extra price support in fruit and vegetables but would rather take its chances in free competition.

On the other hand as a net food-importer Spain has an interest in less CAP protectionism on cereals. Her domestic livestock sector would be badly hit if maize prices rose. The poorest part of Spanish agriculture is Galicia with income levels half the national agricultural average, and very heavily dependent on tiny meat and dairy farms. Spanish milk prices are actually above CAP levels and Galicia would be badly hit if they fell.

In general the poorest regions of Spanish agriculture do not tend to specialise in the same items as the poorer areas in the EEC-9. That is to say Mediterranean fruit and vegetable producers are the most productive in Spain, and so Spain will require regional rather than product-oriented assistance from the CAP.

There are great fears in Europe of massive expansions of Spanish wine and olive oil production. Wine is grown all over Spain, but production is more severely controlled, than in the EEC; it is, for example, forbidden on irrigated land. Spanish spokesmen seem genuine in arguing that they do not wish to let this sector expand. Similarly olive oil is something of an embarrassment. It is mainly grown on large estates in Andalusia, and even in Spain is highly over-priced compared to soya oil, etc. Since the work-force is mainly hired hands,[15] it seems likely that the EEC will be urged to provide alternative employment assistance for Andalusia rather than to support olive oil output more. It is more likely that the future of agriculture in Andalusia lies in the cultivation of early fruit and vegetable products under plastic and in ways that employ the new devices for economising on water.

The performance of Spanish agriculture within the EEC will ultimately depend on two forces, the stagnation that has been typical of the last ten years or so, against the potential that might be stimulated by the higher prices within the EEC. Between 1970 and 1981 agricultural output in 1970 prices rose by about 30 per cent, an increase which was moreover concentrated in the first four years, 1981 being a mere 4 per cent up on 1974. The 1970 figure was itself about the same as the 1963 figure. Consumption has meanwhile been growing faster than this, leading to the rising agricultural deficit. It has to be noted that the balance of expert opinion is that in fruit, vegetable, wine and olive oil sectors where EEC prices are up to double Spanish levels, accession could give rise to an enormous stimulus to production.

Spanish Regions and the EEC[16]

Spain's regional problem is a complex one. It is not a north–south polarisation like Italy, but instead there are three centres of prosperity, Madrid, the Basque area and Catalonia, while in between and on the periphery there are very poor, backward regions such as Andalusia, Badajoz and Galicia. The poorer regions do not have any single feature in common except that they are more agricultural.

The prosperous regions also are somewhat diverse. Catalonia and neighbouring Valencia stand to gain substantially from EEC membership. They are progressive regions with modern industry and the most dynamic elements of Spanish agriculture. The Basque country on the other hand, both because of its industrial structure (steel and ships, etc.) and its political troubles could well become one of the EEC's problematic 'old industrial areas'. The increasing recognition of regional aspirations, and the extreme diversity of Spain's regions are likely to require the attention of the EEC after entry. If anything, membership is likely to exacerbate regional differences. The prosperous parts of Spain no more need treating as underdeveloped regions than do Birmingham or Milan, but Galicia or Andalusia approach Third World conditions. Galicia is almost certain to suffer from accession, but if no trade barriers are erected by the EEC Andalusia could begin to exploit its agricultural potential, though EEC membership will not eliminate the social factors that have held this up in the past.

Spain and the EEC budget[17]

The chances are that Spanish agriculture will not be a great financial drain on the EEC budget, given her major strength in products that receive little financial aid (apart from wine and olive oil) and her status as a net importer. Some parts of Spain will actually lose from CAP membership, and it seems likely that the richer Mediterranean areas will benefit while the poorer northern and central areas will lose, giving rise to an argument for regional aid rather than CAP money.

The EEC's official estimates put the net cost of Spanish membership slightly higher than that of Greece, but rather less in proportionate terms.

The 1978 'Fresco' on enlargement drawn up by the EEC Commission estimated that the net financial cost of Spain's presence would be of the order of 2-300 million units of account (approximately equal to US dollars). The total EEC budget of 1978 was about 13 billion units. Slightly less than would be spent on Greece. Since then it has transpired that Greece is costing slightly more than anticipated, but EEC officials may say privately that the latest unpublished calculations on Spain are of the same order of magnitude. It was estimated that the presence of all three candidates would require a supplementary levy coming from VAT corresponding to 0.13 per cent points of VAT. All these calculations assume of course that there will be no enormous increase in financial support for fruit and vegetables.

EEC Attitudes towards Spain[18]

The French were originally great supporters of Spanish entry to the EEC seeing it as a way of increasing the 'Latin' influence and reorienting the focus of the community in the south. They have recently become aware that what they have in common could well provoke rivalry and their agricultural lobbies have mounted a successful campaign to create fears of Spain's agricultural potential, which are denied by Spanish spokesmen with real or disingenuous modesty about their economy. Italy shares the French fears and has also asked for reinforcement of the CAP policy on fruit and vegetables. These two states argue that import restrictions alone will not be adequate to keep up prices when the main competitor, Spain, is inside the EEC. Since Italy and France could veto Spanish entry unless they got their way on fruit and vegetables and the others could veto any such an extension of the CAP this particular point could well block the Spanish accession. The arrival of the Socialist government in Spain is likely to reduce French hostility, which had in any case become more muted in recent months.

Germany is probably still firmly in favour of Spanish entry. She has investments there and a healthy trade surplus that could be expected to grow with free trade. She also has political capital in Spain. The German SPD has given aid to the Spanish Socialist Party (PSOE) with no apparent strings attached, a gesture of either extreme magnanimity or far-sightedness, most probably the latter. Germany sees political democracy as the key to stability in the Mediterranean region and has an attachment to the EEC as a healer of international problems. At the same time Germany is not looking to pay any large bills for Spain's agriculture: the present CAP suits German agriculture (if not the German Treasury) well but she is not eager to have money spent on olive oil that could go on butter. The Conservative government in Germany is likely to have less of an ideological commitment to the entry of a Socialist Spain into the community, but to keep its eye firmly on the enormous trade surplus Germany has with Spain, a surplus that would grow if she entered the community. Germany does not care about fruit imports but could well see Spain as a market for dairy surpluses.

The UK official attitude seems to be mildly favourable to Spanish entry on the cynical grounds that the more diverse the EEC becomes the more its original ambitions will be diluted. There is another genuine common interest in that Spain like the UK is a net agricultural importer, especially of cereals from the US, and has some motivation for preferring low to high agricultural prices.

The smaller northern EEC states do not seem to have played much role in the debate, though Denmark is apparently anxious to reinforce its own ties with non-EEC Scandinavia as a counter-weight if Spain does enter.

One interesting question is what attitude Greece will take towards Spain. Following the Socialist victory, the Papandreou government in Greece may feel morally obliged to display fraternal as well as geographical solidarity, and it is true that on some foreign policy issues, such as the Middle-East, Greece has more in common with Spain than with the rest of the EEC, but in fact Greek economic interests run counter to those of Spain in many ways. Greece is a net agricultural exporter and likes the CAP which it wants extended to cover her Mediterranean products. She has also asked for generous transitional measures and a favourable treatment that might perhaps be relatively easy for the EEC to concede if they were dealing with Greece alone but could be very costly if applied to Spain (and Portugal) as well. Generous treatment of Greece could make the other nine states more reluctant to accept Spain.

The negotiations on Spanish entry have been moving rather slowly during 1982. Many observers see it likely that Portugal will be admitted before Spain, contrary to earlier expectations, putting the Spanish application on ice for a time, while the community digests Portugal. It appears to be member states rather than Spain or the commission which is dragging its feet. Some commission officials fear that the consequences of Spain's entry could be highly problematic but they feel that an initiative of this kind once started must not be allowed to fail. It would appear that the main unmet demand on Spain's side is for a longer transition period for her industrial goods than the EEC is willing to concede, given that it already feels it has had a raw deal on tariffs from Spain. On the other side the EEC wants a long transition period on agriculture, and, ultimately will probably have to reform the CAP to cope with Spanish membership. Though it might make sense to do so with Spain inside, there are obvious pressures to try and set up a *fait accompli* before she enters. The problem is that the ten cannot agree amongst themselves on how to react to Spain's presence and until they can, progress will remain extremely hesitant. Indeed one exasperated commission official remarked privately that the Spaniards made a tactical error in joining NATO before the EEC. They should have offered to join the military pact only when they were admitted to the political club.

Conclusion

The maturity with which Spain's fledgling democratic government and population have reacted to the economic and political threats to stability after Franco augur well for her capacity to become a useful and positive partner. Those with a more intimate knowledge of the Spanish political system may be more pessimistic than this, but the impression I obtained talking to various politicians and civil servants at the time Spain embarked on her negotiations with the EEC was that she has a sensible and realistic polity, not actually expecting very much in economic terms from EEC membership but fully convinced that participation in the community was an integral part of her democratic evolution.

Greek experience in 1967 shows that membership of NATO is certainly no guarantee that the military will concern themselves solely with external defence, and there is no formal way that EEC membership can actually guarantee the survival of the democratic regime; but fellow members can give direct balance of payments assistance and perhaps more generally keep up Spain's international credit rating. The internal prestige of the new system will surely suffer if she is rebuffed by the community and will go up if she is admitted.

Once inside Spain might well make herself more awkward than she is trying to appear from outside. However, she would very likely be a progressive influence inside the community. The need to reform and modernise her own system is at the top of the social agenda, and will be all the more so with the PSOE in power. Extremism and arrogance are surprisingly absent from the mainstream of Spanish politics; so too are excessive expectations about the effects of EEC membership liable to give rise to disappointment. Spain is likely to make demands for additional assistance for her backward areas, but this will surely be a worthwhile enterprise and could well lead to a shift in the community's priorities towards regional economic development and away from the worst wastes of the CAP.

EEC membership does not seem to have been an issue in the recent election. All parties were in favour of entry bar the ultra-Right. The prospect probably appears to be a logical consequence of democratisation rather than a prospect that is in itself enticing, so the new government will most likely continue to negotiate on the same path as its predecessor. Spain will continue to make demands where interests are at stake while avoiding overall intransigence, but the degree of adaptation she will have to undergo to maximise her benefits from eventual admission is such that if the EEC adopts an extremely tough line to Spain she may refuse the terms.

Notes

1. This point was made to the author (and the editor) in conversation with Agriculture Ministry officials in 1978.
2. See G. Minet, 'Spain and European Diplomacy at a cross road' in G. Minet *et al.*, *Spain, Greece and Community Politics*, Sussex European Paper No. 11, 1981.
3. For the background to this see R. Tamames, *'La Republica; la Era de Franco'*, Alianza Universidad, 1973.
4. See the Report of the EEC Economic and Social Committee, *'Relations between Spain and the Community'*, Brussels, 1979.
5. See A. Wright, *The Spanish Economy 1959–76*, Macmillan, 1977. R. Tamames, *'Introduccion a la Economia Espanola'*, Alianza (various editions).
6. See OECD, *'Spain'*, May 1981.
7. Data in this section from OECD, *'Spain'* and the 1982 Annual Reports of the Bank of Spain and the Bank of Bilbao. Both the latter give excellent up to date information, though the figures often differ slightly between sources.
8. For details see the Economic and Social Committee Report.
9. Data in this section based on Bank of Bilbao Annual Report 1982.
10. Information in this section is largely based on M. Noelke and R. Taylor, *'Spanish Industry and the Impact of the Membership of the European Community'*, European Research Associates, Brussels, 1980, pp. 141–233.
11. OECD *Spain* 1981 reports the Spanish index of industrial product on giving a 28 per cent weighting to these sectors against 22–23 per cent in Italy and Greece and 14 per cent in the UK.
12. Data in this section based on *Anuario Estadistico Agrario*, various issues, and Bank of Spain report 1982.
13. Notably J. Nadal *et al.*, 'El Uso del Agua y las Posibilidades de Regadio en la España Mediterranea', in *Boletin de Información extranjera del Instituto de Estudios Agro-sociales*, May–June 1977.
14. Wheat yields are half the EEC average. Wine yields are relatively even lower (giving rise to fears that they could be raised). Only for a small number of fruit and vegetable items does Spain approach yields in Italy, the lowest in the EEC. In the past the relative productivity levels have not changed much.
15. A detailed, but probably now somewhat dated, study of Andalucian agriculture is contained in J. Martinez-Alier, *Labourers and Landowners in Southern Spain*, George Allen & Unwin, 1971.

16. The Bank of Bilbao produces an excellent biennial report on Spain's regional income data.
17. Data here taken from EEC: *Economic and Sectoral Aspects of Enlargement* (com (78) 200, 1978).
18. See M. Leigh, *Nine EEC Attitudes to Enlargement*, in Sussex European Paper No. 1, 1978.

9 THE SOCIAL STRUCTURE OF SPAIN

JOSÉ CAZORLA PÉREZ AND J. MENTABES PEREIRA

Population

Over the last twenty years the Spanish population has increased in a largely uniform way: from just over thirty and a half million in 1960 to thirty-seven million seven hundred thousand in 1981. The evolution of the population over this time does not show great fluctuations and represents a mostly constant increase. Similarly, the density of population evolved to 74.65 inhabitants per square kilometre in 1980; a figure which is given in Table 9.1. In the context of EEC countries only Greece and Spain have population densities lower than Spain, and France is just above with one hundred per square kilometre.

This perspective changes, however, when we analyse the distribution of the Spanish population by region. This analysis is vital, indeed the 1978 Constitution created a new territorially-organised state. Thus, we find ourselves faced with a new model stemming from what has been called the 'Statute of Autonomies': this concerns principally the organisation of the decentralised state which devolves a high level of administrative and political independence to the different autonomous communities and creates local decision-making organs like governments, parliaments, regional assemblies or supreme legal authorities. This devolution has given rise to a form of state which is unique because it is neither Federal nor akin to the Italian regional model which reduces the autonomy of the regions to a type of administrative decentralisation. In fact distinct autonomous communities function in Spain, although it is necessary to distinguish between the level of autonomy which some of them have at present. Catalonia, the Basque country, Galicia, and Andalusia are the autonomous communities which have been foremost in developing their own powers but this does not constitute an obstacle to other autonomous communities receiving devolved powers at a later date.

All this requires, at minimum, an itemisation of the different facts which are reviewed below, indeed the socio-economic differences between the distinct regions are palpable and substantial. These are the differences which underlie and create the main lines of social structure in each of the

regions and which in their total effect give us the national picture, something which could be misleading without a proper break-down. The
territory which includes the autonomous entities into which Spain is
divided includes the following provinces:

Andalusia	Almeria, Cadiz, Cordoba, Granada, Huelva, Jaen, Malaga and Seville
Aragon	Huesca, Teruel, Saragossa
Asturias	Oviedo
Balearics	Balearic Islands
Canaries	Las Palmas of Gran Canaries, Sta Cruz de Tenerife
Cantabria	Santander
Castille/La Mancha	Albacete, Cuenca, Toledo, Ciudad Real, Guadalajara
Castille/Leon	Avila, Leon, Salamanca, Soria, Zamora, Burgos, Palencia, Segovia, Valladolid
Catalonia	Barcelona, Gerona, Lerida, Tarragona
Extremadura	Badajoz, Caceres
Galicia	La Coruna, Lugo, Orense, Pontevedra
Madrid	Madrid
Murcia	Murcia
Navarre	Navarre
Basque Country	Alava, Guipuzcoa, Vizcaya
La Rioja	Logroño
Valencia	Alicante, Castellon, Valencia.

The area, total population and population density of each of the regions as
well as the national total is given in Table 9.1.

Existing spatial differences in population distribution lead to the
observation that the disequilibrium is not simply of a demographic nature,
but, as we shall see below, is a feature of all parts of the Spanish social
structure. Hence, it can be noted that whilst the Basque Country is 1.44
per cent of Spain's area it contains 5.68 per cent of the Spanish population, Madrid (the autonomous community not just the city) with 1.58
per cent of the area of Spain contains 12.44 per cent of the population;
Extremedura, with some 8.24 per cent of national territory contains
2.83 per cent of the population. Moreover it would be necessary to put
together only Extremadura, Castille/La Mancha, Castille/Leon, Aragon
and Navarre to compose 54.08 per cent of Spain and to equal the population of Madrid and the Basque country which represent only 3.02 per cent
of the surface area.

Such lack of homogeneity in internal demography is certainly not

Table 9.1   Area, total population and population density
in the regions of Spain

Regions	Area		Population		Inhabitants km^2
	km^2	%	Total	%	
Andalusia	87,268	17.29	6,440,985	17.09	73.8
Aragon	47,669	9.44	1,196,952	3.18	25.1
Asturias	10,565	2.09	1,129,556	3.00	106.9
Balearics	5,014	0.99	655,909	1.74	130.8
Canaries	7,273	1.44	1,367,646	3.63	188.0
Cantabria	5,289	1.05	513,115	1.36	97.0
Castille/La Mancha	79,226	15.70	1,648,584	4.37	20.8
Castille/Leon	94,147	18.65	2,583,137	6.86	27.4
Catalonia	31,930	6.33	5,956,414	15.81	186.5
Extremadura	41,602	8.24	1,064,968	2.83	25.6
Galicia	29,434	5.83	2,811,912	7.46	95.5
Madrid	7,995	1.58	4,686,895	12.44	586.2
Murcia	11,317	2.24	955,487	2.54	84.4
Navarre	10,421	2.06	509,002	1.35	48.8
Basque Country	7,261	1.44	2,141,809	5.68	295.0
Rioja (La)	5,034	1.00	254,349	0.67	50.5
Valencia	23,305	4.62	3,646,778	9.68	156.5
TOTAL	504,750	99.99	37,563,498	99.69	74.4
Ceula	18	–	65,264	0.17	3.625.8
Melilla	14	–	53,593	0.14	3.828.1
TOTAL Spain	504,782	100.00	37,682,355	100.00	74.7

a recent phonomenon, it has been the result of a long-term secular trend,
so much so that the increase in the last few decades is a result, principally,
of the following. First, the high percentage of both internal and external
immigration which Spain had undergone, and secondly the internal concentration of the centres of immigration in the industrial zones and the
resultant economic decline of non-industrialised areas. In any case it can
be observed that the population increase of over 10.7 per cent relative to
1970, took place in the cities with populations over 100,000 and the
national periphery has, in general, increased most in size. As can be seen
from Table 9.2 the big cities have continued to expand and the population
to concentrate, to the extent that the situation at the beginning of the
century with over 67 per cent of the Spanish people living in towns of
less than 1,000 people was reversed in the seventies; 65 per cent of the
population now live in towns of over 10,000 and only 35 per cent in
those smaller than 10,000.

Table 9.2   Distribution (percentage) of rural and urban
population 1900-1970

Inhabitants	1900	1970
<2,000	27.5	11.0
2,000– 10,000	40.2	22.5
10,000–100,000	23.2	29.7
>100,000	9.0	36.8

Source: España: panorámica social, INE, Madrid, 1976

An overview of the fifty cities of over 100,000 people shows that these are the conurbations which surround the big metropolitan areas of Madrid and Barcelona and which have been transformed into real 'dormitory towns'. This growth in dormitory towns in the metropolitan areas of these two great cities (to which could be added Bilbao and Valencia) has taken place in the last twenty to thirty years as a result of the migration of manual workers from the countryside to the cities, that is to say, from the agriculture sector to secondary and tertiary ones; significantly over 70 per cent of these cities are in the northern half of Spain. Migration did no more than exacerbate the rural–urban imbalance; indeed as the *Jornadas de Estudios Andaluces III* stated, 'The distance between these two is today greater than ever before . . . Certain regions, like Catalonia or the Basque Country, have practically the same level of prosperity (at western European standards), the same goes for several isolated cities, the sites of services or of industry, the case in almost all southern capitals. At the same time, a large number of Andalusian of Galician areas have not changed much in their basic structure for the last fifty years or so, except for the single factor of depopulation through emigration.'

The inequality between areas is most obvious in regions like Andalusia; even when the region is compared with other more advanced zones of the country. For example, to take a very sensitive indicator like the average level of income per city: the data on income levels have been grouped into cities of under 100,000 pesetas and those of over 200,000 pesetas. Thus we can note, as shown in Table 9.3 (in which only regions of roughly comparable income have been included) that in the case of Andalusia a considerable bunching of the lowest levels of revenue takes place. The percentage of the Spanish population living in municipalities with an income of less than 100,000 pesetas per capita is 30.3 per cent, whilst in

Andalusia it is 53 per cent. This figure can be used as a yardstick of the interregional position in Spain:

Table 9.3   Population (percentage) living in cities in 1975
by income levels

	<100,000 pts	>200,000 pts
Andalusia	53	1.2
Basque/Navarre	7	26.8
Madrid	2.4	82.7
Spain	30.3	19.1

Source: Banesto '78—for 1975.

In the regions of autonomous communities like Castille/La Mancha or Extremadura, this has produced in current figures inferior or similar levels of population density to 'desertization', reckoned overall at 25 inhabitants/km². During this century only three regions have tripled in population (Basque Country, Catalonia and Canary Isles) and five have doubled (Balearics, Valencia, Andalusia, Asturias, and Cantabria). But it was the Basque Country and Catalonia where the most spectacular increases took place, and, indeed, after 1950 these areas doubled in population.

Population Migration in Spain

The progressive movement of the active population from the primary sector to the industrial sector and to construction and services, has in the last three decades provoked the displacement of large numbers of people into foreign countries and into internal zones with high levels of industry like Madrid, the Basque Country, Catalonia, and Valencia. This has in turn, produced the depopulation of other zones or regions, as noted. As has been shown elsewhere, 'The objective motive was the absence of work in places of origin, unemployment and more or less hidden unemployment, and long workless periods'[1] which produced the forced march of Spaniards these last twenty-five years to the most indus-trialised areas. This was caused, by an, 'unequal structure of property, a non-exploitation of natural human and capital resources in the im-poverished regions which impoverished people to the benefits of indigenous oligarchies or of other regions or countries'. It is unfortunate that for the purpose of this work it has been practically impossible to describe in detail the causes which have coalesced to produce this effect, but they are described extensively in the source quoted.

The impact of this phenomenon on the social structure of Spain does not need special study although it is necessary to differentiate between internal and external migration. These have produced distinct repercussions on the social and economic order of the State, because there has been a profound transformation of territorial and political organisation.

The internal migration of the last twenty years, was (according to data taking into account the number of people changing city of residence 1960–75) six million. This has produced a type of unequal development between regions, the great beneficiaries being those areas which received the workers. This becomes clear when the levels of per capita income of the regions are investigated as well as the increases which have been produced in the last twenty years—wage differences within regions become apparent, if the distinction between immigrants and emigrants is made. External emigration, by contrast, has its origins in the same internal variety, and has been considerable throughout this century, although it has not always been to the same places. For the first decades of this century emigration was fundamentally trans-oceanic, but after the 1950s the movement was almost wholly to western Europe: estimates for the 1961–70 period put the number of Spaniards who went to Europe to work at 1,700,000, something which represents 6.3 per cent of the population (1960), who had to migrate to find work.

It should be noted however that there is a decline in the number who choose to emigrate: this process was accentuated after 1973–4 during the nascence of the world economic crisis which hit the host countries, not just restricting the number of foreign workers, but making them the first to feel the effects of the crisis through the termination of their contracts and return to their home country. According to the *Anuario estadistico* census of 1980, in 1979, only some 13,000 emigrated to Europe to look for work. In a classification by professional groups it has to be noted that the largest number were, 'artisans, industrial workers and peasants' along with, to a lesser extent, 'farmers, fishermen, huntsmen, foresters and *asimilados*' (11.5 per cent of these to 76.9 of the former). This tells us that the emigration was largely fuelled by workers from the primary sector which until now has constituted the main axis of the emigration phenomenon. This change, to the extent which has been indicated above, the recession of demand for manual workers in the host countries, shows the level of instability which manual work in the primary sector has reached in Spain. Agriculture was effectively the main exporter of manual workers during the high noon of emigration but it has dropped from 5.3 million in 1950 to 3.6 million in 1980 something which implies that over two-thirds changed their sector of employment. These figures show the rate of real recession which inevitably hits emigration through sharply descending percentages of manual workers in the primary sector who emigrate abroad. Moreover it should not be forgotten that the current Spanish position (profoundly marked by high indexes of unemployment) weighs heavily on the primary sector in which the effects of the recession have been deeply felt.

The Return of Emigrants

The economic crisis which has hit the western world since 1973 produced within only two years of that date, the almost complete cessation of migration to western Europe. In particular, the governments of the host countries to foreign manual workers implemented measures clearly designed to prevent the entry of non-EEC workers. Parallel to this the foreign workers were the first to suffer the consequences of the crisis; in many cases they were thrown out of work at the same time as the economic growth of their own country took off. This provoked the return of hundreds of thousands of workers in many cases to their places of origin, but frustrated their economic and social expectations.

This is presented as the main cause of the massive return of emigrants in recent years but it must also be noted that along with that co-existed other kinds of motivation which contributed to the return of emigrants. Thus CERASE sets out the following forms of returning worker: those returning through misfortune; those returning from conservatism; those returning to retire, and those returning from innovative motives.[2]

Those who returned because of personal misfortune are those workers who occupied the posts which are socially ill-considered overseas, they returned without having been integrated into 'foreign society' and for the most part they came back much as they left (i.e. almost un-changed). Conservatives maintain their local customs and traditional patterns, despite achieving a degree of success. Their main object for returning to their country of origin is to set up a business in the service sector for their own purposes, and on many occasions they simultaneously cultivate land which they already owned before departure or acquired after their emigration. They show the extent to which traditional patterns are extant and maintain their hold overseas. Return for retirement is generally limited and in any case not permanent, due to the fact that leaving usually denotes a certain adaption to a foreign society at the same time as (possibly) entering it through several family ties (matrimony of the emigrant or of their offspring). In any case it is not unusual for them to return to the home country 'to relax and enjoy their savings or their pensions, when they have them'.

'On the latter, the "innovatory returns" in the opinion of Prof. Borreguero are the most interesting and of the greatest social utility', produced by those emigrants who have profited from their stay abroad by developing a form of work, generally of a semi-qualified type, intent on bettering their work situation in their country of origin, creating a small business or looking for a post similar to that which they left.[3] The belief that this type of returned worker is the 'most interesting and of the greatest social utility' is the result of candid interpretation of the problem. The belief that emigrant workers are innovators once they have spent a few years overseas, assumes that they have acquired training, or patterns of behaviour distinct from those of the country of origin. Bohning notes that (if the return of emigrants is to be important and useful) for development to be stimulated the following are necessary: (1) it must be organised and (2) efforts must be concentrated for the return of innovative people so that the desired effect is optimised.

Given this, and applying it to the Spanish experience, we find that it is not simply a criticism of the planning carried out in this case but a criticism of the entire policy. On the other hand the attempt to create poles of development which could, as Bohning showed, serve to concentrate the returning 'innovative workers', has, without exception, produced very little and has created very few jobs. Thus, for example, the pole of Granada, one of the provinces with the largest number of immigrants (not only in Andalusia, which in its own way is the region of Spain which is the most affected by this phenomenon). Hence, in this pole during the eight years of its full functioning only something under 600 jobs were created: in a city of 300,000 people, this number of jobs is insufficient in itself without taking into account the returnees themselves.

In any case, the returned emigrants in these last few years do not fall into the category of 'innovating workers' as drawn up by CERASE, but are more the first three groups particularly in the first of these categories, the disadvantaged, impelled by the economic crisis described above. It needs to be taken into account that the returning emigrant is not just a returning worker, an individual person, but someone bringing back the family which frequently emigrated with him. This raises the problem of the social re-integration of the children of these people who find themselves in an environment which, because they inherited it from their parents, is 'theirs' but which is at the same time 'foreign and distant'.

Sooner or later, the children of emigrant workers, will encounter a labour market to which access is difficult, given the few jobs currently on offer. This complicates the problem, indeed it is not only or simply the situation of returned emigrant workers, but, as was shown above, to a greater or lesser extent they are helped out by the small savings made whilst abroad, although these young manual workers are placed in conditions which others of similar age and qualification suffer from, that is general unemployment.

Evolution of the Workforce

This section will attempt to describe the relationship of the Spanish people to the labour market. We will try to treat the subject from various angles, including the delimitation of the existing active workforce, the distribution of the workforce by sector and lastly, unemployment and the sectors which have suffered it to the greatest extent. The workforce is equivalent to 34.1 per cent of the Spanish population. Given that the working age in Spain starts at sixteen, it can be noted that the active population is 48.3 per cent of those over this age. These percentages have clearly diminished since 1973 when the active population was 38.7 per cent and the active population over 16 years old was 53.1 per cent. This decline has been the result of numerous factors, amongst which can be mentioned, on the one hand, the lowering of the retirement age and, on the other, the increased numbers of young people (during 1973-81) who went into further education, causing a delay of some seven or eight years in the creation of one sector of the active population. It is evident that this drop in the active workforce, was not taken into account in calculating the levels of unemployment, because the active population is not statistically related to the occupied/unoccupied position of the worker. In any case, of the total active population, some 86.5 per cent are in work whereas the other 15.9 per cent are the contemporary unemployed.

It is interesting to look at the distribution of the active Spanish population in each of the sectors of the economy and its development since the beginning of the century. Before taking this up fully, it would perhaps be useful to make some general points on the background, to give perspective to the overall situation. Up to the middle of the decade 1950-60 (the time when a new phase of industrial development started) agriculture was, by far, the most important component of GNP. In 1924, for example, it is reckoned that the agriculture and stockbreeding produced 42.8 per cent of GNP whilst extractive and industrial activities totalled some 35 per cent.[4]

It was not until about 1960 that the industrial workforce exceeded that of agriculture, and until that time it not only exceeded it, but constituted the absolute majority of the workforce. In 1950, the agricultural population, which composed 50 per cent of the active population and was the majority in thirty-six provinces, represented over 80 per cent of the workforce in twelve of them and in eight others, over 70 per cent. Only in four provinces was the agricultural population less than one-third of the total. These coincided, evidently, with the main industries and higher standards of living. They were Madrid, Barcelona, Biscay and Guipuzcoa.[5]

Therefore, once again, it should not be surprising that there has been an increasing transfer of manual workers from agriculture to other sectors of the economy. In 1970 the situation was more balanced with 29.1 per cent of the active population in agriculture and fishery, 37.3 per cent in industry and 33.6 per cent in the service sector.[6] Notwithstanding this, these percentages were deceptive because of one fundamental fact: in industry (including manual workers in construction whose numbers considerably increase the active population) the construction sector is not clearly defined as industry, but has in fact flourished disproportionately in Spain. This is a consequence of the form of development which Spain has gone through and which we have called 'cosmetic development'. The flowering of the economy in the 1970s produced this growth in construction work although this does not constitute a solid base for an economy, and less so when considered as industrial activity.

This can be shown, in Table 9.4 where the percentage of the workforce in each sector of the economy is given.

Table 9.4   Percentage of the workforce in each sector of the economy

	% of active population (34.1% of total population)
Working	86.5
Non-salaried (Employers, independent workers)	26.0
Salaried	60.5
Agriculture/Fisheries	4.7
Industry	21.1
Construction	5.8
Service	28.8
Unemployed	13.6

Source: INE poll of the 1981 active population.

Above, all the low percentage attributed to agriculture and fisheries (4.7 per cent) should not be surprising, these are the wage-earners or labourers although the bulk of people in agriculture are self-employed or independent workers who, in Table 9.4, amount to 26 per cent. In rough figures it is possible to guess that 15 to 26 per cent, should be added to this 4.7 per cent to give approximately 20 per cent of the work-force which could be included in agriculture and fishery.

By contrast we can separate construction from the industrial sector, as we indicated above, and this will considerably reduce the latter to around 21 per cent. This is fundamentally true if we take into account what has really been built (the activity in which the recession of these last few years has been most keenly felt and in which unemployment has been created) it can be reckoned that in 1981 only some 5.8 per cent of the active population was in the building industry. In 1970 this proportion was much higher, if everything is included, as is generally done, in the 'industrial' sector, the distorted image of economic reality, which we talked about under the heading of 'cosmetic' development is produced.

Finally, the service sector represents the largest bloc, reckoned by the section of the active population within it. It is not unusual during the process of industrialisation, for a stage of a concrete business like tourism, to create the greatest inflow of hard foreign currency. Nevertheless, as we shall see, this sector is sensitive to unemployment. In any case one should not be surprised that the percentage of the active population in the service sector is relatively high (28.8 per cent of it) when one takes into account that in the EEC 43.2 per cent are in this sector.

Unemployment

To say at this juncture that unemployment is one of the fundamental and most tragic problems, with which the western countries are confronted is not news. This is precisely the reason for the tragic persistance and diffusion of the problem and the paucity of possible solutions. Lack of work has come to be the principal economic preoccupation of the Spanish people as the facts outlined here substantiate.[7] The unemployment level was around 13.5 per cent of the active workforce according to estimates (FIES—79) and 15.9 per cent according to others (INE): in absolute numbers, over one and a half million are in this position.

The distribution of unemployment by regions is very unequal, creating, in some, a really extreme situation. Thus Andalusia heads the list with 18 per cent of the active workforce unemployed, constituting in this form, as an Andalusian union leader recently stated, 'the region of Europe with the highest unemployment'. Other regions follow in this order: Extremadura, Basque Country, Catalonia, Canaries, Castille, Asturias, etc. The characteristic shape of the phenomenon in each of the regions is distinct given the various activities and industrial sectors preponderant in each one, and at the same time the intensity with which each sector has suffered the crisis is distinct. (Not forgetting the problems of migration in each one which we have already discussed).

An explanation, which is consistent with the above, is that the level of unemployment varies with the size of population centres up to 200,000. By contrast if we take into account the industrial belts of cities like Madrid and Barcelona, we will see that the percentages have reached levels which are really worrying. This can give us an idea of the parameters of the problem, before showing the characteristics of domitory cities and their excessively increasing populations of the last fifteen years—a consequence of internal migration. This is shown in Table 9.5.

Table 9.5   Level of unemployment (percentage) and size of town

	Level of unemployment
<2,000	10.6
2,000– 10,000	11.6
10,000– 50,000	13.7
50,000–100,000	14.0
100,000–200,000	17.5
200,000–500,000	14.5
>500,000	14.6
Barcelona conurbation	15.3
Madrid conurbation	17.6

Source: FIES Survey—79.

By sex, the results show that women are slightly more affected, principally through their massive entry into the labour market in the last ten years. By age, the young, under 24 years, are those who suffer most. Amongst them are the hard core, those who are looking for their first job, and who have no previous professional experience. Looking at the education of the unemployed, the bulk are those who stopped their studies at school leaving age, followed by those of the lowest level, joined by those with university education. On the distribution by sectors, divided by percentages into their previous occupation between distinct branches of activity; construction appears at the top in numbers of workers now unemployed (an estimated 23 per cent of unemployment). None the less industry, as an economic sector (but not in its different sub-activities), overtakes construction to reach 29 per cent. The fact that agriculture, stock-breeding and fishing, or the same thing, the primary sector, do not contribute more to unemployment is principally because of the self-employed character of the workers in these areas and to a lack of a detailed agricultural census which means the lack of precision of the data.

Class Structure

Today in Spain, the dominant mode of production is capitalist, with an increasingly important State role, in social and economic relations; we are in the state monopoly capitalist phase: this is a reflection of the western European situation, in which the interventionist State safeguards the rights of the population, which was created at the end of the Second World War. This mode of production makes the relations between classes in Spain develop around the fundamental contradiction between a capitalist bourgeoisie and the proletariat; the central axis is between dominant and dominating class.

Inside the dominating class-blocs distinct class-fractions can be distinguished which can be allied so that a hegemony is established. Thus in Spain the financial and industrial oligarchy is dominant over the landed oligarchy. Of the landed oligarchy which can be called the 'agrarian bourgeoisie', it is noted that, in the first place, contrary to the image extensively accepted abroad, the work relations in the farms no longer fall into the feudal owner-serf scheme and have been fully superseded, by the clearly capitalist relation. This is why we refer to them as the 'agrarian bourgeoisie' above.

During the passage from feudal to capitalist modes of production in agriculture the presence of a large mass of small-holders was a key transition. In 1970 we estimate that private holdings over 500 hectares, those which could be considered *latifundias*, stood at 5,722 in number. These plots were concentrated principally in Andalusia, Extremadura and Castille. Until 1970 the big farmers of the *latifundias* were the main beneficiaries of credit policies, both public and private; as Naredo has noted, this produced the paradoxical situation that the big enterprises obtained the greatest advantages and in consequence had fiscal aids which also facilitated outer finance.[8]

The transformation is due to the metamorphosis of productive forces in the Spanish economy whereby agriculture has ceased to be the dominant sector. But in any case, it follows that this landed oligarchy holds important sectors of power, coming not from agriculture but from the position that a large number of them held in finance, banks and large industrial enterprises using capital accumulated over the last decades. The financial and economic oligarchy represents, as has been stated, the hegemonic fraction of the dominant classes, a hegemony which became established from the time that industry became better business than agriculture. The industrial bourgeoisie in Spain, which was born in Catalonia and the Basque Country, extended its economic power during this century, and in the banking system they grew and established a monopoly. This gave an extraordinary power to the financial groups which in turn enabled them to control the big industrial sectors.

Autarky was for years a typical feature of the Spanish economy, and it contributed to the power of the financial oligarchy, but once this phase was over, Spanish industry willingly took up foreign capital. Thus in 1971, foreign capital investing in Spanish business represented 13.4 per cent of the social capital in the 300 highest Spanish firms, making 76 of the 138 firms in which it took over 50 per cent of shares to give it absolute control. These are not disproportionately high percentages when compared to other countries of the EEC.[9]

In any case, as a consequence of the economic development of recent decades (weighing on the current crisis which has been a drag on the country since 1973) the position of the dominant bloc in the class structure has been reinforced. On the other hand, the political change which took place in Spain in 1975 (and with the approval of the Constitution in 1978), has introduced a series of political transformations which have directly affected the class struggle such as the recognition of political parties, unions and business associations. This indicated the area in which the struggle for hegemonic power should develop in the class structure, whilst such relations are being rationalised in a way similar to advanced western democracies.

The Working Class and the New Middle Class

According to the most recent data 73.5 per cent of the active population are wage-earners. If we add to this 15.1 per cent 'independent workers', we come to 88.6 per cent as the wider definition of the working class.[10] Undoubtedly the situation of the sectors or factions which make up the working class, are not the same as those of wage earners. In effect the situations of the peasant and industrial worker are different from the journeyman and similarly the technical or qualified personnel are different again from those whose activities which fall into the category of 'wage earner'.

This leads to what is now called the 'middle class' or more correctly the 'middle classes' combining all those social groups which are between the dominant class and the 'working class'. Those are the 'liberal professions' the 'civil servants and workers in public enteprises', 'the middle and upper technicians', 'administrators and employees in commerce' and the 'small industries and businesses'. This 'new middle class', is in being not as a consequence of the 'embourgeoisement' of the proletariat, but is rooted in the transformations of the systems of production, which, in order to function, needs more complicated and diverse work. For this reason it is necessary to distinguish two generically different groups in these 'middle classes': the minority which occupies supervisory or managerial positions and the majority of technical workers and employees who do not participate in managerial tasks and who come to be regarded at times as mere executants although occasionally at a level technically above the others. In both cases it is appropriate to speak of 'class consciousness' although they depend almost exclusively on their labour. Indeed what we meet here are what has been called a 'consciousness of stratum', given their tendency to be located in an intermediate social position which prevents them seeing the basic antagonism between dominant and dominated class.

The working class today is basically composed of industrial workers and is presumably in the region of 34 per cent of the active population.[11] With respect to the composition of the current working class (according to the social origin of its members) we can state that a large part come from agriculture. Effectively 42 per cent of the working class are sons of peasants and agricultural workers: 45 per cent come from working-class families, whilst the remaining 12 per cent come from non-manual occupations, and in general from the lower stratum of service workers and lower employees.[12] Doubtless the origins of the working class has had (and continues to have) its repercussions on the political and trade-union system but it does not operate as the determining element in the dynamic of the class struggle.[13]

Economic development and social transformation in Spain over the last twenty years is genuinely surprising, not just because of the levels and heights rendered (in general it is situated below the average of developed countries if we take these to be the western world), but because it has markedly advanced in the last two decades. This has impelled the disappearance of underdeveloped structures, which until the end of the fifties were dominant in Spanish society. None the less the great regional disequilibria and the very different social structure in each of the regions (from which the economic and social process started) has led not only to the maintenance of differences, but to the increasing disproportion of these inequalities. Thus it is particularly striking that whilst certain regions are above the average income of EEC countries others have standards of living similar in some aspects to those of underdeveloped countries.

Final Considerations on the Standard of Living and Development in Spain of the 1980s

Using diverse indicators of the standard of living and development, it is possible to get some idea of the general outlines based on the facts already given. The economic development of a country is usually analysed through the evolution of national income and its distribution in a given time. In Spain the index of income varies; taking 1961 as 100, 1980 goes as high as 606.1. Similarly the 1977 per capita income was in the region of 346.939 pesetas which puts Spain in a similar position to some EEC members and above others like Greece, Italy and Ireland.[14] Another index which can be used to give the level of economic/industrial development and its evolution could be the consumption of electricity and its distribution in kw/h per person. In a similar way to income, Spain has, moved to consume five times more energy than in 1961. Even so, according to UN data, in 1981 94,500 million kw/h were consumed, that is 2,500 kw/h per inhabitant which makes it the lowest of EEC countries excepting Greece, and above Portugal and Turkey. None the less if we look at the distribution of the total energy consumed in Spain during last year, very great differences could be noted in the level of industrial development between each of the autonomous regions. Thus, setting the national average consumption of electricity of 100, Asturias and the Basque Country are above or around 200 (218.85 and 198.77 respectively): Extremadura, Canary Isles and Andalusia reach only 65, the former coming to only 32.79 of the 100 average. A clear distinction can be traced between the southern half of the peninsula where none of the regions is above the national average, and the north where all are above, except La Rioja (around 80). This gives us an idea of the lack of homogeneity of industrial distribution in Spain that has tended to favour the 'historically industrialised' zones not only in the creation of new industries through the appropriate public institutions but has also impeded the creation of new industries in traditional agricultural areas, even causing the decapitalisation of fishing and farming situated there.

On the other hand the current standard of living in Spain also shows differences, although not to the extent we saw in the last paragraphs. An analysis of different indicators can give as a rough idea of the standard of living relative to the EEC. Taking, first, the total number of telephones per 100 people, in Spain we find a coefficient of 32.59/100. This puts Spain in a similar position to the Community countries, and it is also possible to grasp some measure of the advance made since 1961 when the coefficient was 6.27 phones per 100. Another picture is thrown into relief when we look at the internal distribution of telephones per region: here again Extremadura, Galicia, Andalusia and Castille are those which have the lowest indexes under the 100 average, the highest number of telephones and the areas with the greatest industrialisation also coincide and have the highest standard of living—if this index permits such an interpretation.

Amongst other indexes which enable an appreciation of these features can be found the number of cars per 1,000 persons. Using this index, in 1981 the national average was 270.5 cars per 1,000 which gives levels similar to the EEC countries where the average is 275 cars/1,000. On the other hand this is where there is a much greater internal Spanish homogeneity and in distribution by regions the index only fluctuates around 10 points off the average.[15]

Finally we can look at indexes like health and the presumptive cultural level in Spain. For the number of people per doctor in the country can be used as an index for regional variation: according to the 1981 estimate, for every 474 people there is one doctor and there is a homogenous distribution except in Extremadura and the islands where the ratio increases, up to over 600/doctor. Again, this index takes us to a level roughly the same as the EEC. The cultural level can be reckoned through the number of students who take courses to middle-school level in Spain: from the most recent data, the academic year 1980–81, 10 per cent of people have been through studies. Fortunately this puts Spain above the level of western countries and the *Statistical Yearbook* of 1979 puts only Canada (with 11 per cent) above Spain.

In conclusion we can state that in general, and through the Spanish process of development, a socio-economic position which is not too dissimilar to the rest of Europe has been reached although Spain has been immersed in the world economic crisis since 1973. For this reason Spain's possible inclusion in the EEC will not result in any distortion of the structures of EEC countries. Quite the contrary, entry into the Common Market would contribute to the equalisation of the regions if the zones mentioned (which have the highest underdevelopment indexes) find themselves beneficiaries of the general EEC programme of regional aid to the underdeveloped. Even so Spain finds itself faced by the important rate of unemployment, which should be treated in the same way as in other European countries. This is a problem of such extreme importance and likely to produce considerable economic repercussions, that it will be, and in fact already is, one of the essential points of the bi-lateral talks between Spain and the EEC, and is where Spain's negotiations are sure to encounter the greatest drawbacks.

Notes

1. José Cazorla Pérez, 'El retorno de los emigrantes a Andalucía y El Algarve', *Emigración y retorno. Una perspective europea,* Instituto español de emigración, Madrid, 1971, p. 171. See the excellent work by Antonio Garcia Ferrer, 'Una crítica a los modelos económicos migratorios: algunos resltados empíricos para el caso español', in J. Cazorla Pérez (ed.), *Emigración y retorno. Una perspective europea,* Granada, 1981.
2. Luis Borreguero Gonzales, 'El retorno en la Emigración: Problemas y posibles soluciones' in J. Cazorla Pérez, op. cit., 1981.
3. These percentages come from the Census of the working population by INE (Instituto Nacional De Estadistica) of the first quarter of 1982.
4. Ramón Tamames, *Estructura económica de España,* Guadiana De Publicaciones, Madrid, 1973 (7th edn.), Vol. III, p. 20 et seq.
5. *Anuario Estadístico,* 1962, p. 49.
6. INE, op. cit., 1970, Madrid, 1972.
7. The data here comes respectively from the FIES survey—79 del Dapartamento de Investigaciones sociales de la Fundación (FIES) *Fundación para la Investigacion Economica y Social*—and from the *Encuesta de poblacion activa* of the Institute National de Estadística 1981. Partial results from these can be found in diverse articles in No. 8 of the review *Papeles de Economía Española,* FIES, Madrid, 1980.
8. J. M. Naredo, *La evaolución de la agricultura en España,* Estela, Barcelona, 1971, p. 145.
9. Ministerio de Industria, *Las 300 grandes empresas industriales españolas en 1971,* Foessa-75 (Fundación Fomento de Estudios Sociale Y Sociologia Aplicada) Euramerica, Madrid, 1976, p. 776.
10. Unfortunately these data correspond to the last census of 1970, the census data of 1981 have not yet been published.
11. INE, census of 1970.
12. Foessa-75, p. 795.
13. On this see the excellent work by Jose María Maravall, *La politica de la transición 1975-1980,* Taurus, Madrid, 1982.
14. *Contabilidad Nacional de España,* INE, Madrid, and UN *Statistical Yearbook,* New York, 1979.
15. *Anuario El País, 1982,* Promotora de Informaciones Sociedad Anonima, Madrid, 1982.

APPENDIX: THE ELECTION OF 1982

The New Spanish Government: 3 December 1982

Prime Minister: Félipe González
Deputy Prime Minister: Alfonso Guerra
PM's Minister: Javier Moscoso
Economy: Miguel Boyer
Science and Education: José Maravall
Health: Ernest Lluch
Foreign Affairs: Fernando Morán
Social Security and Labour: Joaquín Almunia
Administration of Territory: Tomás de la Cuadra
Urbanism and Public Works: Julián Campo
Defence: Naris Serra
Industry and Energy: Carlos Solchaga
Culture: Javier Solana
Transport and Communication: Enrique Barón
Interior: José Barrionuevo
Justice: Fernando Ledesma
Agriculture, Fisheries and Food: Carlos Romero

Spanish Political Parties

21,353,996 voters—Turn-out 79.6%*

PSOE (Spanish Workers Socialist Party). Founded by Pablo Iglesias over a hundred years ago and was last in power during the Civil War when Largo Caballero was its leader. It is now led by Felipe González who is part of the non-Marxist dominant group in the Party.

1979	1982
5,469,813 votes (30.5%)	9,836,579 votes (46%)
121 seats	202 seats

AP (Popular Alliance). Led by former Franco Minister and ex-Ambassador to London Fraga Iribarne who founded the Party. Now in coalition with Oscar Alzaga's small self-styled liberal group (PDP) but contains many ex-Franco supporters. The ascension of AP was one of the events of the 1982 elections and it is now seemingly poised to become the major opposition party.

1979	1982
1,067,732 votes (5.76%)	5,412,401 votes (25.3%)
9 seats	106 seats

UCD (Union of Centre Democrats). Founded in 1976 by Prime Minister Suárez from a myriad of tiny centre and centre-Left groups and was largely responsible for the transition to democracy. Its collapse caused the elections to be held early (not as programmed in Spring 1983) and its destruction at the polls by the PSOE and AP is a tragedy for Spanish democracy since it polarises the political scene. Led by Landelino Levilla who ran an active campaign. Outgoing Prime Minister Calvo-Sotelo was UCD.

1979	1982
6,268,593 votes (34.9%)	1,549,447 votes (7.2%)
168 seats	12 seats

PCE (Spanish Communist Party). Led by Santiago Carrillo but has been split very badly over the last two years and was electorally destroyed by the PSOE in these elections.

1979	1982
1,911,217 votes (10.81%)	824,978 votes (3.8%)
23 seats	4 seats

CDS (Centre Democrat and Social). Founded in July 1982 by ex-PM Adolfo Suárez. Has made no real mark.

1979	1982
—	615,540 votes (2.8%)
	2 seats

PNV (Basque Nationalist Party). The traditional Basque Nationalist Party led by Xavier Arzallus and another of its leaders Carlos Garaicoetxa heads the Basque regional government.

1979	1982
275,292 votes (1.54%)	406,804 votes (1.51%)
7 seats	8 seats

Herri Batasuña (Popular Union). The political arm of ETA whose deputies refuse to take their seats in the Cortes.

1979	1982
172,110 votes (0.9%)	206,748 votes (0.9%)
3 seats	12 seats

Euskadiko Ezkerra (Basque Left). Nationalist left-wing coalition connected to ETA-politico-military and led by Mario Onaindia (condemned to death in the 1970 Burgos trial) and J.-M. Bandres a lawyer for the accused at Burgos. ETA p-m gave up the armed struggle in return for amnesty during the campaign.

1979	1982
85,677 votes (0.48%)	98,725 votes (0.4%)
1 seat	1 seat

CiU (Convergence and Unity). Jordi Pujol's moderate Catalan Nationalist Party close to UCD and Pujol is head of the Catalan government.

1979	1982
483,353 votes (3.7%)	794,554 (3.7%)
8 seats	12 seats

Personalities of the December 1982 Socialist Government

Sr Alfonso Guerra: Deputy Prime Minister

Alfonso Guerra is Felipe González' right-hand man responsible for the organisation of the Party and to some extent an *eminence grise* although he has been close to the PSOE leader since they were students together in the 1960s at Seville University. Sr Guerra was a theatre director and an engineer before devoting himself full-time to politics in which he gained a reputation as a formidable debater, an incisive speaker and was, at one time, considered to be on the Left.

Sr Miguel Boyer: Minister of Economics

Sr Boyer was a leader of the Young Socialists in the years of clandestinity, was arrested in 1962 (and spent five months in prison) and then left the PSOE for a short time before rejoining in 1978. He was in the chemical firm Explosivos Rio Tinto from 1974–78 and worked for INI. Sr Boyer is an orthodox economist who will aim at reassuring business milieux and Spanish and foreign banks. Inflation and balance of payments problems are seen as determining factors. Boyer is not keen on a French-style reflation and wants to control wages so as to increase business profits. Boyer is at the head of a super-ministry grouping finance, commerce, and economics and is aided by Carlos Solchaga, Enrique Baron, Ernest Lluc and Joaquim Almunia whose task will be to convince unions of the need for wage restraint.

Sr Fernando Morán: Foreign Minister

Sr Morán has been a diplomat before (under Franco) and was a councillor in London in 1973 but was a member of the Popular Socialist Party until it integrated into the PSOE. Morán was a *critico* but rallied to González and now is classed as a leadership supporter. He is supposed to keep close links with Latin America and their Arab countries but integration into the EEC is not an over-riding priority.

Sr Narcis Serra: Defence

Narcis Serra was one of those who rebuilt the Catalan Socialist Party and became Mayor of Barcelona after the 1979 elections. He was also a Professor of Economics at Barcelona University, a member of the first Catalan provisional government and a good administrator of the Chamber of Commerce (1965–70).

Sr Barrionuevo: Interior

Sr Barrionuevo was a Madrid Councillor after the 1979 elections where he was in charge of the police department and now takes over the government's sensitive problem of terrorism and relations with the Civil Guard.

1982 Senate Election Results

Party	Seats
PSOE	138
Alianza Popular	54
Convergència i Unió	7
Partido Nacionalista Vasco	7

Note

*Although these results were subsequently adjusted by the electoral authorities (the PCE number of seats, for example, fell from 5 to 4), these were accepted on 1 November 1982. There were no 'official' figures obtainable at the time of going to press.

NOTES ON CONTRIBUTORS

José Amodia is a graduate of Oviedo University, was a Nuffield Research Fellow and teaches Spanish Politics at Bradford University. He has been working on the UCD recently and wrote *Franco's Political Legacy*.

Elizabeth Nash was a member of the Labour Party International Depart-. ment, has researched Spanish politics over a number of years, has attended, PSOE congresses, and is now a researcher for Central Television.

Mike Newton is Senior Lecturer and Head of the Spanish Studies Division at Newcastle upon Tyne Polytechnic and has been researching regionalism in Spain (with special reference to Andalusia) for several years.

Dr Peter Holmes is in the European School at Sussex University and has just completed a research project on Spanish entry into the EEC for SERC who will be publishing it shortly.

Dr José Cazorla Pérez is Professor of Political Law in the Law Faculty at Granada University, President of the Spanish Federation of *Asociaciones de Sociologia* and the author of numerous works on Spanish sociology.

David S. Bell of the Politics Department, Leeds University and Visiting fellow of SERC is the author of the *Spanish Communist Party and Euro-communism* (SERC 1980), and Western Europe editor of *Communist Affairs*.

Dr Pedro Vilanova is Professor of Political Science and Constitutional Law in Facultad de Derecho, Barcelona University, a fellow of the Trans-national Institute Amsterdam/Washington and author of papers, articles, and books on Spanish politics.

Dr Pierre Subra de Bieusses is *chargé de Conference* at the University of Paris X (Nanterre) and is author and editor of works on contemporary Spain including *L'Espagne ou la démocratie retrouvée* and *Pouvoirs*, 1979, No. 8, 'L'espagne démocratique'.

Bruce Young was born in 1949. Studied philosophy in the University of Aberdeen (1967-71) and Oxford (1971-73). He has lectured in social science and the history of European philosophy in Wolverhampton Polytechnic since 1975.